Honourable Company

JOHN BELLASIS
(1743–1808)
General of the Honourable East India Company's Service,
and Commander-in-Chief, Bombay.

Honourable Company

by

M. BELLASIS

with a Preface by

ARTHUR BRYANT

LONDON

HOLLIS & CARTER

First published 1952

★

Made and printed in Great Britain
by Jarrold and Sons Limited, Norwich for
HOLLIS AND CARTER LIMITED
25 Ashley Place, London, SW1

PREFACE

by

ARTHUR BRYANT

THE British record in India is one of the great epics of
history. It began with the courage and enterprise of
a handful of merchants and seamen following, in the
face of dangers and uncertainties that today seem almost un-
believable, their "trade of spicerie". It was part of the process
which, in the course of three centuries, transformed a little
half island of four or five million inhabitants into a vast
industrial and commercial power supporting fifty millions
and uniting the greatest confederation of allied and peaceful
nations that has yet existed on this planet. How many of
those fifty millions, whose life in this country is dependent
on that past, take the achievement for granted and are
wholly unaware of the debt they owe to those who opened,
in the face of the tempest and pirate, robber and thug, doors
for their country's peaceful trade where no trade was before!

To do so they had to take their lives in their hands and
fight, not for what was not theirs, but for property lawfully
obtained and for treaty rights freely negotiated, to secure
which they and their predecessors had made vast sacrifices.
India in the eighteenth century, after a series of invasions
and wars of conquest, and of frightful blood-stained
tyrannies, had dissolved into an anarchy to parallel which in
this country we should have to go back for more than a
thousand years, to the dark ages of the Danish invasions.
Surrounded by that anarchy and the many violent despotisms
to which it gave rise, British traders on her coasts could look
for no help from their home country, many months of
perilous sea-voyaging away. The Britain of the early
Georges was as powerless to help them as is the Britain of
today to help a trader or missionary on the far side of the
Iron Curtain. Slavery, mutilation, death in a thousand

v

fearful forms were the lot of British men, women and children who fell into the hands of the savage monsters who tyrannised over the greater part of India before the rule of "John Company" and the British Raj were established. To preserve their trade and their lives, and those of their dear ones, they had to create islands of security, order and justice, and discipline themselves and their native servants and allies to act together in mutual defence.

Thus the establishment of British authority in India was the story of men who made war, not for plunder or conquest, but to restrain monsters of tyranny, bestial cruelty, depravity and treachery from enslaving and destroying them. The tyrants and plunderers who threatened and maltreated them also threatened and maltreated vast multitudes of miserable Indian peasants who, famished, diseased, fatalistic and incapable of combining, were the helpless prey of every military adventurer and freebooter. When, as late as the beginning of the nineteenth century, a small Pindari free company went plundering—a normal seasonal operation and one carried out by similar companies all over central India—they slew in eight days 182 peasants, wounded 505 and tortured 3,033. The favourite and most effective form of torture employed by these armed thieves, as Miss Bellasis points out, was "to tie a bag of hot ashes over a man's mouth and nose and thump his back"; this not only made him divulge, without further waste of his tormentor's time, where he had hidden his belongings but subsequently caused his lungs to rot. Tipu Sahib, the ruler of Mysore, the capture of whose foul and blood-stained capital was the first victory of Wellington's career, drove the miserable Indian Christians of Malabar into the sea chained together in pairs. The tortures he inflicted on his tens of thousands of captives, including many English men and women, are not such as can be set down in print; the walls of his stronghold, Seringapatam, were painted with vast, obscene cartoons depicting their torments. The contrast between the honourable and responsible Indian leaders into whose hands Britain has now committed the rule of India and the men from whom she took it, by degrees and most reluctantly, two centuries ago, would be the justification of her *raj* in history if there were no other. Her sons rescued India from enemies of the human race who surpassed Hitler in despotism and Himmler in sadism. In the fullness of time—and time for such a transformation was necessary— she restored India to the rule of civilised men of goodwill. The gulf between Tipu Sahib and Pandit Nehru was bridged by British humanity and justice. As Miss Bellasis truly writes of the victories of Clive, Cornwallis and Wellesley, "the way was opened for Thames and Itchen and Avon and many a northern burn to flow into Hughli and considerably sweeten it." It is a curious metaphor but, I believe, a true one.

And what a superb courage and military skill went to the British victory over anarchy in the world's greatest sub-continent! The capture and defence of Arcot by Robert Clive, the twenty-five-year-old "failed" clerk from Shropshire, has no parallel in history except the exploits of the Conquistadores and of the young Drake in the Caribbean and Pacific. Nor has his victory at Plassey, won five years later by less than a thousand Englishmen and two thousand Sepoys with 8 guns against an army twenty times their size with 56 guns. If enduring results are any criterion he was a greater conqueror than Alexander; if triumph over over-whelming odds, a greater soldier. Yet even he, "the heaven-born genius", was only one of many in that long procession of young paladins from these little misty islands who in the course of less than a century, under the blazing Indian sun, transformed chaos into order and not so much conquered India for Britain—as up to a few years ago could still be thought—but, as is now clear in the wider perspective of the mid-twentieth century, created the setting for full Indian self-government, unity, sovereignty, and a new and happier future for its many races. "These English are a strange people and their general"—his name was Arthur Wellesley—"a wonderful man," wrote a Mahratta freebooter. "They came here in the morning, looked at the pettah-wall, walked over it, killed all the garrison and returned to breakfast." Yet scarcely one living Briton in a million could name as many as five of the great leaders, let alone of the nameless rank and file, who, in the years covered by this book, made their country the secure guardian and just trustee of a land more than thirty times the size of their own and with a population of two hundred millions—a population which the peace and good administration they gave her has doubled in the last century. Even the immortal names of Rollo Gillespie and John Nicholson are now almost forgotten. Who today has heard of the unlettered Irishman, George Thomas—"Ship Sahib", "George the Victorious"—who, after serving as a pressed seaman in the Royal Navy, placed his sword, splendid person and still more splendid courage at the disposal of an Indian Begum and refounded the abandoned city and ravaged district of Hansi. "One Irish sword", he declared, when insulted by a Revolutionary emissary, "is sufficient for a hundred Frenchmen!" When he died at forty-six at Bahrampur and was buried in an unmarked grave, his epitaph, Miss Bellasis suggests, should have been "One Irish sword!"

These blazed the trail. Those who came after made the highway. Though centred on the annals of only one of the great Anglo-Indian families, whose sons and daughters followed one another in service "as dolphins follow in line across the open sea", *Honourable Company* tells the story of how the factors and merchants, who first went out from Leadenhall Street to "shake the pagoda tree," were transformed in the course of two or three generations into the self-sacrificing, self-effacing public servants who, spending their lives in exile and separation and without hope of worldly reward, gave to the peoples of India sound and just administration, health and relief services, roads, canals, railways and irrigation. "History", wrote Lord Sydenham, "records nothing that can approach the British achievement in India, and the world will never see the like of it again." It was, throughout, a story of men, and of that indefinable quality, character, that makes men. Their epitome can be found on the memorial to Henry Lawrence—the noblest, perhaps, of all the noble men of alien race who gave their lives to India—"Here lies Henry Lawrence, who tried to do his duty." It is to be found, too, in this book. No one who reads it can fail to understand a little better the background of the new India, and to visualise, too, all that it has meant in human endeavour, suffering, triumph and sacrifice.

SMEDMORE,
July, 1952.

AUTHOR'S NOTE

THIS story is mainly based upon family papers, to the chief of which I have to thank kinsfolk for kindly giving me access. Otherwise I have relied upon standard histories and biographies, too many to list, and especially upon contemporary memoirs. The narratives of Tipu's captives, published in the eighteenth century and reprinted in our own, are a vivid supplement to Wilks and Beatson. The strange story of the European mercenaries in native service has been told by Lewis Ferdinand Smith, one of themselves; and by Captain Franklin, the biographer of the astounding George Thomas. A bulky volume of their adventures—exciting, but slightly inaccurate in detail—was collected some half-century ago by Herbert Compton, who also edited the memoirs of Captain Robert Eastwick, under the title *Master Mariner*, and the adventures of John Shipp in the campaigns of Lake and Wellesley. There has been surprisingly little written about East Indiamen, excepting E. Keble Chatterton's excellent book; but then there has been surprisingly little written about anything concerning the Company's rule in India. *The Nabobs*, by T. G. P. Spear, covers the early part of the period, and has a valuable list of authorities; the late Dennis Kincaid's *British Social Life in India* covers its own subject completely and entertainingly; and we have since had *The Sahibs*, a book of extracts, by Hilton Brown, from most of the contemporary annalists— but the period roughly from Plassey to the Mutiny, with all its dramatic history, seems to have attracted few other modern writers. It has attracted me; and I hope it may attract the reader.

DEAL 1951   M. B.

CONTENTS

LIST OF ILLUSTRATIONS

I

STAR PAGODA

IT was the last year of the century, and in a country remote from that in which he had been bred by many centuries in spirit and half a year in travelling time, a gentleman sat dating letters for the English ships. A clerk would afterwards copy them in duplicate, so that if one ship were wrecked, or "catch'd by the French", the letters might reach England upon another. His strong fine paper, his ink of the kind that yellows with age, his sand-box and his quills, were placed upon a writing-table in the broad veranda. We may also see there a little, wild, green parrot or so, with coral beak and black and pink collar, fluttering and perching in the rafters; and we must hear the raucous choir of crows that had begun its discordances at the first glint of dawn. In the huge gardens, half wild, half formal, coconut-palms reared their coarse feathery shocks; when the evening breeze came blowing from the sea they would rustle and rattle like ladies' fans. All the mangoes were in bloom; and there would be a strong sweet smell breathing into the veranda, tuberose and jasmine, like unstoppered scent bottles. Every smell, sweet or foul, was here very strong. Surely this man's first impression, upon landing from the sea, so many years ago, must have been of the smell of the Island, compounded of sewage, sandalwood, dead pariah-dog, burning-ghat, frangipani, spices, and the fish-manure under the toddy groves.

He was a man of past middle age, some five-and-fifty, and had never been handsome. His skin was indelibly coloured by the climate, which had fined his person down to a wiry strength; but there was no languor in his bright, quick eyes. He had heavy, well-arched, black brows; and though the line of his lips was particularly straight and firm, it would be unfair to call it hard. He wore his own hair, accurately powdered, with a trace of whisker below it, in right of the scarlet coat and gilt epaulets that sat across his shoulders. Upon one hand was a ring of black cornelian, carved with his name in Persian characters; upon the other glowed a barbarically beautiful emerald, given him in a khilat from the Queen of Cannanore, who had stripped it from off her own finger.

The great distance, literally and in figure, between the place where these letters were being penned and the place of their destination, could sometimes be forgotten in the nearby town. There it might be possible to cheat oneself with an illusion of contemporary life, seeing so many ladies and gentlemen sweating at the burra khana and the ball in the full rigour of European fashion. When they sat down to dine so hugely, one might disregard the temperature, and the colour of the servants, and think it London; when the fiddles began the minuets, it could be Bath. But the officer who was finishing his English mail had only taken one furlough in thirty years' service, and he knew well enough that the eighteenth century stopped at the settlement borders. Beyond, one might find a chaotic mixture of most past periods: Elizabethan splendour and squalor: Renaissance princes, cruel, brocaded, with a taste in classical poetry and poisons: knights errant, out of Froissart and Malory: the horrid anarchy of the Dark Ages: and, again, slavery and conquest and the games of the arena, as before Rome fell.

One did not, however, come to India to philosophise or to observe: one came for a single reason and pursued a single aim. The soldier with the emerald was of those plain men who have enough unuttered romance within them never to seek for it without, and little green parrots were as common to him as sparrows. The careful handwriting, which time was to oxidise into syrup-colour, never attempted the picturesque. He wrote nothing about the fantastic country in which he had passed a lifetime, nothing about his past employment of the sword by his side, nothing about the gathering of armies in this cardinal year of 1799, when Bonaparte with his immense dream of Oriental empire was looming in Egypt and stretching a hand to Tipu Sultan.

"Dear Brother,—I expect to hear that you are all at work enclosing the Park and Moor; which will make your Estate very valuable. It gives me great pleasure when I reflect how many hundred Years it has been in the Family. I suppose you have got all Studfolds from Kellsike to the Great Tarn. I imagine your boundary goes by the Gullom-holm roadside till it meets Thief-gill-head. I am very sorry Dicky Hill's estate was not laid hold of when it was sold, but perhaps by keeping quiet and going about the Business with Caution it may yet be got, as it will be a very Desirable thing, a delightful Situation upon that fine bank of the Eden in case one might be dispos'd to build there." The consciousness that another lakh would first be needed added: "From pecuniary considerations I must remain, even at the risk of Life, some years longer in India."

Major-General John Bellasis, of the Honourable East India Company's Service, writing from Bombay into Westmorland, could also mention that he now expected his five sons out from England in the Company's ships: "—one after another, as they may be of standing to have appointments."

Two nephews, Joseph and George, had already followed him. Captain George Bridges Bellasis, Bombay Artillery, was by repute the handsomest man in India. He stood six foot of sinewy elegance which might have been made to show off fine uniforms; a devil-may-care geniality lurked usually on his full classical lips and glinted in his eyes; nobody sang a better song after dinner. Dash and elegance are not money-getting qualities. "It would be as Impossible to put you into the nearest road to Wealth and Consequence as to drive a Pig backwards in a strait line across Salisbury Plain", was the lamentation of a friend; what, he inquired, could be done with a man that would so freely give or lend, would marry a woman merely for love, treat a poor man with respect, and be ready to knock down an East India Director? Certainly George tossed away every anna as fast as he made it, and had lately married a beauty with the smallest of portions; but he could raise a black eyebrow and whistle away any care for the future with a Horatian tag, or "I hope soon that infernal Bitch Fortune will begin to smile on me". If any native scryer could have shown to him in the pool of ink or the wreaths of sand or the leaves of the Pali book all that the Bitch Fortune was going to do with him in the opening of the new century, even Captain George might have blenched.

The prospect immediately before him was perilous but inviting. The Bombay Army would soon be on the march under General Stuart, accompanied in the usual manner by ten times as many camp-followers, shroffs, jugglers, nautch girls, traders, palanquin and dhooly bearers, flocks of sheep, droves of bullocks, elephants, camels, horses having each two attendants, a groom and a grass-cutter. Captain Bellasis, with about twenty servants, including those attached to his horses and his dogs, would be taking his guns up the Ghats to strike at a fantastic tyrant, the Tiger of Seringapatam. "The pranks of a monkey, with the abominations of a monster," is the historian's verdict upon Tipu Sahib. Back through the Christian centuries into ancient history the seeker must go to find his like upon European soil. George Bellasis, with his improved artillery, his modern galloper guns, was to take a part in overthrowing Nero, and fight hand to hand with the Praetorian Guard. Shortly he would be able to write: "Where I saw the Sultaun laying, there were upwards of Eight Hundred of his faithful followers and his favourite Woman (past all description fair) in One heap."

"Joseph is a General in Dowlut Rao Scindia's army, with 20,000 men in his pay. He has a salary of £900 English a month, and returning in four or five years will be a man of

immense Fortune"; such was the news reaching England
in this year of 1799, which was to be Joseph's last. Men of
every European nation and of every kind of character—
broken adventurers and first-class soldiers, drunken
deserters, persons of birth and honour fired by ambition,
and ruffians looking for loot—had long been selling their
swords to native princes. In India of the Great Anarchy
the little armies marched, in ever-changing patterns of
enmity and alliance, as the companies of bowmen and
spearmen had moved about medieval Europe. Eighteenth-
century gentlemen, in the character of knights-errant, rode
into barbaric courts and proffered their services to rulers
who might heap their hands with jewels, and punish by
murder the crimes of failure or of too great success. The
heads of Vickers, Dodd, and Ryan grinned and blackened
upon Holkar's spears; and the great De Boigne left Scindia's
service a millionaire.

Joseph Harvey Bellasis had chosen to sit down in Siege
Perilous. Had Sir Lancelot's epitaph been phrased by a
polished writer of the Age of Reason, it could have been
something like his. "He combined in his character and
person all the excellent qualities which can adorn human
nature; his courage bordered on temerity; his integrity was
irreproachable; his generosity unbounded; and his liberal
mode of thinking rare and honourable. He was a fine
Greek and Latin scholar; . . . in music he was perfect, and in
painting much above mediocrity. He was an excellent
engineer, uncommonly skilled in military tactics. In his
manners he was not only affable, open and conciliating, but
inchanting . . . Recorded virtue and excellence act as
stimulants and as examples to noble actions; and though
poor Bellasis' fame is not engraved on polished marble or
recorded in the dubious page of history, yet his memory
will be cherished and respected by every person who was
acquainted with his many amiable, useful, and dignified
qualities. His person was tall and handsome, and there was
something very engaging in his countenance. He was a

man of uncommon ingenuity; and we may justly mourn his
loss in the language of Horace:—

> *Quis desiderio sic pudor aut modus*
> *Tam cari capitis.*"

The ditch of the fort in the Datia State which was to hold
his bones was not within the prevoyance of Joseph Bellasis,
but he was well used to expect such a fate. Upon its alterna-
tive, the return across the seas with lakhs of Indian gold,
and upon ties which bound him to India, personified in a
Rajputni lady, we may suppose him to be meditating: sitting
in his armed camp in 1799, a lonely but impressive figure:
"The High-in-Rank, the Favoured-of-the-Maharajah, the
Well-Wisher, the Valiant-in-Battle, and the Wise-in-
Durbar."

He, indeed, was not to leave his name upon polished
marble, though his brother was to do so, and his uncle.
For General John there was to be a very fine monument in
Bombay Cathedral, all marble cannon-balls and furled
standards; with the more enduring immortality of having
built a famine-relief road to be known after his name more
than a hundred and fifty years later, and having constructed
the landing-pier called the Apollo Bunder, to be famous
when Bombay took its right place as the gateway of India.
But it was the five sons of John Bellasis, with their sons and
their sons' sons, soldiers and civilians under Company and
Crown, who were to keep his memory alive.

These kinsmen upon whom we pause in the year of
Seringapatam can be taken as the type of scores and
hundreds more: of all the men who left the mild airs and
green fields of their own civil land for a vast, burning, and
dangerous country, there to shake the Pagoda Tree. More
ancient than the Rupee or the Mohur, the Star Pagoda was
named by Albuquerque's men from the likeness of a
temple upon one face of it. Moslem contempt called the
temple *But Khana*, Idol House, and Portuguese tongues
garbled the sound. When the English took possession of

Bombay the coins they found were the Pagoda, Shahi, and Xeraphin. The jest or cant allusion of "Shaking the Pagoda Tree" began early; and the Star Pagoda twinkled, a Star in the East to which generations made pilgrimage.

The land where grew the Pagoda Tree had in it mountains and deserts and great wildernesses full of savage beasts, but its peculiar terror was not that of a country uninhabited by man, that air of something at once virgin and dangerous, which is to be felt in the new continents even yet. It seemed on the contrary that men had swarmed there from the beginning, that the dust of it was powder of forgotten cities and dead men's bones. Every crumb of that earth must have gone through the full cycle of transmigration into grain, into human flesh, into earth again, as countless a number of times as the transmigrating soul of which the Brahmins taught; and the terror to oppress the fancy was that the people were so many, living on this earth in such swarms, and dying on it in such heaps when the rains failed to fertilise it: so many, dwelling under a tyrannous sun and tyrannous rulers, that it mattered not how many thousands should die by famine, or how many thousands the king should slay for his diversion. Dynasties of jewelled rulers, generations of priests, wonderful city after city, had passed away before Rome was mistress of the West or Christ had walked in Galilee; the invading Alexander was become a vague name, the great King Asoka a legend, when Islam carried the crooked sword into India.

Every cold weather, Sultan Mahmud of Ghazni would come slaying and sacking down from the North. "Jewels and unbored pearls, and rubies shining like sparks or like wine congealed with ice, and emeralds like fresh sprigs of myrtle, and diamonds in size and weight like pomegranates" did he loot from the temples; and in the year of the Hegira 414 he slew 50,000 at Somnauth, carrying thence the gates and treasure. In the Christian year 1187, when St. Francis was a small child in Assisi, when Frederick Barbarossa was

Emperor, and when Richard Lionheart was preparing his Crusade, the chieftain of Ghori, near Herat, came conquering down through Sind and the Punjab into the rich Ganges plain, peopled by heathen "fit only to be sent to hell". The Hindu host was overthrown at Tarain; Bihar was destroyed, with its temples and libraries and great calm Buddhas—and with it Buddhism in Upper India; Bengal was subdued to a rule that lasted until Plassey; and thereafter one terrible Sultan followed another at Delhi. It was Alaud Din who sacked Chitor, about 1300, because he desired Queen Padmani; and Hindu poets told how the Rajput chivalry died defending the walls, while their women— Queen Padmani and several thousand others—died ceremonially upon funeral pyres in the cellars below: the rite of the jauhar. . . . Murdering or blinding their relations to secure the throne, the Lords of Delhi culminated in the parricide Tughlaki Sultan, so pious, austere, and cruel that the empire broke away from him piecemeal, and half a dozen independent kings continued the harrying of the heathen. Of one, Humayun, it was written: "The nobles and generals when they went to salute the Sultan used to bid farewell to their wives and children and make their wills"; a poem of celebration upon his death began: "Humayun Shah has passed away from the world. God Almighty, what a blessing was the death of Humayun!"

The one great Hindu power which had dammed the advance of the Delhi conquests and survived to fight with these Sultans was the strange southern empire of Vijayanagar, a marvellous city of forts and palaces and temples, which astounded the traveller Paes, who viewed it in the reign of the English King Henry VIII. It was so wealthy that the immense populace all wore jewels, and every pot and pipkin in the king's palace was of gold; moreover, there were rooms in the palace made wholly of carved ivory; and when Deva Raya I propitiated Firoz Shah Bahmani with the hand of his daughter, he carpeted the wedding-route for six miles with cloth of gold and precious stuffs. The King of Vijayanagar went barefoot and dressed always in white, with a high brocaded cap; he had 12,000 wives, of whom some 3,000 were required to burn at his death. There were 500 elephants in his stables; and very few thieves in the land, because a theft, however trifling, meant loss of hand or foot. For more serious crimes a culprit would be suspended by a hook beneath the chin, or torn between the royal elephants. Architecture, art, and poetry flourished. Everything was on sale in the splendid markets, including bouquets of fresh flowers, which were considered a daily necessity. Much of the revenue was provided by the courtesans, who occupied the best streets and were highly respected, having the right to go and chew betel-nut with the royal ladies. But Vijayanagar fell before the combined Mohammedan powers at the battle of Talikota; they made it a depopulated ruin, smashing up its carved wonders with maces and hammers; it took them five months.

Now India had again a master from the North: the cat-eyed Moguls were come. Contemporary with Elizabeth of England, the greatest of their race, Akbar, was conquering and remaking the land. The Jesuits whom he entertained at his court, and who described so clearly his short, strong person, loud voice, kingly bearing, and eyes "vibrant like the sea in sunshine", set him down as *"gloriae percupidas"*: avid for conquest and renown. They never made a Christian of him, though he incorporated their teachings in a synthetic religion of his own, and reverenced Christian holy things, as did Jehangir, the heir who poisoned him with dust of diamonds. None of his successors equalled him, though all had the family talents. Jehangir, who would go into raptures over the wild-flowers of Kashmir, delighted in watching barbarous tortures, to the dismay of Sir Thomas Roe, ambassador from James I, who had brought him an English coach for Queen Nurjahan. Shahjahan constructed the Peacock Throne, entirely of jewels and resembling a very ugly cot-bedstead; he also loved one woman, Mumtaz Mahal, until she died in bearing her fourteenth child, when he built for her the most famous and lovely tomb in the world, and consoled his old age with dancing-girls, in Agra fort, where his son had imprisoned him. Aurangzeb Alamgir, "World Seizer", took over a realm that had been thirty years at peace, and in a reign that lasted from Cromwell to Queen Anne shook its stability fatally by a grand persecution of Hindus. He destroyed several thousand temples, knew the Koran by heart, trusted nobody, lived as an extreme Moslem ascetic, and died at the age of ninety. Apart from this puritan who had renounced all the pleasures of art, the Timurid Moguls encouraged in architecture and painting the making of masterpieces that still refresh the world. The charm of those paintings, the beauty of the Taj and the Pearl Mosque, and the blazing magnificence of the court, partly blinded European observers to the extreme misery of the common people tilling the soil, and blocking the roads with their corpses in years of famine.

The coming of Europeans in ever-increasing numbers had coincided with the rise of the Moguls. First came the Portuguese with their double motive: to deal a blow at Moslem power and spread Christianity, while capturing the spice trade. Then, a century later, came the English and the Dutch, with their simple motive of profit; then the Danes, and last the French. The "Great Mogoll" generally regarded these humble traders with magnificent tolerance. It occurred to none—except a crazed Sikh prophet—that India's next masters had not arrived by the traditional route. It was not any European threat that troubled the later days of the Mogul Empire, but the sudden emergence of the Mahratta power under the chieftain Sivaji. After 1707, the year of Aurangzeb's death, the great Empire, the nearest thing to unity that India had ever known, was to come unstuck in every direction, and throughout the succeeding period, the "Great Anarchy", the Mahrattas were to be dominant.

The Mahrattas came from hill country, the Western Ghats, "Mountain rats of the Deccan", Aurangzeb called them, and were Hindus of the lowest, or Sudra, caste: small, sturdy men, as vulgar in appearance as the Rajputs were naturally noble. Bold fighters, they were particularly endowed with cunning, and particularly proud of it. Sivaji, who had set up as a robber chief at an early age, scored his first great success in 1659, by parleying with the general of an outnumbering Moslem army, and while they were ceremonially embracing, disembowelling the man with the weapon called "tiger's-claws"; ambushed Mahrattas then attacked, and made booty of horses and weapons. From then on, Sivaji, who was as devoutly attached to cows and Brahmins as his adversaries were to the Koran, became an independent king and a great menace to the Imperial dominions. He founded an hereditary dynasty of Rajahs at Sattara, but these presently became mere puppets of the Prime Ministers, or Peishwas, who were also heredi-tary, and seated at Poona. The Moguls had soon been compelled to pay *chaut*, or danegeld, to the Mahrattas, as their own ancestors had been bought off by the Delhi Sultans; and it was the Mahrattas with whom, in the violent confusion that was eighteenth-century India, the English had to deal.

"The new trade of spicerie" had first interested England in the reign of Henry VIII, when it was a fiercely guarded Portuguese monopoly, by right of discovery: "For out of Spaine they have discovered all the Indies and Seas Occi-dentall, and out of Portingall all the Indies and Seas Orientall." At last, however, the route was detected "by which go the Portingalls to their Spicerie", and a few Elizabethan merchants began their bold venture, not forgetting the advice of an experienced Venetian: "Those parts of the Indies are very good, because that a man that hath little shall make a very great deal thereof; alwayes they must govern themselves that they be taken for honest men."

This the English merchants commonly did. They were

not at all grand people, despite the fact that they organised their little trading stations in a hierarchical manner, with strict grades from Writer up through Factor and Junior Merchant to Senior Merchant, great respect for the authority of the President or Governor, and even greater respect for their "Honourable Masters" at the India House. They were tradesmen, and rather resented the advent of impoverished gentlemen, such as Cavaliers ruined by the Civil Wars. Also, despite episodes like Captain Keigwin's rebellion at Bombay, and the attempt of Sir John Child to pursue an aggressive military policy, they were not at all military-minded, and had no notion of making any conquests in the increasingly disordered land of Hind. They plodded quietly along with their trading, seeking with gifts in hand the friendship and protection of the "country powers"—"the Moors"—and fortifying themselves against their possible ill-will by timid and inadequate defences, such as the "Mahratta Ditch" at Calcutta.

As the eighteenth century advanced, India was coming to pieces all round them; vast territories were here ruled by an usurping governor, there by a conquering stranger, and elsewhere by no one at all, so that men lived as in a tiger-haunted jungle, in daily fear. This was not good for trade; but the Company was neither desirous nor able to do anything about it. What changed the whole complexion of matters, and turned the English in India from anxious little shopkeepers into imperial conquerors, was the fact that the French desired to assume the latter character. There were no bounds to the ambition of Dupleix, the Governor of the French settlement at Pondicherry. His colleague, La Bourdonnais, proved at the battle of St. Thomé that an army of 430 Europeans, with 700 trained sepoys, could rout a Mogul army of 10,000; and when he took the English settlement at Madras, Dupleix cancelled the merciful terms allowed to the English merchants, and had them marched in triumph through the streets of Pondicherry. It was his bad luck that one of them was Robert Clive.

A young clerk, attempting to live, like all Company's Writers, on a salary of about twopence-ha'penny a year, the fires within him banked up and self-consuming, the genius which he might suspect in himself quite unemployed, Robert Clive had done nothing as yet but be shipped away from home as incorrigibly idle and mischievous, attempt suicide, risk his life with public intrepidity in a duel, and become a thorn in the flesh of his official superiors. But this was the moment for which he was born. He tossed away his pen, girded on a sword, led a tiny force through incredible tropical thunderstorms, and took the enemy's fort at Arcot. No more surprising and inspiring story than that of the siege of Arcot is likely to be told, even in English history. Having achieved his aim of drawing large enemy forces— the armies of the adventurer whom the French were setting up as Nawab of the Carnatic—away from besieged Trichinopoly, Clive held Arcot with his starving handful: his sepoys begging him to give all the rice to the white men, and let them subsist merely upon the water in which it was boiled: and after fifty days, he routed an attack so decisively that the thousands of attackers broke, fled, and raised the siege. The fighting Mahrattas were delighted to ally themselves with such a man. With their aid, Clive rolled up half a dozen victories, and razed to the ground the pompous city and monument which Dupleix had built, after the Eastern fashion, to proclaim the conquering pre-eminence of France.

When this young man went home to England at the age of twenty-seven, with the bride whom he had commissioned out, sight unseen, on the strength of her portrait, he had altered the whole face of affairs in India. When he returned again, he won the battle of Plassey. Surajah Dowlah, the Nawab of Bengal, a vicious stripling, had taken occasion to plunder Calcutta; he enjoyed inflicting torture, but it was his guards who packed 146 English prisoners into the garrison black hole overnight—twenty-three somehow came out alive in the morning. Clive "waited upon the Nawab" before the rains, on June 23rd, 1757, on the plain of Plassey. He had 800 Europeans, 2,000 sepoys, eight guns, and no cavalry; he was opposed by 55,000 horse and foot, and more than fifty guns, some served by a highly trained French party. It is true that one wing of the Nawab's army was commanded by Mir Jaffier, who was waiting to join the winner. Clive was the winner, within an hour; and England had gained Bengal. The Company now ruled a territory bigger than Britain, under the nominal suzerainty of Mir Jaffier, whom they set up as Nawab.

With the acquisition of Bengal came a wild scramble to shake the Pagoda Tree. The scene which developed was not a pretty one, and caused a deal of righteous indignation. The "Nabob, or Asiatic Plunderer" was a cockshy for English satirists during the next two or three decades: some typical verses with that title began with spirit:

> *Concerns it you who plunders in the East,*
> *In blood a tyrant, and in lust a beast?*

A contemporary observed more reasonably: "Those men must have more than a moderate share of virtue, who, considering the universal veneration in this country paid to men of wealth, will return with a moderate fortune . . ." and a modern historian has commented that only an angel of light could have done much good in that place at that time. The tradesmen, with suddenly turned heads, and the rush of worthless adventurers whom Clive disgustedly recommended the Company to buy off on arrival, were not angels: though indeed they almost look like them by the side of most of the native rulers. Barwell losing £40,000 at cards, or Francis having to pay Rs.160,000 for being caught up a ladder at the window of Mr. Grand's wife, were disedifying spectacles; but though wrong is always wrong, there is a difference in degree which is almost a difference in kind: and India's destined new rulers were at their first and worst something better than the sub-continent had ever known before. The Barwells and Smiths scrambled ignominiously for the wealth of Bengal: they did not construct solid thrones of emeralds while the poor died at their gates. They kept a luxurious table, but they did not feed elephants on rice and butter while mothers were eating babies. They would keep a native mistress or two: not two or three hundred, with a guard of eunuchs; nor did they demand suicide by burning on the part of their women when they died. They might be corrupt; but they did not put up justice openly for sale. They might be harsh masters: but they did not divert themselves with tortures, or mutilate an entire captured garrison, or make a public holiday to celebrate each holocaust of 20,000 infidels. They might be arrogant: but they did not, like the Brahmin, regard millions of their fellow creatures as entirely destitute of all human rights. Philip Francis and Warren Hastings were deadly enemies: they went out one misty morning and shot at one another in a fair and correct fashion; neither of them procured the other's secret assassination and gloated over his severed head, as did Aurangzeb with his brother. In effect, although Englishmen returning home with Indian gains were bitterly decried and distrusted, and there was talk of Hughli flowing into Thames, the way was opened for Thames and Itchen and Avon and many a northern burn to flow into Hughli and considerably sweeten it.

The reforms of Clive, and—after he had finally returned to England to be questioned by Parliament, as he indignantly put it, "like a sheep-stealer"—those of Warren Hastings and Cornwallis, ended the misgovernment of Bengal; and amazingly quickly, the get-rich-quick generation was succeeded by persons of genius and responsibility, who began to realise that there was an Empire here to manage, and not a shop. The greatness of Warren Hastings passed into that kind of immortality to be secured by ballad and nursery-rhyme: generations of mothers sang to their children, and ayahs to their little white charges, about the glories of that wonderful Governor: the inflexible little

man who had made his dreams come true. For the reason
why Warren Hastings had come, at seventeen, to the land
where "a man that hath little shall make a very great deal
thereof" was his driving wish to become rich and repur-
chase the ancient seat of his family, lost because of their
ruin in the Civil War. Daylesford seemed hopelessly beyond
the reach of the shabby and ill-fed little boy who went to the
village school; as well beyond his reach seemed the woman
with whom he fell in love, when he returned to India after
losing his first modest fortune. But he got Daylesford, and
he got "elegant Marianne". When Hastings, who knew
and loved the people whom he ruled—he spoke their
tongues, as Clive never did; and desired to found a faculty
of Persian poetry at Oxford—had gone home to as ill a
requital as Clive's—impeachment, and a seven years' trial
—there came Cornwallis, the brave and honourable soldier
turned administrator. With no intention of enlarging the
Company's dominions, he did so as a consequence of his
victorious encounter with Mysore under the arrogant
Tipu; and when Lord Wellesley took his place, the Company
was well on the way to greatness, and the old humble days
lay far behind. Wellesley it was who started the fashion
of referring with brisk contempt to "Our Honourable
Masters"—late so worshipfully regarded—as "Those
cheesemongers in Leadenhall Street". The picked young
administrators whom he encouraged, Metcalfe, Elphinstone,
Malcolm, and their like, devoting the best of their lives and
energies to India, have been described as the nearest
approximation to Plato's ideal of the philosopher-king.
Steadily rising standards of government kept pace with
steadily increasing territory—sometimes ill-acquired, but
always well ruled; until the thing that had started as a
modest trading venture grew into fantastic greatness. A
hundred and fifty years from Plassey, a Viceroy could say:
"Oh, that to every Englishman in this country, as he ends
his work, might be truthfully applied the phrase 'thou hast
loved righteousness and hated iniquity'. No man has, I

believe, ever served India faithfully of whom that could not be said. All other triumphs are tinsel and sham. . . . To feel that somewhere among these millions you have left a little justice or happiness or prosperity, a sense of manliness or moral dignity, a spring of patriotism, a dawn of intellectual enlightenment, or a stirring of duty where it did not exist before—that is enough, that is the Englishman's justification in India."

To stand and look forward and back in the year 1799 is to see one way that new nineteenth-century India of secure dominion, peace and law, fading beyond John Company's cognisance into an immensity of administration and armies, colleges, hospitals, missions, roads, bridges, railways, irrigation, sanitation, and famine-relief: with boys made men by huge responsibilities, and devoted officials at so little *per mensem* wearily sweating over files. Looking the other way, in the past lies that dangerous eighteenth-century India to which men came only to earn gold, shaking it from the Pagoda Tree.

> *For thee, for thee, vile yellow slave,*
> *I left a heart that loved me true,*
> *I crossed the tedious ocean wave,*
> *To roam in climes unkind and new.*
> *The cold wind of the stranger blew*
> *Chill on my withered heart; the grave*
> *Dark and untimely met my view—*
> *And all for thee, vile yellow slave.*

Most commonly it could only be earned by many years of hard plodding or hard fighting. The slowness of promotion in the Company's Army particularly was such that if a man escaped the perils of the battlefield, or the worse daily perils of the climate, he must grow old before he could go home: and delaying to save a little more money, to gain one more step in rank, would finish by joining that often-quoted Mynheer Wandermere, "who was to have gone home next year".

c

In the last year of the century the Company's dangerous
neighbours were the Mahrattas, under the two great chiefs
Scindia and Holkar, and Tipu of Mysore. Hyder Ali, the
ruthless adventurer who had turned the Hindu dynasty of
Mysore off the throne, had been trouble enough, with his
scouring cavalry; but his son Tipu was not only bad but
mad, and had recovered from his humbling by Cornwallis.
France and England had resumed their traditional fight;
and there had uprisen the Corsican, "the modern Alexander", who had turned his eyes, like Alexander, upon India,
with plans and ambitions fit to stir the ghost of Dupleix.
Pondicherry had been long captured and rendered harmless;
but now men were calling the Doab "the French State",
because the powerful mercenary brigades in the service of
Scindia were French trained and officered, and ready to the
hand of Bonaparte.

The three Presidencies drilled their little armies watchfully, carried on their little law-courts, followed the daily
round of trading. Outside the bounds of their governance
still raged the Great Anarchy. By the custom of the country, the Suttee walked forth to burn, ceremonially printing
her handmark in vermilion on the gatepost of her kinsmen's
house; and terrified little girls were given in marriage, or
murdered as infants in the Rajput forts; and travellers were
strangled with the rumal, or poisoned with datura, by the
consecrated brotherhood of Thugs. These things were as
yet no business of the Company's servants; who must only
slowly become aware of the full extent of the destiny to
which they had been led by the twinkle of the Star Pagoda.

The story could anciently have been done into an epic
poem; modernly, perhaps, into a full-length romance.
For the purpose, a novelist might invent an English family
who should be mingled in the affairs of India onward from
the earliest trading days: Esmonds, or Forsytes; servants of
the Company, to end as servants of the Empire. Being
chiefly designed as types of their very numerous kind, and

links between sequent pictures of periods and events, they
should be unremarkable persons; but as a family, it would be
well that they should derive from some background having
in it traces of colour and poetry—an association with some
particular patch of English earth, perhaps with some
particular passages of English history. Let them come at
first to India for motives also that have a touch of romance:
one seeking gold enough to marry his true-love, or to rebuild
a shattered house; such a dream as the poverty-bitten little
Warren Hastings dreamed of Daylesford. Let our family be
chiefly soldiers, for that India was got by the sword; and let
us connect them not with the showy glories of Calcutta, but
rather with quiet Bombay. Beside our Company's officers,
let us have one of those free-lances in native service who
were often able to even themselves with kings. Let us have
storming of forts, and death in battle; and, perhaps, as an
illustration of manners, a fatal duel. Let us have love-
stories; and at least some mention of the huge amount of
promising young life gobbled up by the Indies—a muslined
bride to meet the fate of Rose Aylmer, a hopeful cadet cut
short in mid-prospect. Let us hear about the great wooden
ships whose approach was signalled by a blue flag at Malabar
Point: the *Grosvenor*, the *Lord Camden*, the *Scaleby Castle*, the
Hindostan. Let us meet those potentates their captains, along
with great merchants, writers, collectors, and persons with
famous names: Wellesley, Lake, Elphinstone, Malcolm.
Let there be a glimpse of the years beyond the Mutiny,
when the Honourable Company had passed away; and then
an end upon some significant modern picture—if we dare, a
coincidence.

Such a tale would not be difficult to put together, and it
would be easy enough to invent the family that should be
the peg for the panorama, the string for the beaded events.
But it would not be necessary. Very many such families
exist; and to the annals of one of them, John Bellasis has
been adding as he sits on his veranda penning with a quill
that treacle-coloured handwriting.

It is to be tried whether those worn old slips of letter-paper will be accepted as tickets of admission to the past. . . .

> *Unfathomable sea, and time, and tears,*
> *The deeds of heroes and the crimes of kings*
> *Dispart us. . . .*

II

BELLASIS AND BOMBAY

"THE Portugalls have choused us, it seems, in the
island of Bombay, in the East Indys," observes
Mr. Samuel Pepys, in May, 1662; "for after a great
charge of our fleets being sent thither with full commission
from the King of Portugall to receive it, the Governour, by
some pretence or other, will not deliver it to Sir Abraham
Shipman, sent from the King . . . which the King takes
highly ill, and I fear our Queen will fare the worse for it."

With the other moiety of the swart little Queen's dowry,
Tangier, Mr. Pepys was to be much intermixed; and by the
beginning of '64, his labours upon the Tangier committee
had brought him acquaintance with John, Lord Bellasis,
who was to be the new Governor. He records elatedly that
he was "accosted and most highly complimented" by that
nobleman—"and I may make good use of it". A few days
later, when he called to pay his respects at the Bellasis house
in Lincoln's Inn Fields, my Lord was even more gracious.
Pepys was soon dining with him at the Sun tavern, and
hearing tales about the Civil War.

Bombay and the Bellasis family, which thus enter together
upon Mr. Pepys's stage, were destined to be linked for the
better part of the next three hundred years, now by freakish
coincidence, now by the closest of lifelong ties.

The glories of the East Indies were brought home to
Pepys when he went down to Erith to inspect a captured
Dutch East Indiaman: "My Lord Brouncker and Sir
Edmund Pooly carried me down into the hold of the India
shipp, and there did show me the greatest wealth lie in
confusion that a man can see in the world. Pepper scattered
through every chink, you trod upon it; and in cloves and
nutmegs I walked above the knees; whole rooms full. And

silk in bales . . . as noble a sight as ever I saw in my life."
There was a tale also of eight bags of diamonds and rubies
"taken from about the Dutch Vice-Admirall's neck".
Obviously, any additional foothold in the Indies was
desirable; Bombay might yet prove a grand acquisition,
though an island so poor and sandy, unhealthy and unprofitable, to all seeming, that most persons continued to think
that England had been sold a very bad bargain—"choused
by the Portugalls"—even when put into undisputed
possession. The current jeer:

> *Three things to be seen,*
> *Dunkirk, Tangier, and a barren Queen—*

might well have named Bombay, for nobody accounted
much of the place.

As for the Governor of Tangier, John Bellasis was fifty
years old when Pepys began to serve under him, and was
also Captain-General of the Forces in Africa, Captain of the
King's Guard of Gentlemen Pensioners, Governor of Hull,
and Lieutenant of the East Riding of Yorkshire. He came of
an ancient family in the North Country, which in the
previous few generations had acquired great possessions
and been ennobled, but had made no mark on the page of
history until the wars between the King and the Parliament.
Suddenly then the name of Bellasis came into the histories
and memoirs, no two agreeing how to spell it. John spelt
it "Belasyse", in an admirable clear handwriting, more like
a scholar than the soldier that he was; but it was also spelt at
different times in a score of other ways, from Belasius,
Bellysse, Bellizes, to Belas, Bellers, and Bellowciss—this
last in a deed where "interchangeably" is spelt "inter-
chaungehablye".

However spelt, the name was clearly good Norman
French, as was the family motto: *"Bon est Bel Assez"*: "Good
and Beautiful Enough"; while the arms, argent a chevron
and three fleurs de lys azure, had the simplicity of all early
coats. Indeed, the founder of the family had come to

England with Duke William and carved himself with his sword a portion of the County Durham. In that remote and barbarous country between Tyne and Wear, a country of rude speech, old songs, long traditions, grey stones, hard knocks and hard riding in Border foray, the Bellasis family flourished and spread. Of their stronghold of Bellasis, and the town about it, nothing would remain in future centuries but some indestructible walls converted to the uses of a farmhouse, a grassy trace of moat, a vague memory, and a persistent tale of hauntings. Then would come the roaring tide of industrialism, and these relics would be drowned in Middlesbrough. Beauly, Wolveston, Houghton-le-Spring, Henknoll, and other manors of the Bishopric, were early in Bellasis hands; under Wolsey the butcher's son, and Henry the butcher, would come manors too many to name, and an abbey. Pending that time, however, Sir Ralph followed Sir Rowland, and Sir Robert followed Sir William, and Sir Brian followed Sir Roger, doing their knightly duty, putting on their armour at the behest of their feudal lords, and marrying their neighbours' daughters—Lambton and Strickland, Smythe and Thirkeld ladies, very commonly named Margaret. It was the second Sir Rowland who married the heiress of Houghton-le-Spring, in the reign of Henry III; he got his spurs at Simon de Montfort's victory of Lewes; and in the church of Houghton-le-Spring he lies in stone, armed, with praying hands. It was Sir John Bellasis who, being commanded to take the crusade, exchanged all his lands of Bellasis and Wolveston for those of Henknoll, held of Durham Abbey—so bad a bargain that a rough country distich was made upon it:

> *Johnny t' th' Bellas',*
> *Daft was thy powle*
> *When thou changed Bellas' for Henknowle!'*

At Henknoll, then, the family continued, living quietly under the grey northern skies, without glory or infamy, until the advent of the brothers Richard and Anthony

Bellasis, who may be considered to have brought it both. For neither of these gentlemen was at all daft in the poll; and between them they got a whacking share of the plunder when Henry VIII robbed the Church. Anthony, the younger, was a Doctor of Laws and a Master in Chancery; his pen cut better than his ancestor's sword, for he—"prudent, wary man", says Surtees—was the true founder of the family fortunes. He was one of the Council of the North, and also one of the King's commissioners for the visitation of religious houses. He and his brother stripped the lead off the roof of Jervaulx Abbey, and sold it for a goodly price; and Newborough Abbey, at Coxwold, in the fattest, fairest part of Yorkshire, fell into his clutch entire. He died with "vast estates" to leave to his nephew William, Richard's eldest son, who had succeeded his father at seventeen. Richard had not done so badly; he also had been of the Council of the North; Wolsey had granted him the Manor and Grange of Great Morton, Co. Durham, and he had eight or nine other manors in Durham and in Westmorland, besides Henknoll. Thus at a stroke, and in one generation, the family became immensely rich, and of corresponding importance in their country. At least, however, they were well-born, unlike some of the promoted tapsters who made that era one of "so many gentlemen and so little gentleness"; and Sir William (knighted when High Sheriff of Yorkshire, during the 1564 visitation of Philip and Mary) underlined the fact by having his tomb at Coxwold adorned with a series of shields forming a complete heraldic pedigree from Norman times. He married a Fairfax, and so did his heir, Sir Henry, the first baronet, who kneels with his wife very handsomely in marble in York Minster.

The long lifetime of William Bellasis, who lived to be eighty-one, not dying until 1604, had seen the family firmly settled into Newborough. The countryside—that countryside which had risen so bravely against these changes, under the banner of the Five Wounds, and been so cruelly cheated by the King—must have thought Anthony Bellasis to be

certainly damned on his departure; but by the time William
occupied his heraldic tomb, murmurs about the curse on
Church lands must have died down. Moreover, despite the
tightening of the Cecil screw, the priest-hunting pursui-
vants, executions and fines, the Bellasis family held to the
Old Faith, with whatever politic veerings and tackings.

Newborough being now their principal seat, Morton, in
the parish of Houghton-le-Spring, was reserved for a
younger line, stemming from Bryan, the brother of Sir
Henry, along with lands across the Westmorland border.
It is under Elizabeth that we first find a Bellasis—Stephen—
at Marton in Westmorland: called Long Marton, to distinguish it from Morton and Murton, both nearby. Over
the Cecilian persecutions, and the Civil Wars of the subsequent generation, the Long Marton records are somewhat
confused; but the George Bellasis who took possession
during the Commonwealth may have been the sixth and
youngest son of Sir William of Morton House, and seems
to have been heavily fined as a recusant.

The name was grown familiar in the recusant lists, and
also among Royalist composition papers: for no sooner
had King Charles raised his standard against the Parliament
than almost every Bellasis had ridden to draw the sword for
him. Sir William and his sons received the King in 1633, at
the head of the gentry of Durham; they melted down their
plate, and came cheerfully close to ruining themselves.
Meanwhile, Sir William's first cousin at Newborough,
Sir Thomas the second baronet, was created Baron Fauconberg of Yarm, for his faithful adherence to the King, and
presently advanced to be a Viscount. He was a good deal
too rich and grand to be ruined; but along with his great
friend, that remarkable character the old Marquess of
Newcastle, he was forced to flee the country after Marston
Moor. He, however, died at Coxwold at the age of seventy-
five, three years after the killing of his King, and was
succeeded by a grandson, for his elder son had predeceased
him. In addition to numerous daughters, all married to

irreproachably Royalist and Catholic husbands, old Thomas
had one other son—that John Bellasis whom Pepys was to
serve, and who was to be ennobled on his own account,
as Baron Bellasis of Worlaby.

To retrace all that John Bellasis did for the Royal cause,
after raising six regiments of horse and foot and being
placed in command of a Tertia of the Royal Army, would
be to fight the Civil Wars over. He was at every battle; he
held Newark, he held York, after the famous quarrel with
Prince Rupert; and he made a name as a gallant and
chivalrous cavalry leader—with only the persistent draw-
back of being very unlucky. What he felt about his nephew's
marriage, in 1657, is not recorded, but can be guessed: for
young Thomas, second Viscount Fauconberg, espoused
"with great pomp" Mary Cromwell, the Protector's third
daughter.

Cromwell, for his part, had no exceeding trust in the
noble and gentle husbands whom he had hastened to secure
for his daughters; he had them married, not only by his
official rites, but also privily by ordained clergy; agreeing
with that Independent minister who saw his daughter
married with Prayer Book and ring as "he was loath to have
her whored and turned back upon him for want of a legal
marriage".

Clarendon observes that the Protector's "domestic
delights were lessened every day, he plainly discovered that
his son Fauconberg's heart was set upon an interest destruc-
tive to his own, and grew to hate him perfectly". Worse
than a Royalist son-in-law was a Royalist daughter: Mary
felt as did her sister, Mrs. Claypole. Beautiful and very
spirited, Lady Fauconberg would have made a far better
successor to her father than did her wretched brother
"Tumbledown Dick": "According to a saying that went of
her," says Bishop Burnet, "that those who wore breeches
deserved petticoats better, but if those in petticoats had been
in breeches, they would have held faster." She is credited

with securing her father's head after the Restoration, for safe and secret keeping at Newborough; but she certainly did a great deal to bring the Restoration about. It was, however, her husband who was hustled into the Tower by the Committee of Public Safety, and subsequently loaded with honours too many to mention by the restored Charles.

Pepys notes these public figures very often: Lady Fauconberg at the play, in a vizard; Lord Fauconberg positively wallowing in Court favour. Somehow, the portrait of Thomas Bellasis, arrogant, pop-eyed, over-weighted with an immense periwig, does not please the beholder like that of his Uncle John—painted by Vandyke as a young cavalry leader. To be sure, Vandyke always made his sitters look noble; and the long fair face of John, Lord Bellasis, handsome and solemn, with his own fair hair curling down upon lace cravat and armour, suggests the perfection of chivalry. With unswerving firmness, John had kept to his religion; Fauconberg had not. It could not be pleasant for the uncle to see the apostate nephew, who had actually mingled his blood with that of the regicide, far more caressed at Court than himself. Perhaps John's face was too long for that Court, and his character too irreproachable; at least, the several formal posts of honour which he would have to resign upon the passing of the Test Act in 1673 were poor requital for a lifetime's arduous service. He was to receive further requital in his old age: five years in prison. When Father Huddlestone was smuggled in to shrive the dying Charles at last, a heavy item in the King's confession must have concerned the guiltless Catholics whose lives and liberties were sacrificed to Titus Oates in 1678.

Before that time, tragedy had removed John Bellasis' eldest and only surviving son, Sir Harry Bellasis, who was in many respects unsatisfactory. Although M.P. for Grimsby, he was a ruffling courtier, and had already con-trived to get himself tried for murder—having, with other gentlemen, pursued and slain a guiltless tanner whom they mistook for a highwayman. He had also married a girl, Susan Armine, from a Protestant and Parliamentary family. Pepys records the manner of his death—horrid, dramatic, ridiculous, but undeniably with a certain touch of nobility— in a duel with his best friend, Tom Porter, after they had been drinking together, and had quarrelled about nothing at all. ". . . finding himself severely wounded, he called to Tom Porter, and kissed him, and bade him shift for himself, 'for', says he, 'Tom, thou hast hurt me; but I will make shift to stand upon my legs till thou mayest withdraw, and the world not take notice of you, for I would not have thee troubled for what thou hast done'. And so whether he did fly or no, I cannot tell; and Tom Porter showed H. Bellassis that he was wounded too; and they are both ill, but H. Bellassis to fear of life. And this is a fine example!" Having enjoyed both the drama and the moralising, Pepys later finishes: "Sir Henry Bellassis is dead of the duell he fought about ten days ago, with Tom Porter; and it is pretty to see how the world talk of them as a couple of fools that killed one another out of love . . ." One cannot suppose a more literally bloody silly case; and yet there is that touch of the noble.

Harry Bellasis left behind him one little boy, who was to inherit the title of Bellasis of Worlaby, and extinguish it by himself dying childless; and an ambitious widow. Susan Bellasis was reputed both witty and learned, but all authorities agree that she had no beauty at all: nor can the conventionally flattered portrait by Lely at Hampton Court contradict this. She was thus excellently fitted to become mistress to James, Duke of York; for it will be remembered that Charles always vowed his brother's mistresses were so ugly that they must be imposed as a penance by his confessor. Poor James, most temperate in other matters, had found his fatal addiction to Court harpies most weakening to the mind. Nothing but doting weakness could have induced him to give Susan Bellasis, as he did, a written promise of marriage. At the same time, he strove to make her a Catholic: efforts which Susan ostentatiously withstood —like Nell Gwyn when hooted in mistake for Louise de Kerouaile, she might have exclaimed, "Good people, I am the Protestant whore!"

All this was most dismaying to Lord Bellasis. If nobody else at Court liked his long face and high principles, the Duke of York did so: the two men were great friends. The old Cavalier could not see his master ensnared by a woman who was probably a tool of the Protestant party, without great perturbation. Meanwhile, the violent and well-subsidised propaganda against James spattered every Catholic at Court; a particular pasquinade, too dull and too dirty to quote, attacked John Bellasis: "This Hero once got Honour by the Sword"—and had lost it by turning pimp. Nothing could be more unjust; so far from having elevated his daughter-in-law to her position of favour, it seems to have been Bellasis who tumbled her down from it, by informing the King of the secret marriage contract. Charles sent for his brother, and told him—as Burnet unkindly phrases it—"That it was too much to have played the fool once: that it was not to be done again, and at such an age." The lady, although "recalcitrant", was induced to give up her bond, and consoled by being made a peeress in her own right. She married a Page of the Backstairs; and James married Mary of Modena.

Four years later, Bedloe and Oates, the worst rogues who ever dirtied the page of a history book, fed the British public its fill of calumnies; judicial murder was done; and five Catholic Lords, Arundell of Wardour, Powys, Stafford, Petre, and Bellasis, were clapped into the tower. Oates had named Lord Bellasis as the proposed leader of a Catholic Army. As he was now sixty-four, and nearly crippled with gout, my Lord was as little fit for the battlefield as he was for the amenities of the Tower. It did not, however, kill him, as it did Petre, though he and his fellow victims, impeached without trial, were kept in prison until 1683; except Stafford, who was beheaded.

What amends James could make when he came to the throne, he did make, and John Bellasis became his First Lord Commissioner of the Treasury. Fauconberg, who was openly disaffected, was disgraced. Then the see-saw swung again, nephew up and uncle down: the little Dutch usurper was invited over, James must flee, Thomas Bellasis was made Earl Fauconberg, and John Bellasis went home to die: 1689 was no year for public tribute to his virtues. Not until the new century was well come in did his two surviving daughters, Barbara Webb and Catherine Talbot, raise a marble monument at St. Giles-in-the-Fields to commemorate the "Loyalty, Prudence, and Courage" of the man who had lived and died for his Faith and his King.

So the Stuart era goes by, in a drumming of cavalry charges, a glitter of steel and hatred, a wanton riot of satin and flesh and pearls, an intricacy of treachery, nobility, tragedy, and Mr. Pepys's shorthand. For the Bellasis family of Morton House, Co. Durham, it left nothing behind it but an autographed letter from Charles II acknowledging that they had ruined themselves in the Royal cause.

Morton was sold, coming finally to the Lambtons. Under Queen Anne, the head of that branch took up his sword, commanded a regiment at the taking of Vigo, and became a general in Marlborough's wars. At the same time, two cadets of the family, Thomas and Charles, having no fortune to inherit, set out to make one. They went to Bombay.

In 1668, King Charles had been glad to hand this doubtful bargain over to the East India Company. It was the only territory which the English ruled, as distinct from "factories" in the domain of native princes; and it was in a state of disease and decline. Ovington sketched it in 1689: "The island lies in about Nineteen Degrees North, in which is a Fort, which is the Defence of it, flanked and Lined according to the Rules of Art, and secured with many Pieces of Ordinance, which command the Harbours and the parts adjoining. In this one of the Company's Factors always resides, who is appointed Governor to inspect and manage the Affairs of the Island; and who is vested with an authority in Civil as well as Military Matters, to see that the several Companies of Soldiers who are here as well as the Factors and Merchants attend their various Stations and their respective Charge. The Island is likewise beautified with several elegant Dwellings of the English and neat Apartments of the Portuguese, to whom is permitted the free exercise of their religion." At that time, the trade of the place had suffered very badly from Sir J. Child's injudicious attempt to wage single-handed war with the Great Mogul; the English population had been literally decimated, there were "not above sixty left by the Sword and Plague", and only one horse and two oxen among them. Matters mended in the course of another decade or so; but still the ground was sterile, the water scarce, and the air unhealthy—mostly owing to the local custom of manuring the coconut trees with stinking buckshoe fish. The vapours which steamed up at morning and evening, with a choking smell of fish-glue and corruption, were at their worst in September and October, after the rains, when Europeans were observed to die most generally. Hence came the saying that "Two Monsoons are the life of a man".

The crowded groves of these fish-manured toddy trees produced so rich a crop of coconuts that the merchants were very reluctant to make any damaging changes. As for the mortality, to be sure—"They drink very strong Portugall wines at the hottest time of day"—and—"The Common Distemper that destroys the most in *India* is Feavers, which the *Europeans* with difficulty escape, especially if they have boil'd up their Spirits by solemn Repast and been ingag'd in a strong Debauch."

Whether or not this was the case with Charles Bellasis, Writer and Factor, he fades from record at once. Thomas, however, is secure of all the immortality to be attained by having his name in Governor Aislabie's subscription list for the building of Bombay Church, later St. Thomas's

Cathedral. Of course, there had been a Christian church in Bombay for many generations, but it had been built for the saying of Mass. Still "permitted" as this was, the doorway of the Catholic Cathedral, also dedicated to the Apostle of the Indies, must be passed with head-shaking, and a condemnatory sniff at the incense. As it is more than probable that Thomas Bellasis had been bred up to go to Mass, he may have been bowing in the house of Rimmon when he gave in his subscription of Rs.40, or £5, towards the English church. However, he was a middle-aged man at the time, and must have known what he was about. For so pious a confederation—and in Bombay Castle, as in the factories of Madras, Surat, and Calcutta the Company's servants held prayers twice a day—the neglect to complete a suitable building for public worship was surprising. Probably it was intended to show a superiority to vain ornament that St. Thomas's Church was such a plain barn when Governor Oxenden set it up originally; but it then had languished unfinished for many years, a blot on Bombay Green, affording shelter to rogues after dark, and disgracing the prosperous merchants. At length, the Rev. Mr. Cobbe, the chaplain, made a truly fervent appeal for funds, and Governor Aislabie headed the subscription list. Perforce, the Senior and Junior Merchants, the Factors and the Writers, all contributed according to their position. In 1718, the improved church was opened, adorned with the oyster-shell windows which were considered to filter the light with agreeable coolness, and with a floor of stamped cow-dung. Everyone went after service to a feast of celebration in the Castle, with music; and a salute of twenty-one guns was fired, answered by the ships in the harbour.

Thomas Bellasis, having contributed his forty rupees, is no more heard of. If he scraped together his little pile of Indian gold, he never lived to carry it home to the North. He, it would seem, wagered his bones against the golden stake, and lost, and left them in the dusty little settlement, where the sea sounds for ever at the base of Bombay Castle.

Elvaeal Pinxt

THOMAS BELASYSE, VISCOUNT FAUCONBERG.
Born 1577, Died 1652.

John Lord Belasyse.
From an Original by Van Dyck.

SUSAN, LADY BELLASIS
from an engraving after the portrait by Lely.

While Bombay, the Company's Cinderella, awaited its
eventual recognition, in the due revolvement of time and
season, as the true gateway of India, Madras flourished
extremely under the rule of that superb "Interloper",
Thomas Pitt; and in 1721, Governor Pitt married a son to a
Bellasis lady.

The Company had been fighting Thomas Pitt for twenty
years before it gave in, and bribed him into its service
with the Governorship of Madras; and then it was not
able to stand his "haughty, huffying, daring temper" for
very long. Ever since he, the younger son of a younger son,
born at a Blandford parsonage, had set out to seek fortune
in the Indies as an illicit merchant, an "Interloper", that
daring and that temper had had full rein. "A roughling
immoral man", protested some of the stock-holders weakly,
when the Company handed over Fort St. George to him in
1698. There, in kingly state, under a scarlet umbrella, with
a personal guard of 400 blacks, fifes, drums, trumpets, and
his own flag, he received the emissaries of the Great Mogul.
In his high-handed way, he governed very well until the
year 1709, when he carried his enormous wealth back to
England, sending the famous Pitt Diamond ahead of him,
concealed in the heel of his son's shoe—although there are
two family portraits of himself, one with the Diamond in his
own shoe, and one with it in his hat. This "great concern",
as he calls it, this notable gew-gaw, he had acquired for
£48,000, and later sold to the Regent of Orleans for the
French Crown.

It hall-marked him, he was "Diamond Pitt", the first and
most famous Nabob to buy with his Eastern spoils English
lands and political influence—and thereby to change English
history. In his great descendants, Chatham, and "Young
Mr. Pitt", the strain of genius which the old Governor
undoubtedly possessed burst into full blaze; but the strain
of madness which also undoubtedly burnt in that blood
came out repeatedly in others of the family. They were a
volcanic breed, and he the most so. His letters from India

to his squabbling sons and daughters were hardly calculated to make peace among them. "Have all of you shook
hands with shame," he bellowed, "that you regard not any
of the tyes of Christianity, humanity, consanguinity, duty,
good morality, or anything that makes you differ from
beasts, but must run from one end of the kingdome to the
other, aspersing one another, and aiming at the ruin and
destruction of one another?" "Not only your letters but all
I have from friends are stuffed with an account of the hellish
confusion that is in my family." To his eldest son, Robert,
he writes, on suspicion of Jacobitism: "It is said you are
taken up with factious caballs, and are contriving amongst
you to put a French kickshaw upon the throne again."

The Governor was indeed a furious Whig, and would
never have permitted his third son, John, to marry Mary
Bellasis, sister of Lord Fauconberg, if that nobleman had
not conclusively demonstrated his devotion to the house of
Hanover—and been rewarded for it. The earldom conferred by Dutch William had lapsed, as Thomas Bellasis had
got no children by Mary Cromwell; he had died in 1700, and
been succeeded in the viscounty and estates by the eldest
son of his brother Rowland. Now, Rowland had not
apostatised, and had spent most of his life on his mother's
estate of Smithells in Lancashire, which was honeycombed
with priest's-holes; of his sons and daughters, Anne became
a nun, of the English Dames at Pontoise, Rowland married
a daughter of Christopher Roper, Lord Teynham, and
Thomas, the heir, married a daughter of another great
Catholic house, Gage of Firle. Both the Gages and the
Ropers were going to conform, pretty soon; and when this
Thomas died abroad—significantly soon after the failure of
the 1715 Jacobite rising—his eldest son, another Thomas,
thought it best to make his own allegiance to George I
quite plain. Subsequently abjuring his religion, he received
the same reward that his great-uncle had once received, and
was made an earl. He was also to enjoy the happiness of
being Lord of the Bedchamber to King George II.

This Lord Fauconberg's sister Mary is recorded by the Pitt family biographer to have been a young woman "whose personal talents and accomplishments distinguished her as much at least as her birth, and much more than her virtues". She was probably quite virtuous enough for John Pitt, who was the black sheep of that singular flock: "An amiable vaurien, a personal favourite with the King, and indeed with all who knew him as a sort of Comte de Gramont, who contrived to sacrifice his health, his honour, his fortunes, to a flow of libertinism which dashed the fairest prospect, and sank him for many years before his death in contempt and obscurity." When John was at home, Governor Pitt slept with the keys under his pillow; one understands why, on hearing how John replenished his purse on one occasion. Upon a day when an agent was due from the country with rents, John waited outside his father's house in Pall Mall: watched the agent in and out: thrust his own way into the presence of the secretary or steward who was counting the gold: swept it all with his sword into his hat, and escaped, laughing heartily. When Thomas Pitt died in 1726, he bequeathed nothing at all to his son John, stating explicitly that that was what he was worth.

One more purely coincidental link with the island of Bombay belongs to this generation. Lord Fauconberg was, of course, the patron of Coxwold living, and he had conferred it upon the Rev. Laurence Sterne: though he might have been affronted to learn that this was his sole claim to the notice of posterity. Yorick, up from Yorkshire to court and be courted by the fashionable great in London, was to die miserably in a London lodging in 1768, alone but for somebody's footman who had dropped in with his master's inquiries; but six years earlier, the parson with the skull-like face and the febrile, unhealthy genius burning in his eyes, had met with the last of his Platonic paramours, Eliza Draper, his fair *Brahmine*. Enthusiasts for Sterne and his works, particularly the French, who made as much fuss about him as they earlier had done about Richardson, were to gush over Eliza's birthplace at Anjengo, the remote factory where also had been born Orme, historian of India; also over her haunts in Bombay, where she had shone at assemblies as the young wife of a rich elderly merchant. Perhaps it would have been better for Eliza if she had never come to England in '62 and entered the hothouse atmosphere of the Rev. Laurence Sterne's devotion. The experience of being his soul-mate seems to have made her as dissatisfied with her own loveless marriage as he always professed himself with his; for when she was got back to India, she eloped from her merchant—who had set up an unplatonic female friend—with the first man who came along. She died in Bristol in 1778, but her pensive, too-romantic shade seems to hover about old Bombay.

Sterne's patron died at Newborough in 1774, and was succeeded by his only surviving son, for two had died in childhood. Henry Bellasis was fifth baron, fifth viscount, second and last earl of the new creation. He was, of course, bred up a Protestant, though his sisters made Catholic marriages; and he was a special favourite of George III—they were of the same age. He had been made to marry suitably, in 1766, although he was badly in love—as that old Court gossip, Mrs. Papendieck, tells us—with a certain Miss Cheshyre. Poor Miss Cheshyre's chances of marriage had not been increased by one of her sisters having stooped to folly and very properly died of it; and Henry was forced away into the well-dowered embrace of Charlotte Lamb, sister of the first Lord Melbourne. The Lambs of Brocket Hall were of no family, but they had a great deal of money. In four-and-twenty years of matrimony, however, Charlotte gave her husband only daughters, four of them; and when she died in 1790, he waited but six months before marrying his early love. A quarter of a century is a long time; they were not happy years, for a younger sister—perhaps resembling what my Lady had once been—seduced my Lord's affections.

Whether such example had any effect upon my Lord's daughter Elizabeth cannot be said, but in 1789 she had been married to Bernard Edward Howard, the Duke of Norfolk's heir: and in 1794 she eloped from that gentleman with Lord Lucan. Bernard Howard—"Barney"—does not cut a very pleasing figure in Creevey's pages; but then Creevey, though he lacks Greville's cold sniff, took a poor view of so many people. The marriage was probably one of convenience, because a Howard must have a Catholic bride. The particulars are not worth retracing; suffice it that she was divorced, in the usual costly and elaborate manner, by Act of Parliament; and was enabled to marry Lord Lucan, and give him two sons and four daughters.

Elizabeth Bellasis was thus, in a way, responsible for some of the worst disasters of the Crimean War, for the succeeding Lord Lucan, her son, together with his brother-in-law, Lord Cardigan, bungled that command in a way at which history still shudders.

She was certainly responsible for the continuation of the noble line of Howard, for she had left an heir behind her, who was to succeed his father as thirteenth duke. She had thus, at least, done better than her mother: Henry Bellasis, dying in 1802, saw his earldom become extinct, and his estates descend to his eldest daughter Charlotte, whose husband, Thomas Wynne, had consented to take her name. But no more Bellasis' were to reign at Newborough, even by this expedient: Charlotte had no children, and must leave all to her nephew, the Yorkshire baronet Sir George Wombwell, son of her sister Anne.

The barony and the viscounty of Fauconberg died out also, for they went to two elderly second cousins, of the branch which had been living in France for the free practice of their religion. The first, Rowland Bellasis, never had married; the second, who outlived his brother by five years, dying in 1815, was a priest. With this Abbé Charles Bellasis, D.D. of the Sorbonne, "all these ancient honours became extinct", as one record puts it.

There had been talk about a curse—the curse that comes of snatching Church property:

> For evil hands have Abbey lands
> Such evil fate in store;
> Such is the heritage that waits
> Church robbers, evermore.

Those who cared for old stories, and the countryside in general, for such memories are long in the North, could look back upon the cumulative ill-luck of many generations —so many barren marriages, so many dead children: titles and lands going down cater-cornered to nephews and cousins: the double extinction of the earldom that had twice been bought at such a price: the career of John Bellasis, for all its gallantry and distinction marked *Infelix*: Thomas Bellasis, for all his full-blown prosperity, getting no heir from the bride who had brought the head of the regicide to Newborough. . . . In the new century, there was to be no Bellasis left at Newborough, only the posturing marble figures above the Fauconberg tombs in Coxwold church— wearing Roman habits, with full marble periwigs.

True it is that families do go up and down; perhaps it was not extremely remarkable that the family of Bellasis, once so numerous and flourishing in three or four counties, should dwindle and ebb, first from one and then another. With the sale of Brancepeth Castle, by the last Viscount—this having come down through a daughter of the junior line, being once part of the Tudor acquisitions—the name vanished out of its original county of Durham, and was only left about the Palatinate here and there: in monuments and brasses, distich and ballad, in the name of a bridge, or the site of a cross.

But in Westmorland, the name persisted, with the younger branch of a younger branch, which had taken root at Long Marton about the time when the senior branch began to rise in the world like a well-flown kite. And in 1768: when the famous incumbent of Coxwold was dying:

when Henry Bellasis had got two disappointing daughters of his loveless marriage: when the Abbé Charles was a young priest: when Warren Hastings was applying to Robert Clive for a reappointment to the Company's service, stating through a friend that "he must return to India, or want bread": young John Bellasis of Long Marton set out for Bombay, with the aim of retrieving his family's fortunes and making his own.

III

THE THREE BROTHERS

"BEYOND the farthest parts of Lancashire, more northward lyeth another lesser country of the Brigantes, called by modern Latin writers West-moria and Westmorlandia, in our tongue Westmoreland. The air in winter especially is a little sharp and piercing, yet very healthful; the soil for a great part of it is but barren, being full of great moors and high mountains, called in the North Fells, yet there are many fruitful valleys in it, abounding with good arable meadows and pasture ground, and commended for plenty of corn and cattle. . . . Its division according to the temporal government therefor is into two great baronys, the one being divided from the other by a ridge of mountains, our Appenine growing here broader, through which there are three common but not very good passes, called Grayrigg Hawes, Crookdale Hawse, and Kirk-stone, containing the south part of the country called Kendal Barony." Thus Sir Daniel Fleming, in the seventeenth century, concerning his native county.

The families tucked up in this back pocket of England were long as notoriously Jacobite and Catholic as their Lancashire neighbours. The Flemings themselves, the Stricklands, the Parrs, the Bellinghams, the Leyburns, were no strangers to harboured priests; and neither, we may suppose, was the household of Long Marton. The ennobled portion of the Bellasis family had made its own compromises, sons being reared as Protestants, daughters being encouraged to add the family name to the records of Radcliffe, Petre, Stonor, Gage, Talbot, Neville, Roper, Eyre, and Howard. Moreover, however publicly Protestant the Lords Fauconberg, they maintained Catholic chaplains for the women of the family, and for the country congregations which clustered about the chapels of great houses, and which were doomed to miserable extinction as one by one these families conformed. And perhaps Mr. So-and-so, the chaplain, in his sober lay clothes, would be finally summoned to the death-bed of more than one Protestant master of the house.

For the small gentry, however, matters were more difficult. The Penal Laws had been devised with the greatest ingenuity to take order that there should be no Catholic gentry, and to begin that immense gap, to be apparent in later generations, between those who were too great to be successfully persecuted and those who were too small to be worth the trouble: so that Catholics would presently display no medium between dukes and hod-carriers. When a squire of middling means has to pay double land-tax and a quantity of nagging fines, at the same time being forbidden to ride a proper horse, or wear a sword like other gentlemen, or to push his fortunes in the army, the navy, or the law, or even to become a physician or a schoolmaster—the day comes when he gives up either his Papistry or his gentility.

It was a system which achieved large and lasting effects in Ireland, of course; and in England, together with the dynastic wars, it caused many of the best names in the Catholic north to be found among mechanics and artisans. The Bellasis family seems, despite all, to have been fairly fortunate in this regard. Weavers and innkeepers of the name of Bellas', descended of the youngest sons of who knows which youngest sons, come vaguely into view in the eighteenth and nineteenth centuries; but the Long Marton inheritance passed down unmolested from generation to generation. No doubt there was a little contrivance; the family would go quietly to Marton or Appleby Church, and as quietly hear Mass when they got the chance; they could probably find a schoolmaster of similar sympathies; their neighbours understood them. If they might not make a great figure in the world, it is likely that they did not wish

to do so. Their ancestral fields for the tilling, the sheep on
the fell, the round of the seasons, the little grey towns of
Appleby and Kendal, must quite suffice them. The George
Bellasis whose seventeenth-century will is preserved was
pious enough: "I bequeath my soule into ye handes of
Allmighty God, my Maker, hopeing for salvation through
ye merits of Jesus Christ, my onely Savior and Redeemer."

Their manner of living at Long Marton must have been
plain and primitive as that of their original ancestors in the
little stone towers or unfortified manors of the misty past.
Over the Border, they would have been bonnet-lairds;
under Dufton Pike the distinction between squire and
yeoman was so vague that most of the local families wrote
themselves indifferently either. As to pedigree, the Flemings,
Stricklands, and Maudes, with whom they intermarried, had
as long a one as any Bellasis; and other neighbouring names
had been there when the Normans came and built Marton
Church. Nobody troubled about display; there was probably no piece of silver greater than a seal at Long Marton
with the family crest upon it—as there certainly was not at
Morton, after the melting-down for the King's cause.
When a new house was to be built, for the benefit of George
Bellasis, who had married Elizabeth Furnas of Dufton, no
arms were placed above the door, but only the initials of the
couple, and the date 1715. It was a long grey stone building,
a plain fell farmhouse; and though it contained a muniment
chest full of Tudor parchments and the like, these were
seldom disturbed. Joseph, the only son of George and
Elizabeth, began even to write his name Bellas'. This con-
traction had been always common, as witness the fourteenth-
century distich about "Johnny t' th' Bellas'"; and in all
probability it was usual to clip oneself in common country
speech, and sign oneself at full length in any document,
with whatever variation of spelling. A son of Sir Thomas
of Morton signed himself "Hen: Bellas" in 1642; and there
were documents at Long Marton signed "Bellas" and en-
dorsed by a cautious lawyer "Bellasis".

Howbeit, Joseph Bellas', Gent., born 1691, was the first to send a son to Oxford: clear measure of the fact that the family had no longer any secret Popery about it. The lad, of course, went to Queen's College, like all Westmorland men, and like his Furnas cousins. His mother was Margaret Hill of Crackenthorpe, in Bongate parish; and her uncle and brother were both Fellows of Queen's.

It is with the children of Joseph and Margaret that we have here to do. They were married in December, 1727, and had a daughter, Elizabeth, a year later: she would grow up to marry the Rector of Dufton, and live to be ninety years old. Then, in 1730, they had a fine boy named George; then three girls in succession—Emma, destined to marry the Rev. Nathaniel Springett, of Goring, Co. Oxon., B.A.; Hannah, who married a Crosby of Kirkby Thore; and Margaret, who married Cousin Hill of Crackenthorpe. At length came two more sons: Hugh, born January, 1740; and John, born July 16th, 1743.

Two of the sons, it was settled, were to be bred for professions, and one was to inherit the estate—diminished by the dower of sisters and the education of brothers. The parts and talents of the eldest early marked him as fitted to distinguish himself in the world beyond little Westmorland, and there were prospects for him of preferment in the Church. The youngest should be a soldier; and the middle son, plain plodding Hugh, should have the land.

Probably heads were shaken, and the North Country proverb quoted that when once land is left away from the eldest, all goes wrong; but as the boys grew up, the arrangement jumped well with their inclinations. George, so much the senior, must have thought the meagre heritage of a Westmorland squire well lost for Oxford and London. At eighteen he left for his three days' journey south to matriculate at Queen's: he was very tall, very handsome, and must have seemed incredibly old and important in the eyes of six-year-old John, to whom he had always been another father.

He would one day speed the younger to India with a most stately letter of fatherly advice. Meanwhile, one supposes John a sturdy little urchin, silent but bright-eyed, noticing and thinking. Plainly, beyond Kirkstone Pass, beyond those mountains—"magnificently rude", as tasteful people began to say—lay another and most different world.

John was to go south himself to finish the education which Appleby Grammar School began; but the Westmorland childhood never left his memory or his heart, as the Westmorland burr never entirely left his tongue. The long grey house with the stone mullioned casements, the pollard trees along the courtyard wall and the green before it, the arched gateway to the stables and farmyard, the neighbouring thatched cottages, the horsepond and the pack-road, the trout-stream and the fields and the fell-pasture, and Dufton Pike—here would always be home for him. In the stone-floored kitchen the boy would beg for buttered sops or curds-and-cream, or jump for joy at the visit of the ginger-bread-seller. Beside the keeping-room hearth in winter he might listen to his mother reading aloud, or hear his father's voice engaged in interminable farming discussions about prize-winning "lamb-sucked ewes" and "shearling tups". Then there were the village Merry Nights, with the square eightsome reels and the kissing dances, and all the winter and summer ploys of "so many happy days", which he was to recall from very far away, in years to come.

The principal figure at Long Marton one feels to have been Mrs. Bellas', born Margaret Hill: "my dearest and best of Mothers", as John wrote to her. Margaret Bellasis—as she ought properly to have signed herself—was a notable woman, growing in her old age to be even formidable. She was born with the century, and at past eighty is recorded to have shot at a poacher, and, moreover, jumped a brook. From whomever she inherited the high aquiline nose and resolute mouth to be remarked in her silhouette portrait, she perhaps got some of her spirit from her uncle, the Fellow of Queen's. He was also Rector of Charleton-on-Otmere, but was commonly known as "the Major", from having laid aside his clerical character to become a major in the Oxford University Volunteers at the time of the '45 Rebellion—having no mind for the victory of that Papistical Pretender, Prince Charles Edward.

The Hills were of good Westmorland stock, intermarried with the Machells, the old Lords of Crackenthorpe. They had a long connection with Queen's, and patronage in Oxfordshire and Berkshire. Livings in those fat, fair counties did often fall to sons of the fell, for the Fane family, Earls of Westmorland, had a seat at Basildon and controlled several advowsons. Howbeit, the Hills owned the advowson of Yattenden in Berkshire, which is said to be the "Ethandune" where King Alfred fought the Danes; and the Rev. Benjamin Hill, D.D., Margaret's brother, was Rector there in 1754, and ready to take his nephew George Bellasis as his curate. George had come down from Oxford a Doctor of Divinity, having indeed taken with high credit the degrees of B.A., M.A., B.D., and D.D.

Four years later the Reverend Benjamin resigned the living in George's favour, on the occasion of that young man's marriage, and himself became Vicar of Monk Sherborne in Hampshire. Thither came to him his nephew John Bellasis, now a lad of fifteen, to be polished up in his *Arma virumque cano*.

The whole character and feeling of the countryside just south of Oxford and tending to the south-west edge of England is extremely remote from the pure gauntness, sharp airs and rainy skies of Westmorland. There is a rich peace about the water-meadows by Thames, a rich assemblage of slumberous huge trees in the New Forest, and the rolling dairy country over the Dorset border is richly gilt with buttercups. Here are fine houses and gardens, and noble wealthy towns, surprising to one who has seen no greater place than grey Kendal, with its dye-works and hand-looms. Here with his Uncle Benjamin was to be the home of John Bellasis until he should go to the Indies; and here did he early fall in love with a Dorset girl. Anne Martha Hutchins was the only child of the Rector of Wareham and Swyre, and her portrait proclaims her a beauty, with a deer-like throat, a lovely bosom, and large bright eyes.

This passion must have put the finishing edge upon John's ambitions and resolves. A steady young man, not so tall nor near so handsome as his elder brother, he did secretly entertain such ambitions to even a romantic extent. He knew well that in fitting him out for India his family were taking a ticket in the lottery and expecting him to turn up a prize; and he wished not only to make a fortune sufficient to benefit them all, but one large enough to restore their ancient name to its proper consideration in the world.

Now he must grow rich before he could marry, for Anne Martha could bring no dowry. For another reason also he desired to heap gold in her lap: her father—"a reserved man, and but little known"—was Hutchins the antiquary, who had been labouring all his life upon an immense and learned "History of Dorset". His proposals for publishing the work of thirty years "met not with the reception they merited", further to quote Dr. Cuming, of Dorchester, who was to receive the subscriptions when a meeting "of the first persons of the county" had at last decided to encourage the publication. But in the years when John was courting Anne and waiting to set forth upon his fortune-hunt, the wonderful great book remained hopelessly in manuscript—a burning shame, as John must think, for his reverence for this work and its author is very plain. His vows to Anne about what he would do in the matter when he was a rich man may be guessed from what he actually did in future years.

There is no record of how his nomination to a Cadetship was obtained, but probably through the Chichele Plowdens, who were friends of his uncle. Nor do we know why he did not start for India until he was five-and-twenty; possibly his father's death in 1765 had caused delay, besides adding the

pathetic figure of a widowed mother to those whom his
success was to benefit. Of his ability to achieve that success
his portrait, painted in his new uniform, shows no doubt.
It is not a picture of artistic merit, but one would swear it
was a startling likeness. The young man looks out under
his black brows, solemn but not depressed with responsibility, and the firmness of his mouth is matched by the
firmness of his grip on the sword set before him. The sword-
sash in this picture was a parting present from a friend, Mr.
Lyford of Basingstoke. John's eldest brother gave an
equally valuable present of valedictory advice. The Doctor
had now acquired two other livings; he had also got two
sons and a daughter. In his letter he quotes Aristotle about
the young affecting to know all things, and being vehem-
ently positive: also Horace as to their being *monitorium asper*,
impatient of advice, and *sublimis*, proud of their own talents.
He continues: "I wou'd inculcate on your Mind (my dear
Brother) in the first Place a strict Regard and Attention to
the Precepts and Duties of Religion. . . . A proper Regard
and Attention to your superior Officers—a condescending
good-natured behaviour to your Inferiors, a diligent application in the severall Qualifications of your Profession, a
careful improvement at all Opportunities of your Learning,
will infallibly gain you Honour, Friends, and Preferment.
This will put it in your power to be useful and serviceable
to the Publick and your Relations—and *this* is the most
likely method whereby to gain a *General's Staff*. I have fore-
borne to mention anything of Courage, as I think it not
wanting in your Constitution, however, as *That* is absolutely necessary in your Profession, I pray to God to support
you, and I make no doubt but that you will stand with a
becoming Resolution all the Deaths and Dangers of War. Not
apt to degenerate into rashness or Folly, as little inclined to
give an affront as to receive one, disposed as much to avoid
the meanness of a *Bully* as the imputation of cowardice."
Further, the Doctor disagrees "that youth is an available
Excuse for vicious Indulgence"; and sees no reason why

"Drunkenness, Fornication, or Profaneness shall damn a man of 40 years of age and be indulged in one of 20". John probably carried a charm against these latter evils in the shape of some token from the Dorset girl, when with his sword and his silent resolutions, he set foot aboard ship.

As there is no record of which ship, it is tempting to suppose that he sailed on the *Duke of Grafton*, fellow passenger with Warren Hastings. That quiet inflexible little great man spent this voyage falling in love with Marianne Imhoff, wife of a miniature-painter, a dubious German baron; and making up his mind to possess her legally and respectably. It is well known how a bargain was struck: Imhoff, for a handsome consideration, was to obtain a divorce through some Franconian court: Marianne, after a year or two of blameless waiting, was to become lady paramount of Calcutta. However, it is improbable that John Bellasis ever beheld the red-gold ringlets and infantile graces of "beloved Marianne", or the small spare form and tight mouth of the future Governor-General; for the *Duke of Grafton* was bound for Madras, where Mr. Hastings had a task to accomplish before proceeding to clean up the corruption of Calcutta.

John landed at Bombay in September, 1769, and was commissioned Ensign of Artillery. What he had expected the place to be like, one does not know; but if he arrived after the rains of that year, he saw a short-lived greenness about Malabar Hill and the compounds and garden suburbs of the quiet little town; withal, an air of being at the hither end of nowhere. It sat upon its swampy peninsula, bastions and a deep ditch about it, largely given up to fortifications and powder-mills; with already one Parsee shipyard where mallets rang as though it were Deal or Portsmouth. Between two marine gates, above the moaning sea, stood strong Bombay Castle; it was reputed to be haunted. Behind it Bombay Green held room for the manœuvres of many

ANNE MARTHA HUTCHINS
wife of General John Bellasis, with her daughter
Helen Hutchins Bellasis.

GEORGE BRIDGES BELLASIS
(1767–1825)
"The handsomest man in India."

more troops than the 2,000 or so that were stationed there. People generally lived in and about the fort, close to their occupation; not many garden-houses were yet to be seen on Back Bay, none on Malabar Hill. The Governor had a large house of stone and chunam in Apollo Street, but not yet a retreat at Parell: indeed it was to fall to John Bellasis' son to superintend the building of this. The houses of the few hundred Europeans were modestly unlike the pillared palaces which the nabobs were building at Calcutta; they were low, plastered inside and out with the brilliant white chunam, had tiled roofs, deep verandas, and windows commonly glazed with oyster-shell. In the wide sandy streets, Europeans were carried, languidly bedded in curtained palanquins; or more briskly, seated in the favourite local bandy-cart, drawn by great white oxen. These creatures with their wide horns could go fast for a short distance, until they smothered their muzzles in choking foam. Walking round the walls between the Apollo gate and the Bazaar gate, one saw here black slaves from Madagascar, here Christian Goans and Malabar Hindus almost as dark, here wheat-pale prosperous Parsees—it was just a hundred years since they had petitioned to erect their first Tower of Silence on Malabar Hill, here martial Mohammedans swaggering in whiskers, here a sombre Portuguese priest, here a cross-belted soldier in scarlet; everywhere a jostle of glossy brown nakedness, a clash of pure colours in drapery, a glare of muslin as white as the chunam.

That intolerable weariness which could creep upon the hearts of the English in India was less felt in Bombay than in Calcutta—the "hell well stocked with bread". It was in Calcutta that Philip Francis fumed: "The waste of spirits in this cursed country is a disease unconquerable, a misery unutterable. . . . I hate the thought of dying of the spleen like a rat in a hole . . . stretched with a damned *hic jacet* upon my heart." This was the black *Accedia* which caused Clive to clap to his head the pistol that twice misfired; which caused Charles Metcalfe, shipped out at sixteen, to write a

miserable petition to be taken home. In Bombay, a milder
boredom, a less violent impatience with the slow communi-
cations delaying news of some venture in which one's
fortunes were embarked, would send a man to the native
astrologers. Fat Thomas Hodges, the reigning Governor
when John Bellasis arrived, had been told by a wizard that
he would die in Bombay; and this indeed shortly came to
pass. Whether John Bellasis consulted any such soothsayer
to learn whether he should achieve the desires of his heart,
and whether his death should be soon or late, naturally
among friends, or bloodily and ringed with swords, one
cannot tell. The prophecy could have been that he should
achieve all that he looked for, but with that touch of the
bitter and the hollow which attends all human success;
and that his death would be of both manners, and not
soon.

Cards, coursing the hare on Malabar Hill, arrack punch,
the Assemblies at which Eliza Draper had lately figured, the
evening promenade along the Esplanade, were the simple
diversions of a small society, largely military. A soldier
could scarce suffer from brooding, with daily duty to do,
and a strong expectation of being soon called into action.
For the threat of the "country powers" overshadowed the
little settlement almost as much as in the old days before
Clive and Plassey. There was Hyder Ali, who had come off
winner in his first clash with the Company, and but just
dictated a peace under the walls of Madras; there was the
Nizam of Hyderabad, much under French influence—and
despite the failures of Dupleix and Lally, the French still
had designs upon India; above all, there was the new
Mahratta empire. The Company was bound to come to a
full-scale clash with the Mahrattas sooner or later. This,
however, did not occur for some five years after the arrival
of John Bellasis, when the Presidency was to attempt
securing Mahratta allies by backing a candidate to the
disputed succession of Peishwa. Meanwhile, John first
saw service in 1771, when he was appointed Lieutenant

Fire-worker of Artillery and dispatched on a little jaunt with Colonel Kaye, to abate the nuisance of some troublesome piratical little states which lay northward of Bombay. He played his part well, for he had learnt his business, and was no raw lad, but a courageous and determined man. He sent no description of this or of subsequent actions home to his family until 1779, when he broke this rule for sufficient reason, observing: "I never before this time mentioned to any of you anything relating to our Expeditions as I feared it might make you uneasy."

There was reason enough for uneasiness in December, '74, when the Lieutenant Fireworker was storming Versova and Caranjah with Colonel Keating. The Presidency had decided that it could no longer exist without possession of Tannah, Salsette, and, if possible, Bassein. These forts and islands neighboured Bombay far too closely to remain in alien hands. The Portuguese had clung to them till 1739, being then dispossessed by the Mahrattas; and from the Mahrattas—that is, from the would-be Peishwa Ragonath Rao—the president and council attempted to obtain them in 1774, as the price of their alliance. Unsuccessful haggling was interrupted by the news that the Portuguese, the original possessors, were sending a fleet to retake them. The Bombay government rushed to equip a military expedition that should get in first, which it did by just one day, for immediately after its departure the Portuguese fleet anchored at the mouth of Bombay harbour and lodged a formal protest. Moreover, the Regulating Act had just been passed in England, which constituted Bengal the supreme Presidency, and forbade Bombay or Madras to make war without permission from Calcutta. Bombay had got round this by supposing that the new Act was not in force until formally proclaimed; but before the expedition was complete, letters to that effect had arrived from Bengal, and a demand to know what was happening. Bombay, blessing the fact that it took at least two months to send dispatches to Calcutta by sea, went ahead with its dashing and illegal plans.

Thus Tannah was stormed, a bloody business, with a hundred English casualties among the 620 whites with the sepoys, and a subsequent massacre of the garrison. Then the fort of Versova, at the northern end of Salsette, must fall after a lively action; and then the island and fort of Caranjah. John Bellasis, doing his duty, made no song about it, but with "a *becoming Resolution*" as his brother had put it, stood to his guns, and used that "Cut and Thrust Artillery Sword" which we find in a list of his possessions. But it must have been an unwelcome juncture at which to be risking his life: for Anne Martha Hutchins was to sail for Bombay in the New Year.

Six months earlier he had bidden her come: six months before that, she had written him news of her father's death. 1773, long looked forward to by the old Rector as the publication date of his life's work, saw his death before the folios were in print. He had been toiling upon them, despite a recent stroke, his gout, and his seventy-five years, for certain antiquarians had set a subscription on foot to defray the publishing. It was hard indeed that he should not see it. So Anne must feel, the only child of her parent's middle years; remembering how all her own life and all the family's best energies had been reverently devoted to that great book: remembering all the copying she had done and how her mother, in the Wareham fire of '62, had rushed into the burning rectory and rescued the MSS. at the utmost risk. 1774, which was to make Warren Hastings the first Governor-General of British India; which saw Parliament doubting and debating and dubiously acquitting the honour of Robert Clive, who had handed them an Empire—and saw him, unable to endure the idea of their injustice, and the physical pain which he was stupefying with opium, kill himself at the age of forty-nine—saw Anne Martha Hutchins making ready to sail for India. It appears that she took with her, to furnish her new distant home, a large chest-of-drawers and a dressing-table of Wareham oak, with a "Monk Sherborne triangular Looking-glass".

She sailed in the spring of '75, on the *Talbot*, Captain Snow, and arrived at Bombay in August. It was more than six years since she had seen her lover; nor would she see him now for the better part of another year, for he was absent in the field. She must still wait, but now among the dangerous discomforts of an alien climate, among strangers, and with the knowledge that John Bellasis was likely enough to be killed before they could meet.

In England, the other two Bellasis brothers pursued their separate paths, which were not by way of crossing. Hugh is never recorded to have stirred from his lands, or to have spent thought or time upon anything but their cultivation; while in the civil South, the Doctor of Divinity acknowledged no home-sickness for Dufton Pike. Fate was to take him into the North again, and thus to change and renew his life entirely; but not for some years yet.

There is something in the figure of the eighteenth- and early nineteenth-century divine which is quaintly paradoxical, compared with his reason for existence. Where, in the largest temple in Christendom, the Successor of the Fisherman worships the Son of the Carpenter among all the splendour that can be devised by man, the scene appears not paradoxical but seemly; not so, the idea of the buzz-wigged, shovel-hatted pluralist, capped by the villagers, intent upon tithe-pigs. Such reflections can certainly never have occurred to Dr. Grant of Mansfield, or Archdeacon Grantly of Plumstead: or to George Bellasis, Rector of Yattenden, and Vicar of Basildon and Ashampstead. A handsomer Doctor of Divinity, or one in whose person ancient blood appeared more nobly, would have been hard to find. His large clear features, black brows and bright eyes, were well set off by the full powdered wig and rosetted hat; and he enlivened his spruce black with yellow silk stockings, and a kind of bishop's apron, to which he asserted himself entitled by reason of his academic distinctions.

These had been great; he could have made for himself a

High-Table Oxford career, had not the family living been awaiting him, and had he not desired to marry. He was twenty-six when he married Mrs. Land, born Margaret Harvey, who was five years his senior, the daughter of one clergyman and widow of another. Her mother had been a Lybbe of Checkendon and Hardwick, whose descent could be traced back to two English kings. Margaret Harvey Bellasis thus also could bequeath good blood to her children, but not very much else. Her fortune appears to have been moderate; and though her young husband was inducted as Rector of Yattenden the year after their marriage, and obtained first Basildon and then Ashampstead as the children began to come, they were far from being a wealthy couple.

For the unfortunate truth was, that these livings had been planned to fit an earlier ruder age, an age when the parson was a species of menial, and married the serving-maid. Any one of them could have been colossal wealth to Parson Adams, but all put together they did not amount to as many hundreds as would properly suffice a scholarly cultured gentleman with many great acquaintance to live in the style that came naturally to him. The great acquaintance appeared at christenings: although the eldest son, Joseph Harvey Bellasis, born in May, '59, had but two clerical godfathers, Charlotte, born in March, '61, was godmothered by Lady Fane, and her mother's aunt, Mrs. Breedon of Bere Court; and George Bridges Bellasis, born August, '67, was accompanied to the font by the Honourable Peregrine Bertie, brother of the Earl of Abingdon, and Lady Gibbon, eldest daughter of Admiral Watson—Clive's coadjutor in India—with the very wealthy Mr. William Bridges of Wallington.

Cowper was expressing the contemporary view that scholarship will not advance a man half so much as patronage: "The parson knows enough who knows a Duke"; but George Bellasis, who had the one, and access to the other, seemed none the better. It became clear that whoever would remake the family fortunes, it would not be he. Men with far fewer advantages, but with that lucky touch with money, analogous to the gardener's green fingers, might have done it in his place; but his was the contrary touch, to be inherited by his otherwise brilliant sons. With all his abilities—and he was not only a scholar, but with some skill in painting, and a remarkably fine amateur musician—he must spend his days fussing about disputed tithes, and taking pupils to make ends meet. By the time his eldest boy was rising twelve, ends could not be made to meet.

Steventon Parsonage comes at once to mind, as we observe the tall handsome doctor with his pupils. His exact contemporary, and not so very far distant neighbour, Dr. George Austen, had just undertaken the charge of a son of Warren Hastings by his first marriage; and was soon to increase his own large family with a little girl—"She is to be Jenny" . . . but she was always Jane. A small society in one corner of England, everybody knew everybody else of the same standing; and if the Bellasis did not know the Austens, they had a quantity of common acquaintance. The little links are endless, from Mrs. Lybbe-Powis, connected both with the Austens and with Mrs. Bellasis, to the Lyfords of Basingstoke, John's friends. The doctor, as he grew older, and his fine sons, as they put on uniform, must be unaware that they looked like illustrations to *Pride and Prejudice*.

There are, however, no financially embarrassed clergymen in Miss Austen's novels; we must visit the later *Framley Parsonage* to see how such folk may easily get out of their depth. Whether Dr. Bellasis managed it with some such single act of imprudence—it is briefly recorded that he was "too generous"—or merely by maintaining a civilised standard of living, refusing to harry parishioners who paid tithe unwillingly, and repairing and adorning the churches in his care—certain it is that by 1772 his debts were so serious that he must leave Yattenden, after preaching a farewell sermon so pathetically eloquent that even the tithe defaulters were in tears, and it was subsequently printed.

By 1774, there was no help for it, his other livings must also be sequestrated, and his home broken up. Margaret Harvey Bellasis was now getting on for fifty and could hardly subside into some cottage; she went to kinsfolk at Pangbourne. The doctor was presently able to join her, between engagements to preach at the University and elsewhere: to prepare Joseph for Queen's, whither he went in '75, and to tutor his other two children.

In that first winter of his ruin, while John, far away, was storming Versova, it must have been great comfort to George that his children would have an uncle to look to so very likely to be "useful to the Publick and his Relations".

John was expressing every wish to do his duty in this regard. Before going upon Keating's expedition—and mentioning no word of it—he had written to Hugh at Long Marton a letter full of intense interest in the lives of all there; the mutual quarrels between his brothers-in-law, Kilner, Crosby, and Hill—Mr. Kilner "whose conduct was ever imperious and haughty to the highest degree", seems to have been lording it over the others; and Hugh's own farming discontents. Hugh had recently taken a wife, Miss Mary Ellwood—"whom I have not yet the happiness of knowing, yet esteem and respect her in every degree as my sister"—and she had brought him a dower which he seems instantly to have put into the land. He had not Midas fingers, either, though he was plainly a penny-pincher. To any largeness of plan or boldness of attempt it would prove impossible to spirit him up; and yet he was to be little the better for all his grubbing. If he was too cautious, and his elder brother too expansive, it would appear that only the youngest brother knew when to be prudent and when to be generous. "Providence at present has situated me at a great distance, but I am yet not without hopes of one day having it in my power to return so situated in circumstances as to repay in a grateful manner the many obligations I am under amongst you. . . ." This was no empty compliment, as time was to prove. Particularly, the so-far-distant man expresses anxiety for his "dear and best of mothers. For God's sake take care of her, make her life comfortable. . . . I wish I was situated with my present income within the circle amongst you." There were grounds for anxiety on this point, as John must know, in helpless absence. What with these preoccupations, and the expectation of the sweetheart for whom he had waited so many years, he must have carried a weight of cares into battle with him.

Ragonath Rao, commonly known as Ragobah, had succeeded as Peishwa of the Mahrattas when his elder nephew, Madhoo Rao, died of consumption, and his younger nephew, Narrain Rao, was assassinated in his apartments, and probably with his connivance. The puppet Mahratta Rajah at Sattara had invested him as Peishwa, he had forced acknowledgment and tribute from neighbouring powers, Hyderabad and Hyder Ali, when a number of Mahratta chiefs combined against him, proclaiming the pregnancy of Narrain's widow, Gunga Bhai, and their allegiance to her son, if she should have one. The politic Nana Furnavis— who has been variously called the Metternich and the Machiavelli of India—made tolerably sure that she should, by placing her in an inaccessible fortress along with several Brahmin women in the same condition as herself. It was improbable that they would all bear daughters. The son was duly born, in April, '74, named Madhoo Rao Narrain, and proclaimed Peishwa. Nana Furnavis and the other ministers of this unconscious infant, at headquarters at Poona, now succeeded in detaching the two most powerful chiefs, Scindia and Holkar, from Ragobah's cause; and Ragobah, hastily retreating into Gujerat, became suddenly ready to make a bargain with Bombay Presidency. The terms he offered were very lavish: perpetual possession of Salsette and the other islands which had been stormed, also of Bassein, which had not, and other territory, affording more than nineteen lakhs of revenue; also a guarantee against Mahratta incursions into the Company's possessions.

Of course, the Bombay council were no longer legally entitled to conclude any such bargain, however tempting, but they did it, signing the treaty in March, '75, and at once providing the troops which it bound them to furnish. No sooner, however, had Colonel Keating departed, with John Bellasis for his A.D.C., and a detachment of 1,500, than news arrived of a crippling defeat inflicted upon Ragobah by the Poona army. His cause now appeared so little hopeful that some of the council were for giving up, and not ratifying the treaty; but Colonel Keating was taking a bolder, indeed more foolhardy view, and congratulating his government on finding Ragobah so destitute as to be entirely dependent upon them. Governor Hornby thought likewise, seeming to suppose—as one historian has impatiently observed— "that his 1,500 men would be a match for the whole Mahratta army". Against the Mahratta army the 1,500 were now hurled, in combination with an undisciplined, disorderly mob of some 20,000, Ragobah's troops. An undeserved and very costly victory resulted, mainly due to the admirable European artillery. The Brahmins at Poona must feel persuaded that the gods could never award final victory to one who leagued himself with unclean Europeans; but certainly the campaign ended with Ragobah in a position of advantage, and Scindia, Holkar, and the Gaekwar of Baroda preparing to join him.

Meanwhile, a wonderful muddle began, due to the slowness of communication between Bengal and Bombay. Calcutta heard in May of the March treaty with Ragobah, and sent a furious dispatch—which reached Bombay in August—pronouncing it invalid, telling them to withdraw Keating and his troops at once, and adding that they themselves were sending an agent to negotiate with Poona. Then they heard of the victories, and wavered; and when their agent sent back word that he could make no headway with the Poona ministers, they about-turned and began heartily supporting Ragobah. However, Nana Furnavis having climbed down as soon as he saw the Calcutta emissary giving up, a treaty had been concluded, in February, '76, known as the treaty of Purandhur, from the hill-fort where it was signed: it bound the Company to annul the treaty with Ragobah, and disband his army, under an amnesty. Calcutta had to ratify this, though now regretting it; and it threw Bombay into the utmost dismay, especially as Leadenhall Street had now heard of their treaty with Ragobah, and written to approve it—in direct defiance of the Regulating Act as it was.

This comedy of slow-motion cross-purposes led only to a sort of deadlock; but for John Bellasis it meant something else. After more than a year in the field, he was enabled to return to Bombay; and on the evening of the 3rd June, 1776, Lieutenant John Bellasis of the Artillery was married by the Reverend Mr. Burrows to Anne Martha Hutchins, only child of the Reverend John Hutchins, M.A., Rector of Wareham and Swyre and Author of *The History and Antiquities of the County of Dorset*. Pride in that great book was to find its way into the marriage notice, as it was one day to find its way on to a tombstone.

All things come to him who can wait. The patience of John Bellasis received reward for the past and promise for the future when he turned away handfasted with his early love, as beautiful as ever he remembered her.

"Bombay May 1st 1779.

"My dear Brother. . . . We have had several Expeditions within these last few years, I have been peculiarly fortunate, having never received the least hurt, though repeatedly and repeatedly in the utmost dangers. I have been returned but three months from our last . . . though a short yet a very warm campaign it proved, we lost many valuable officers and a great number of men, the enemy and us kept a perpetual cannonading for two and twenty days successively; and the last engagement we had, we were in immediate and perpetual action from three o'clock in the morning (the 12th Jany.) till four in the afternoon. I had the honour to command the Artillery in the advanced corps and in consequence where the weight of the Action was, it proved a lucky day to me, as it gave me an opportunity to distinguish myself, for which I have had the honour to be publicly rewarded. On our return to Bombay, some were rewarded, others censured, agreeable to merit. I will here insert that part of the General Orders of this Garrison which respected myself, as it will no doubt give you all joy to know the honour and preferment I gained on that occasion. 'Captain John Bellas' of Artillery having acquitted himself on the late Service much to the satisfaction of the Governour and Select Committee, and having shown great knowledge of his Profession, he is appointed Director of the Laboratory, which will be vacated for him by the promotion of Lieutenant Colonel Dagon, who is to be Commandant of Artillery.' . . . I never before this time mentioned to any of you anything relating to our Expeditions as I feared it might make you uneasy, but this circumstance as it turned out well, I could not omit, particularly as the offices I now hold will in future prevent my going on any more, and will I flatter myself in a few years put it in my power to come and settle amongst you, in as independent Circumstances as I wish for. Besides the honour the Governour etc. have been pleased to pay me here, I was shown a paragraph a day or two ago by the Secretary wherein they have in the General Letter to the Company, been pleased to pay me some very handsome compliments. I must confess to you, my situation on the late Service was so ticklish, that I felt a great deal for my poor Wife and Children, as I should have left them in worse circumstances than I could wish; how distressed do you imagine her situation must have been during my absence; however thank God, I came off safe, and now think it a happiness that I had an opportunity of gaining that honour, which every ambitious Soldier wishes for, to make himself a respectable Character."

The simple, brave, and competent John certainly was that, on or off the field of battle; and his first and last account of his professional exertions is of peculiar interest as illustrating how an ill wind may blow good to selected individuals, for the action so tersely described in this letter to Marton was the disastrous business of Wurgaom.

After a lull, due to the fact that neither side was sufficiently satisfied with the treaty of Purandhur to carry it out more than very imperfectly, the Bombay government received from England strong encouragement to break it, if the Mahrattas could be found to have broken it first, and to take the field again in support of Ragobah. Moreover, they were approached by a dissident party at Poona, where Nana Furnavis had been encouraging a French envoy. In all these circumstances, Bombay applied confidently to Bengal for money and troops to assist them in recommencing hostilities. The Council at Calcutta had for a long time been quarrelling like an amateur dramatic society, but Warren Hastings had prevailed over Francis and his tail, and his casting-vote as Governor-General imposed his policy. In this instance, it was to help Bombay. Daringly, a long voyage at an unfavourable season was avoided by sending the troops overland, although through much unfriendly territory. They several times had to fight, as they crawled towards the Nerbudda, under an incapable commanding officer who presently died of fever. He was succeeded by a far more competent person, Colonel Goddard, who went briskly forward, and halted to await instructions. He got plenty. Warren Hastings desired to make an alliance with the Bhonsla Rajah of Berar, by supporting his claim to succeed as Mahratta Rajah—although, as the Rajah intended to be a real ruler, and not a cardboard fiction, this would have cut out any necessity for a Peishwa; the Bombay government were agreed—giving way to some compromise —to have Ragobah installed as regent for the infant claimant of Poona; and the pro-Ragobah party at Poona had suffered a sudden collapse into chains and dungeons, which

had induced Warren Hastings to think twice about backing
the plans of Bombay. He therefore sent to withdraw Colonel
Goddard from the authority of the Bombay government,
also empowering him to treat with the Berar Rajah. At the
same time, Bombay sent to tell Goddard that he was not
wanted—following this up with a most urgent message
ordering him to come at once. Confronted with this cat's-
cradle of confusion, Goddard marched, covering 300 miles
in twenty days. It seemed to him that something was very
wrong.

It was. Once again Bombay Presidency had hurled its
little army against the Mahratta Empire, desirous of showing how much it could do unaided. This time, however, it
sent a sick man, Colonel Egerton, in command, with two
members of Council to do all the actual commanding. One
was old Mr. Carnac, who had once campaigned with Clive,
ranking as brigadier, and therefore fancied he knew all
about war; the other, who might have been useful, having
been lately resident at Poona, died almost at once. The
expedition set forth in November, '78; it mustered 3,900
men, of whom 591 were Europeans; and marched slowly
through the Ghats—the flat-topped mountains of western
India—towards Poona. . . . By the 11th January, at Tully-
gaom, only eighteen miles short of its objective, the army
found itself surrounded by 50,000 Mahrattas, and debating
between surrender or retreat. Sick old Colonel Egerton had
handed over command to Colonel Cockburn, but, being unable to leave, he and dithering old Mr. Carnac were still able
to impose despondent counsels. They began a night retreat;
but at dawn on the 12th were compelled to stand, near the
village of Wurgaom. Then began the battle that John
Bellasis describes as lasting more than twelve hours: his
guns, strategically placed in the village, were what kept the
enemy off. He does not describe, though he was never
likely to forget, the clouds of furious Mahratta horsemen
with their lances, perpetually charging, the deafening
din and smoke of the cannonading, the shower of rockets

which sent droves of screaming camp-followers panicking about, the shocking casualties. Certainly the situation was "ticklish". The bold and efficient Captain Hartley, whose sepoy grenadiers had been fighting enthusiastically, pleaded for a planned retreat; but Cockburn and the others would not agree, and sent to treat with the enemy.

They had, in point of fact, no power to conclude a treaty; and no self-respecting government could have ratified the terms to which they assented. They gave up everything, promised a large indemnity, sent to countermand Colonel Goddard's advance, and would certainly have handed over Ragobah, had he not made his own terms with Scindia. However, the moment they were released from their discomfortable position and on the way back to Bombay, they sent off the second message to Goddard, which brought him posting along.

"On our return to Bombay, some were rewarded, others censured, agreeable to merit. . . ." Egerton and Cockburn were suspended, and as soon as the Directors heard the tale, they lost no time in sacking Mr. Carnac, too. Captain Hartley—always to be a friend of John Bellasis, and godfather to one of his children—received proper praise, and was at once promoted to Lieutenant-Colonel. It did him little good, however, as so loud a howl arose from those who lost a step in seniority that the thing had to be virtually cancelled. There was, however, no ambiguity about the excellent staff appointment which was bestowed upon John Bellasis; and his promotion, though specially antedated, was due. If few other people might think with satisfaction of Wurgaom, he was able to do so.

Soon, Hyder Ali would be storming terribly through the Carnatic—supplying Burke with one of his most effective passages—and withdrawing attention from the operations elsewhere, which would see-saw from victories under Goddard, Eyre Coote, and Popham, to a final stultifying treaty, arranged because the Company, so hard beset, must be at peace with the Mahrattas. One day, Ragobah's son would be Peishwa, but he himself never won to Poona.

Captain Bellasis concluded his dispatch home, of May, '79, by describing his style of life in his new position. "It's true I have liv'd in a genteel and respectable manner ever since my arrival in India. . . . I am now absolutely obliged to do many things you will think me extravagant in, and yet not, in support of my situation, to be avoided; I keep a Chariot, a Palanquin (a method of being carried about by four people), and a Chair (something like the Sedans in London). . . . I'll give you a list of my Household; imprimis, Mrs. Bellas', two children and myself, that's four." And he goes on to number a score of Indian servants: not that he then or ever refers to them by their Indian designations—except for the "Massole or flambeaux" —to him, they are coachman, butler, or cook. This is somewhat characteristic of Bombay, where people never grew as Orientalised as they did in Bengal, and would talk of breakfast, not of *chota hazri* or *tiffin*. Double the number of servants, too, would have been necessary in Bengal of the Nabobs; but what was the simple rule in the poor and unpretending Presidency of Bombay must strike Westmorland with amazement. "And besides this I pay £100 a year house rent: this will astonish you. . . . Notwithstanding, I hope in a few years I shall lay by sufficient to come and settle amongst you in a neat genteel comfortable way, without all this parade, shew, and nonsense."

The two children in the "Household" referred to with such patriarchal pride were Helen Hutchins Bellasis, born on 2nd December, 1777, and George Hutchins Bellasis, born 23rd October, 1778. John's reverence for the intellectual standing of his wife's family—that same feeling which was bowing the polite world at the feet of Dr. Johnson, and had brought young Mr. Boswell down from Auchinleck for the purpose—was to bid him endow all his children with their mother's surname. Little George was rather delicate, but Helen had been a very fine infant and was thriving; she had been painted with her mother—a picture in which the seven years of waiting, the heats of India, the anxieties of a soldier's wife, do not show as having dimmed the radiant beauty of Anne Martha. Happiness and love are great cosmetics.

These children had three first cousins at Marton, George, Fanny, and William: William, born in the same year as Helen, was destined also to follow the twinkle of the Star Pagoda: and it now began to become clear that so were the three much elder cousins in Berkshire. Of George Bridges Bellasis, indeed, it could not yet be pronounced that he would seek his fortune in that direction, for he was but a handsome promising schoolboy; but Joseph Harvey Bellasis, having left Oxford with credit, had just been commissioned in the Berkshire Militia, and the profitable prospects of the Company's service, especially with a successful uncle to smooth his way in it, were to beckon him. As for eighteen-year-old Charlotte, it is probable that she was already engaged to the officer of Bombay Engineers who was presently to summon her to his side. Three handsomer young people were not to be found in their neighbourhood; Charlotte in particular had a head of remarkably beautiful hair, inherited through her mother— 'Lybbe-Powis hair', as it came to be called: curling and thick, of a hot beech-leaf brown, too lovely to be hidden by powder; a ringlet of it, tied with a blue ribbon, still catches the sunshine with the gleam of life, when her young bones have been for more than a century and a half part of the dust of dusty Bombay.

For when the seventeen-eighties were come in, and the Company was engaged with those terrible foes Hyder and his son Tipu, while Mr. Warren Hastings was quitting India, to find his services recognised by an impeachment, Charlotte Bellasis received the summons to the long voyage, and said good-bye to her friends. Her uncle, she was aware,

F

had now prospered exceedingly; he had built a fine garden-house outside Bombay, known as Randall Lodge, and from this she would be married. Her elder brother, when he embraced her, gave her hope of an early meeting: he was coming out with next season's ships to make his fortune in the Land of the Pagoda Tree.

IV

THEY DIED YOUNG

THE *Lord Camden* East Indiaman lay in the Downs, in March, 1784, when the changeable lights and colours of English spring weather were striping the sea with glittering bands and picking out chalky, pearly details of the lovely sweep of coast between the forelands. It is a view with a great deal of sky, perhaps furnished on March 17th with those enormous shining clouds locally known as "Kent Fair Maids", which the great Indiaman was shaking out her canvas to rival, for a fair wind blew. Boats of all sizes, but all looking small enough by the side of the great ship, were certainly plying briskly up and down: Deal luggers, manned by the famous Deal hovellers; and little cockboats that had just conveyed the last passengers aboard—charging them, it is to be hoped, no more than the regular five shillings. When passengers were in an urgent hurry, and the sea was choppy, it was too much the habit of Deal boatmen to lie upon their oars and demand five guineas.

The people of that extremely maritime town, "for the most part bred to the sea, and rough though not rude in their manners", as a contemporary observes—half pilots, half boatmen, and all smugglers—must take the deepest interest in the movements of an Indiaman. Glasses would be levelled at the *Lord Camden* all along the shore. To be sure, the greatest interest would ever be reserved for incoming vessels, their holds stuffed with such richness as Pepys marvelled at when he paddled in pepper, and their decks thronged with Nabobs, yellow as their own pagodas, who had not seen England in a quarter-century, their pale children, who had never seen it before, their languid ladies, and their shivering dark attendants. From the impressive sides of such a ship, the boats would row away and ground on Deal shingle with much profit unknown to the Excise—for every sturdy rower in wide canvas trousers or boat-petticoat would show a certain additional and temporary stoutness, due to a cunningly contrived inner suit of calico bags, which would be presently ripped up to pour out a dry and fragrant stream of expensive smuggled tea. Silks, shawls, bandanna handkerchiefs—commonly known as "gays"—and fairy-fine muslin would somehow leak away also from a returned Indiaman in the Downs; while the captain in his cabin entertained with East India sherry the Customs officials and the Company's Deal agent. About such a vessel, there was always the rejoicing atmosphere of a perilous voyage safely behind, profits secure, the shores of England gained—unalterably home to the exiles who viewed them with delight.

About a departing ship, on the contrary, there is always a melancholy to be felt, even in the case of a huge modern mechanism which appears as large and lifeless as the quay from whence it departs: at sight of the widening seam of water between liner and quayside, the least sensitive traveller is touched with a primitive emotion. How much more would this be felt with such a creature as a sailing vessel, beginning to make ready and stir, feathering out her shining wings to a rhythmic old chant, and presently coming about with all sail set, and travelling her salt road.

All in the Downs the fleet was moor'd,
The streamers waving in the wind . . .

The Company's ships were extremely like the frigates of the Royal Navy; they also wore a pennant at one mast, and a square flag at another; the flash and flutter of these must have been a pretty sight through the shore glasses, as the *Lord Camden* got under way. The passengers must surely have lined the rail that spring morning of '84, including the six ladies who were to share the roundhouse. "The Three Castles that watch the Downs", the little red-roofed houses full of simple English comfort, the chalk, the greenness of the wholesome county of Kent, all were to fade away as the ship stood out clear of the Goodwins; it would not be the last view of England, but it was the moment of parting, the start of a long, long voyage with an unknowable destiny at the end of it.

Charlotte Bellasis kept her twenty-third birthday two days out at sea; she must have wondered how and where she would keep her twenty-fourth. It cannot really have seemed possible to her that she would never keep it, for that kind of possibility has no reality to the young—and she was going to Bombay to marry her lover, from the fine house of her rich uncle.

"A most amiable young lady, and generally beloved. I shall ever cherish her memory with affection": that is Mrs. Fay's portrait of Charlotte; whom we can see otherwise growing very pale as soon as the ship was got into mid-Channel—the paler for the glowing contrast of all that lovely hair—and lying down upon her cot, to hope that Captain Walker's prophecy of her soon becoming a hardened sailor would be fulfilled.

Mrs. Fay, who was making her passage upon reduced terms, in consideration of chaperoning Miss Bellasis, a Miss Fisher, a Miss Turner, and a Mrs. Pemberton, was an excellent woman, unfortunate in having married a bad husband. She presently gave to the world a volume of her adventures, which had been remarkable. Mr. Fay, who was by profession a lawyer, and by inclination a ne'er-do-well, had set out for India in 1779, carrying his bride with him, and making the journey overland. This involved every possible uncomfortable complication with robbers, storms, mountains, deserts, and finally a shipwreck, upon sailing from Suez to Calicut. Worst of all, they were here taken prisoner by Hyder Ali, and carried up country. Through all these hardships and perils, Mrs. Fay had borne herself almost too well; for reading between the lines of her record, one may see that she was so clearly and consciously a better man than her husband as to breed aversion in him before long. Resentment on his side and contempt on hers had undermined their marriage by the time they were liberated and able to proceed to Calcutta. Here Mr. Fay seems to have fribbled away his excellent prospects, offended those whom he should have courted, come home to bed in his boots, and finally brought in a native mistress, so that his wife was obliged to leave him. She had returned to England in 1782, but finding nothing there to equal the opportunities promised her by influential sympathisers in Calcutta, she was now going out there again to establish herself in trade; if men could make their fortunes thus, why should not women? She carried with her a young person to act as assistant, Miss Avis Hicks, who made a sixth in the roundhouse.

"To guard against imprudent attachments, which are more easily formed than broken", Mrs. Fay had carefully arranged with Captain Walker that the young ladies should very seldom come on deck; indeed, they were not on deck more than half a dozen times during the whole voyage. Probably nobody wished to quit the roundhouse for the first fortnight or so, for the weather was shockingly rough. Charlotte Bellasis certainly might not even quit her cot. She had not turned into a sailor: she was wretchedly, hopelessly, pitifully ill. If there is any human ailment more horrible to endure, more prostrating, and more ignominious than acute sea-sickness, it would be hard to name. Hope of her ever growing used to the motion of the vessel must early have left the poor bride; and she had in prospect month upon month of such torment, which nothing could shorten except some catastrophe that should be far worse.

To the sufferer, nothing can seem worse—not death itself; but shocking things enough could happen to an East Indiaman. Every hopeful Cadet, every Miss in muslin who stepped aboard the Company's great ships, bound for the golden East, committed themselves to a throw of the dice with uncomfortably high stakes. They could not tell if they were to have five or six placid months of shipboard

flirtations and tiffs and boredom, or if they were to be
whelmed for ever in unknown seas, bloodily engaged by
enemies or pirates, cast naked ashore to be speared
by savages or enslaved by Oriental princes. The further
horrors of death by thirst or cannibalism must lurk round
the corner of the imagination.

Mrs. Fay must know all this very well: had she not very
nearly sailed for home in the fatal *Grosvenor*?

At the beginning of 1782, Mr. William Hosea, who had
been seventeen years in the Company's service, had booked
his passage in the *Grosvenor*, Captain Coxon, for twenty
thousand rupees; he was returning to England with his
fortune and his family. Mrs. Fay, a great friend of theirs,
recorded in her diary at the time that Mrs. Hosea was in
"charming spirits" at the prospect; though delay and
expense were caused by her being confined just before they
were due to sail, so that they must proceed to Madras on a
country boat and join the *Grosvenor* there. The newly born
child must be left behind, as unlikely to stand the voyage:
"Poor Mrs. Hosea was dreadfully affected at parting with
her infant . . . but it must in all probability have fallen a
sacrifice." She, however, took with her another little girl
of sixteen months, and two seven-year-olds belonging to
friends: little Miss Shore, and little Tommy Chambers,
eldest son of Sir Robert Chambers, the judge, "a charming
boy," says Mrs. Fay, commenting that it was late to send
him home. There was at least one other child being sent
out of reach of the climate that filled so many tiny graves.
The *Grosvenor* sailed, leaving Mrs. Fay disconsolate that she
could not travel with her rich friends; there was no passage
available, save at nabob's prices; she was obliged to leave
later in a ship with a swearing Welsh captain, who found
himself far too near the coast of East Africa one afternoon,
when he had supposed himself to have rounded the Cape.
She must have recollected this circumstance months after,
when she heard what had happened to the *Grosvenor*. . . .

In rough, thick weather, but with no least alarm, the *Grosvenor* on August 3rd, 1782, was at least a hundred miles from land, according to the Captain's reckoning—the coast of Pondoland, in savage and semi-desert South Africa. The ship's invoice included nineteen boxes of diamonds, rubies, sapphires, and emeralds, half-a-million-pounds' worth of gold and silver bars, and specie to the value of £717,000. When she had left Madras she was listed as carrying "Star Pagodas, 162,378, and her register of diamonds in Star Pagodas, 24,444"; she shipped the additional treasure before she left Trincomalee, when her cargo was valued at a round two million pounds. A letter is in existence, written to a friend in England by Mr. Hosea, stating: "I have handed over to the purser my parcel of rough uncut diamonds for safe-keeping". . . . That night, the Captain went below, as usual; but just before daybreak on the 4th, the officer of the watch received a report from the look-out of "Breakers ahead!" Confident that no breakers could be there, he put it down to the kind of delusion which besets a man who has been watching many hours with strained senses. But the alarm came again: this time the officer must share it: he sent below for the Captain. There was no room for doubt when Coxon came on deck, no time for his shout of "Wear ship!" to be obeyed. At the next moment, she struck, with a rending force which carried despair to all on board.

By the brightening light it was seen that the shore was no more than three hundred yards away; but the surf was ravening like a pack of white wolves, and *Grosvenor* was battering her life out among it. Three seamen volunteered to swim ashore with a line, and successfully, although one was drowned; a hawser was hauled after, and several gained the land by this means. It was, however, of no use to the women and children; and two boats and a hastily constructed raft were smashed to matchwood as soon as launched, killing four seamen. The vessel itself now split fore and aft. All had crowded upon the starboard quarter, which drove into shoal water; as a result, everybody reached land except the cook's mate, who was drunk in his berth. Sailcloth shelters were made for the ladies; some drowned hogs and poultry were cooked, and some casks of beef and flour, with "a leaguer of arrack" salvaged. But then came down a horde of natives, quite naked and black, and plundered all that came ashore, though without yet attacking the castaways. Captain Coxon now proposed that he should lead his crew and passengers towards the Dutch settlements at the Cape, which he fancied they might reach in about a fortnight. They set out accordingly in hopeful heart, carrying the first mate, who was ill and had his wife with him, as had the captain.

. . . It was one hundred and seventeen days before six wretched survivors reached a Dutch farmstead. The party had split up and split again, as first some remained behind with the slow-travelling women and children, and then of those who hastened ahead some must fall out exhausted. Constant attack by natives and peril of wild beasts were overshadowed by the greater horrors of starvation and thirst. One of the children, little Master Law, eight years old, was with the foremost party and was kept alive a long while by the men who died off one by one. The survivors had come down to debating who should be killed that the others might drink his blood.

The Cape government sent out an expedition to search for the rest of the one hundred and thirty-five persons who had been wrecked. Only twelve were found, seven being lascars and two black serving-women. However, there was a persistent rumour that some of that large ill-fated company still dragged their lives out in remote kraals. Friends in England dispatched another search-party—but it did not even find any bones. The great land of Africa had swallowed those men, women, and children, as the sea had swallowed their treasure. But as gold and jewels endure, search continued for the treasure, and was to continue for generations: keeping alive the memory of the most unhappy of all wrecked East Indiamen, when the fate of the *Halsewell* was half forgotten, wherein Captain Pierce sank in his roundhouse with his arms about his two daughters, and the fate of the *Abergavenny*, which gives the name to Deadman's Bay near Weymouth, and was commanded by the poet Wordsworth's brother, who refused to save himself—"he seemed indifferent about existence, and perished at the age of thirty-five". The *Doddington*, the *Dartmouth*, the *Winterton*, the *Asia*, and so many more of the Company's great ships went to their doom in circumstances of various distress; but the pitiful details of the wreck of the *Grosvenor* would be remembered for more than a hundred and fifty years, and men would then still be seeking and diving for the lost diamonds, rubies, Star Pagodas; for that treasure, guarded by sands and surf and great cruising sharks, which may never be beheld again until the sea gives up the treasures of every wrecked Indiaman—and the dead.

Mrs. Fay would be wisely sparing of such tales to her female companions, no doubt; though she could hardly forbear giving them the details of her own first nightmare journey to India. She would describe to them what to expect of Bombay or Madras, and tell them of Calcutta, now known as the City of Palaces, and ruled at the whim of Hastings' "beloved Marianne", who had startled the brocaded and whaleboned ladies by wearing the simplest muslins and a cloud of unpowdered ringlets.

The past receding fast behind her, the future clearly sketched, Miss Bellasis had but to endure the present. Most wearily familiar must she have grown with her surroundings. The furniture had not, of course, been provided by the Company; each passenger had been recommended to procure "a sofa, with mattress, a pillow and a chintz covering for the daytime, a Hanging Lamp, a looking-glass with sliding cover, a swing tray, a chest-of-drawers in two pieces, foul-clothes Bag, an oil-cloth or carpet (this merely for the sake of Appearances), a bucket and rope for drawing salt water". The ladies were particularly advised to bring a

good supply of hair-powder and "papillote paper", harts-
horn, aromatic vinegar, aperients and "Cologne water".
Also, silver knitting-needles, as steel would rust in moist
fingers. Dabbing her brow with Cologne water, poor
Charlotte must have viewed the Canaries, Tenerife, and the
Cape Verde islands with a helpless longing for land; the
Lord Camden touched neither there nor at the Cape. Off the
Cape, although there was a heavy swell, and the ship was
going eight knots, the young passengers would have the
cuddy cleared for a dance: they tumbled about unsteadily,
singing and laughing, but it may be supposed that Charlotte
was not among them. Soon the weather grew worse, heavy
seas were shipped which put out the galley fire and led to
cold dinners; but by the 24th of June, the ship dropped
anchor, under tropical sunshine, in the Bay of Johanna, an
island north of Madagascar. Charlotte might go ashore and
feel firm earth beneath her foot again. All found it a pleasant
interlude, there was luscious fruit for sale, and the inhabitants were civil though thieving. Every black had a grand
title, which amused Mrs. Fay: "The Duke of Buccleugh
washed our linen; H.R.H. the Duke of York officiated as
boatman; and a boy of fourteen who sold us some fruit
introduced himself as the Earl of Mansfield." In a week's
time they sailed again, and on the 20th of July at daybreak
viewed Old Woman's Island; the blue flag was hoisted at
Malabar Point; by eleven o'clock the *Lord Camden* had
dropped anchor before Bombay and saluted the Fort: one of
the gunners injured himself by reloading an uncleaned gun.
In the roasting hot-weather glare, the passengers landed
and were overwhelmed with hospitality. "We dined at
Mr. Nesbit's, Chief of the Marine, who gave us a repast in
true old Indian style. . . . We had every joint of a calf on the
table at once, nearly half a Bengal sheep, several large dishes
of fish, boiled and roast turkeys, a ham, a kid, tongue,
fowls, and a long train of etceteras. The heat was excessive,
the hour two, and we were thirty in company in a lower-
roomed house. . . . It is, however, the fact that they ate with

great appetite—to my astonishment, who could scarcely touch a morsel."

Undoubtedly Charlotte must have agreed with Mrs. Fay in this particular. After she had done her duty of "setting up"—a ceremony retained in Bombay, though exploded in Calcutta, and requiring newly arrived ladies to be at home to company until late into the night—Charlotte would be conveyed, with a palanquin and many servants, to her uncle's garden-house on Back Bay. There she must try to regain the roses which a gentleman expects in a wife newly imported from Europe. On August 21st, she was married to Captain Daniel Beat Christie, Bombay Engineers.

Mrs. Fay came to the wedding and said farewell before departing for Calcutta and her business struggles—in which she immediately lost the assistance of Miss Avis Hicks, who found a husband. She must have been sorry to part with poor pretty Charlotte, that "most amiable young lady", and perhaps felt also a pang of wistful envy of one so young, fair, and happy, so surrounded by love and prosperity . . . Two months later, Charlotte was dead.

At evening, the slow white oxen drew her body to burial.

> *Nature around assum'd a solemn Grace;—*
> *Blanch'd was each fading Cheek with Sorrow pale;*
> *O'er each attending Mortal's Woe-fraught Face*
> *Dull Melancholy threw her dimmy Veil!*

—such were the expressions of "the Physician who attended her", in an Elegy of thirty-one verses, addressed to the bereaved husband. "Check not, my Friend, thy Sorrow's gushing Tide", this work begins; it ends with a compliment to local beauty:

> *And thou, sweet Maid! whose ev'ry future Joy*
> *Hangs on the Die of matrimonial Chance,*
> *May varied Bliss alone thy Life employ,*
> *And with thy Years thy Happiness advance.*

> *Like thy lost Charlotte's may thy Nuptial Vow*
> *Meet from a Husband's Worth its full Return!*
> *In either Breast responsive Kindness glow,*
> *And long as Life the Torch of Passion burn!*

Of the dead girl, the physician who could not save her life from the tiger heat and the deadly monsoon vapours, further records:

> *How great and yet how Modest was her Worth!*
> *How full of gentle Virtues was her Mind!*
> *There is not in the Space of peopled Earth*
> *A soul more pure, or softness more refin'd.*

> *Her nervous Sense, by sparkling Fancy dress'd,*
> *Teem'd with convictive Force upon the Ear;*
> *In each Decision Judgement shone confess'd,*
> *Her Taste was signal! Her Discernment clear!*

> *Yet with those rare endowments was she born*
> *Most fondly to endear the name of Wife,*
> *And form'd to Bless while gifted to Adorn*
> *The humble circle of domestic Life. . . .*

> *Such was thy Charlotte, rear'd by Caution's Hand,*
> *Foster'd beneath a Father's jealous eye,*
> *Such those Perfections which our Praise command,*
> *And in our wakeful Mem'ries ne'er shall die.*

These verses, which perhaps will hardly be considered equal to Gray in the same form, or Landor upon the same theme, must have pleased their writer, but can scarce have consoled Captain Christie for the loss of his bride of a few weeks. They, however, together with Mrs. Fay's praise, are all that remain to tell of young Charlotte Bellasis, except for one curl of beautiful hair.

Joseph Harvey Bellasis arrived in India in 1785, and must have had time to learn before he sailed that there could be no happy meeting with his sister. For himself, he was determined that the dice should fall more luckily; and he seemed well qualified to succeed, with his energy, brilliancy, charm, and uncommon distinction of manners and person. If birth gives a right to these things, he had such right, not only through his father's ancient stock: a family friend, Edmund Lodge, who was Bluemantle at the Herald's Office, and later to become Lancaster Herald, had taken pleasure in tracing the Harvey descent through Lybbe and Burnell, Hungerford and Fitzalan, Delapole, Stafford, and Audley, to the Plantagenets. Lodge, with his passion for the trappings of a chivalrous past, certainly liked his friends the better for their blazonry; it must, for him, have thrown an air of romance over the two tall brothers adventuring to the East; when George followed Joseph in a few years' time, Lodge was to prove his principal correspondent, ally, and admirer: together with the cheerful spinster sister who kept house for him.

As Joseph was a very infrequent letter-writer, his friends and family now heard little of him; and pretty well all that has been preserved in his hand are scrawled memoranda about money matters, for which he had an inherited incapacity. "Mr. Bellasis is a very irregular man in points of business," lamented one agent. Far more characteristic is a Glee for three voices, words and music both of his composition. The trifling thing brings back not only a personality but an age:

> How happy we Soldiers, thus destin'd to rove
> From danger to glory, from glory to love:
> But happier still is the Fair for whose charms
> We forego all the danger and glory of Arms.

Joseph's "Fair" was named Juliana Williams, and he married her so immediately upon arrival that one fancies he must have met her on shipboard. She had some fortune— her father, a retired Company's officer, was a banker; and to judge from a drawing made by her father-in-law on her visiting England, she was extremely pretty. In his profession, Joseph relied upon his uncle, it seemed, less for influence than for example: for he proceeded not to Bombay but to Bengal. Tipu Sahib had just succeeded his father, Hyder Naik, as the Company's chief antagonist; and a campaign against him, thoroughly mismanaged by Madras, had just ended in a most humiliating peace: the commissioners who negotiated it at Mangalore having to proceed with a gallows suggestively set up before each tent. Plainly, such a peace could not endure; and indeed Tipu broke it in 1790 by an attack upon the Rajah of Travancore, who was under the Company's protection. Meanwhile, Lord Cornwallis had arrived, as combined Governor-General and Commander-in-Chief; and he was to beat Tipu back to his island capital of Seringapatam and force from him a treaty by which he ceded one half of his conquests, paid three crore and thirty lakhs of rupees, released his prisoners, and gave up two of his sons as hostages.

These were busy years for the Company's soldiers; but Joseph sent home no record of his campaigns—nor, according to custom, did his uncle, beyond a few curt references to "the situation of public affairs" preventing his returning on furlough as soon as he had hoped. Yet it must have been in the winter campaign of '90 that he earned his gifts from the grateful Queen of Cannanore. Colonel Hartley, with but a small detachment from Bombay, and apparently with his friend Bellasis commanding the artillery, then did a very good job of clearing Tipu's troops out of Malabar. As great cruelties had been practised upon the people, it was no wonder that the local rulers should welcome their deliverers. The Queen not only gave John Bellasis the emerald off her finger, but also a carved ebony chair, lately belonging to Tipu.

Due and overdue for his three years' leave at home, Major Bellasis—he was got so far up the long slow ladder of promotion, and would be a Lieut.-Colonel next year—sailed for England in 1791, with his wife and their youngest

children. They had been miraculously fortunate, and only
lost one baby; but the parting with each child in turn must
have been almost as bad, when they might not learn for a
year whether their children had not met such a fate as those
aboard the *Grosvenor*, or how they fared in England. After
Helen and George had come Joseph, Edward, and Daniel;
and Anne was to be confined in England of another son,
John. Her portrait, painted with her first-born, with a
companion picture of her husband, had been packed off
ten years before to old Mrs. Bellasis in Westmorland. This
determined old lady had been suffered by her kinsfolk to do
a very shocking thing; having apparently spent most of her
slender jointure upon favourite grandchildren, she had
resolved to be a burden in no one's household, and had
withdrawn herself into the Earl of Thanet's almshouses at
Appleby; news that John could not hear with patience. He
pointed out that this was a gross abuse of a charity not
meant for gentlefolk, and that "no doubt the neighbourhood
cry out (privately) shame at it . . . I do not mean to intimate
that it was any of your faults, for I am persuaded it was her
own choice." This could be confidently guessed by anybody
viewing the old lady's fierce aquiline profile; but when John
hastened to send over sufficient money to ensure her a
comfortable income, her haughty spirit was softened, and
she returned to her friends. At Christmas of '85 John
wrote encouraging Hugh and Mary to make much of her:
"You are on the very spot where we altogether passed so
many happy days, and where I hope we shall yet meet again
and be as merry as we ever were (I believe I can dance
a jig still). The present season puts me in mind of all those
merriments. Mrs. Bellas' makes us a Christmas cake, and we
drink all friends round Dufton Pike." Compelled still to
postpone his departure, though "I long to be amongst
you", one dream must perish—that of seeing his mother
again: Margaret Hill Bellasis died in the summer of '87.
John's bitter disappointment shows through his restrained
style.

He must be the more resolved upon his other plans. As soon as he reached England he arranged for the publication of a new and complete edition of that great book about Dorset, by the late Rector of Wareham and Swyre; he cleared off the debts on his brother's sequestrated livings; and he saw Sir Isaac Heard, Garter-King-at-Arms, about resuming the proper spelling of the family name. The parchments at Long Marton were routed out, and copies of the parish registers, to prove that the name had not been clipped until the last generation. Moreover, the Heralds pronounced the Long Marton branch fully entitled to bear the Bellasis arms: adding a martial tent behind the azure lion couchant that was the crest, with the same in chief upon the shield. The three brothers and their children now began to use the proper mode of spelling their name: Joseph Harvey Bellasis, indeed, had always done so. It was probably a matter of indifference to Hugh. His brother's letters from India had contained frequent mild admonitions to him not to make a mere drudge of himself: "You are yet but a young man, and I would seriously recommend you to ride about and inspect your work-people, without in the least putting your hand to it, but I know well that both you and my sister labour harder than you ought to do for your health's sake." One sees Hugh's wife scolding in the dairy, and herself panting at the churn; while he, perhaps sullenly conscious of the contrast with those two men of the world, his brothers, continued to be as awkwardly rustical as he could. He sent hams down to Wareham, where Anne Martha was having her baby in her mother's house, happily surrounded by other children; but he would not promise to destine his own youngest son to Oxford, though his brother begged: "By no means turn him to husbandry."

The second son, William, however, it was presently determined, should go out to his uncle and be placed aboard an Indiaman. George Bridges Bellasis, the doctor's youngest, who was now five-and-twenty, had been an officer in the Portsmouth Marines for some years, turning

G

the heads of young ladies at Portsmouth and Basingstoke Assemblies, though whether he ever danced with Miss Jane Austen is not known. He had now transferred to the Company's service, and sailed for Bombay in the summer of 1792, his pleased uncle commenting: "I will venture to say a more accomplished fine young fellow never went to India." In the spring of 1793 John Bellasis must himself return, to the great chagrin of such brother-officers as had hoped he might remain in England and clear the way for their promotion. He of course left his young sons behind him, including the one English-born baby; they were under the care of friends, Captain and Mrs. Carpenter, living at Potters Bar. Helen, however, accompanied her parents; she was now fifteen, and ready to be married. She had spent the last years being finished at boarding-school: her father had sent her a long, tender, serious letter, exhorting her to make the most of her opportunities, not to be puffed up at being a parlour-boarder and ever to preserve a mild and gentle conduct. She was always, indeed, her father's especial favourite; and was growing up with much of her mother's beauty, dark hair and brows, and, long, bright, grey eyes. Her cousin Emma Springett came too; and two other young ladies travelled under the Bellasis protection: here was quite a bouquet of expectant brides. The *Barwell*, Captain Welladvice, was detained at the Isle of Wight, waiting for a convoy; and the party enjoyed themselves riding about the island: "We have a black boy and three black girls to attend us, and Captain Welladvice has his cook and other servants on shore, so that we make it out very well. . . ." It is a period picture, the sketch of a summer scene, with all those laughing girls in muslin, attended by blacks, with the Indiaman riding in the roadstead. It begins to cancel out the less happy voyage of Charlotte Bellasis; and perhaps her forlorn ghost may be dismissed at two happy weddings soon after arrival at Bombay. Miss Springett shortly captivated General Brownrigg, commander of the Bombay forces; Helen Hutchins Bellasis was married, two months after her sixteenth birthday, to the senior partner in the great house of Bruce, Fawcett & Co.

Matrimony was toward in another, and unexpected, direction. The wife of Dr. Bellasis had long been failing, she had perhaps been missing her children; in 1795 she died at the age of sixty-nine; and in 1796 the widower married Miss Leah Viall, a young governess whom he had first met in 1789 when preaching a charity sermon at Kendal. Leah Viall was an elegant creature, dazzlingly fair, with regular features as calm as her temper, many accomplishments, some demure dimples, a genteel descent, and a character which impressed all who came in contact with her: but unfortunately with no money. Hers, therefore, must be the pitiful fate that overhung Jane Fairfax: fortunate for her that it proved to be more nearly that of Miss Taylor, later Mrs. Weston. At eighteen, she entered the household of Mr. Joseph Maude, a wealthy banker of Kendal. He was of excellent family, for the Maudes, anciently De Montalt, bore the lion rampant of Scotland debruised two bars sable to signify captivity, in remembrance of Andremar Montalt who took the Scots King prisoner in 1174. Joseph Maude had married Sarah Holme, daughter of a local ironmaster whose forge at Force Bridge, with its blast and hammers moved by water, had been wonderingly toured by the poet Gray in 1769. They had nine sons and three daughters, who all appear to have doted on Miss Viall for the fifteen years that she spent with them, certainly "less as a governess than as a friend". Had she not been penniless in a particularly mercenary age, her sedate charm would early have got her a husband; as it was, her favourite pupil, Anna Maria, showed an Emma-like readiness to forward the match which eventually presented itself. Dr. Bellasis had caused a stir upon his return to the scenes of his boyhood; his preaching—warmly commended in the *Cumberland Pacquet*—his connection with the great world, his fine person and manners, and the rumour that his wife was old and sickly, had induced the spinsters and widows of Kendal to entertain him at many tea and music parties; nay, several insisted upon his sitting for his likeness; and it is not improbable that they set down the texts of all the sermons which he preached in those parts, like Mr. Elton's female admirers. They would have been dismayed to read another composition which he penned in 1790: "Dear Miss Viall—The dimple next me last night has produced the following lines:

> *Young Cupid, being simple,*
> *Fell into a dimple,*
> *Where he caper'd and flutter'd about;*
> *In a thousand new fancies*
> *Shot his shy glances,*
> *And his mother could ne'er get him out.*
> *The Graces in duty*
> *Threw three lines of beauty*
> *To help remove Venus' woe,*
> *But the rogue lik'd his quarters,*
> *So he snatch'd all their garters,*
> *And now shoots with three strings to his bow!"*

When the divine ceased to have two strings to his, and could replace gallantry by serious addresses, his brother John, who had met Leah and thought her "a wonderful, excellent, accomplished woman", offered a thousand pounds toward her dowry: Mr. Maude gave another thousand; and they were married in London, with the approval of everyone except the spinsters of Kendal. The confidante Anna Maria wrote a very long letter on the occasion, full of double-refined sentiment, laced with genuine feeling. "This is the day I shall feel for you and think of you through every hour of it; may you possess your wonted composure and presence of mind; and sincerely do I wish that this day, in its anniversary, you may regard as the happiest of your life. All good attend you. All evil I pray heaven avert."

The marriage indeed was a perfect success, although the groom was sixty-six and the bride not half that age. Leah of the bright, fair face was not a north-country woman—she came from Norwich—and after so many years in ungenial Kendal, she felt herself got into a paradise at Basildon Parsonage. She wrote with ecstasy to Anna Maria of the "lilachs", the "little songsters", the serpentine evergreen walk, syringa and sweet briar, and all the beautiful fruit. Happy herself, she made the doctor very happy: completely so when a little daughter was born in May, '97, and named Anna Maria. In 1800 George Bridges Bellasis was to explode with pleased laughter at the news that he now had a little half-brother Edward, as well; and to swear that "they ought to make my father a bishop, for getting children at his age." It was a pleasant, smooth-running household, and included two of Leah's old pupils: the doctor's curate, Joseph Maude, newly ordained, who had also found southern England so highly agreeable that he was resolved against ever taking a northern cure; and poor little Charles Maude, who had been born, like one of the Austen sons, without his proper allowance of wits, but was very amiable and fond of digging the garden. The Vicar, pacing in his powdered wig the church path they called "the Doctor's Walk," was not to see much of the new century, in which it was fated that his youngest son should be extremely successful, and even famous; he wrote to his brother John with the greatest gratitude for all his bounty, praying God to protect him and restore him to his native land: when he gave his little children anything that pleased them, he would teach them to say "Uncle John, Bombay!"

Uncle John, Bombay, wrote into Westmorland in July, 1797, to describe the arrival of his nephew William, in perfect health and good spirits; but must continue: "I am distress'd to say my Situation has been such as to make his Arrival not so pleasant as it otherwise would have been; from a very unexpected and heavy stroke of Providence falling upon me. Mrs. Bellasis is no more! She died on the 14th of May of a short illness, and which even the doctors who attended her thought was no danger. You will easily conceive this has perfectly Unhinged me, and thrown me all into Distress and Confusion; and it must be Time alone that can bring my Mind and feelings to usual Calm.

"We were living in the utmost Happiness: an excellent House with a most beautiful Garden, horses, carriages, and in short every Comfort, I may say to what might be call'd one's utmost Wish! My only Daughter most comfortably and happily settled, Miss Springett married and happily settled also, to Major-General Brownrigg. One of my sons appointed a Writer, and expecting him out in the latter Ships, looking for the rest one after another, as they may be of standing to have appointments: having got perfectly the Better of a set of Enemies who had conspir'd against me in the hope to Effect my ruin. . . . Appointed a full Colonel, and at the head of the Regiment I have rose up to by regular gradation, from the bottom to the high and honourable Rank I now hold, with every prospect of further Advancement. . . . But so uncertain is all Earthly enjoyment. . . . It is our duty to Submit, therefore, good God, Thy Will be done! If purity and virtue was ever Perfect, it was in her. . . ."

If misery ever confused a stilted phrase, it can here be noted. John Bellasis might have added to his grounds for resignation that they had so long been happy together: she might so well have died, not at forty but at twenty. But just in a day or two she had gone, they had taken his Anne away from him, and put her in "a brick'd grave" in Bombay burying-ground . . . and all his success was bitter in his mouth. The references to his enemies concerned those officers who had been disappointed by his return from England: these had accused him of bargaining to resign his commission while the army was in the field in 1790, and breaking his word of honour by returning. Of these charges a court martial had fully and honourably acquitted him, and he had been made Commandant of Artillery. With an effort, his letter resumes the subject of young William, who has received an excellent character from Captain

Wordsworth of the *Abergavenny*—doomed to go down in Deadman's Bay—and for whom he has obtained free mariner's indentures from the Governor in Council. William's prospects are now very fine indeed.

Every Indiaman carried, according to size, from four to eight officers, working the ship as strictly as a man-of-war. They wore fine blue uniforms faced with black velvet, and gilt buttons, with cockaded hats. The Captain was an absolute potentate, and so great a man that upon his landing at Bombay or Madras he was entitled to a salute of thirteen guns, like a Member of Council, and the guard would turn out at the Fort, as to a general. In the course of two or three voyages, he would be able to make a handsome fortune. Beside his pay he had a right to export fifty tons of freight free of charge to the Indies, and bring twenty tons back; if he were a good business man, the profit could be immense. The Company had a fixed scale of charges for passengers, ranging from £95 for a mere subaltern or assistant-surgeon, who was allowed one-and-a-half tons of baggage, to £235 with three-and-a-half tons for a general—plus the charge for bedding and cabin furniture; but if the Captain chose to resign some of his own spacious quarters to people who could pay top prices, he could do so. With all this, he could hardly clear less than £2,000 on a voyage, and sometimes as much as £12,000. It was no wonder that such sums were paid to the owners for the nomination to a command; though the custom of such sales was abolished about this time. The Captain earned his grand position: not only had he an immense responsibility, but he must work his way up; he must be over twenty-five and have made one voyage as chief or second mate; the chief must not be younger than twenty-three, and must have made at least two voyages, one in other service. It was a ladder worth climbing; and Colonel Bellasis set his nephew upon it by arranging for him to make a preliminary voyage in a country ship.

In October, '97, just before his twentieth birthday, the

young man wrote home all his news, dating from "Ship *Betsey* on a Voyage from Bombay towards the Cape of Good Hope."

"My dear Father and Mother—I have great pleasure to inform you of my safe arrival in Bombay. . . . I got leave to go on shore, I enquired where Col. Bellasis liv'd, and his House was soon shewn to me. As I was advancing towards his House I met my Uncle going out in his Carriage. I spoke to him and at the same time gave him my Letters, and then he did not know me, he look'd at the Letters and when he saw your Handwriting, He with a pleasant Smile said, I suppose you are my Brother's son William. . . . He then came back with me to his house, and he told me to stay there, in that room, till he came back, it would not be long, and in about a ¼ of an hour He came to me Again, he then said, I suppose you have not heard of my great Loss, I said no I had not, he then said that his Wife Mrs. Bellasis was dead about six weeks before my arrival at Bombay, she went off very sudden and unexpected death. Before her death they liv'd in the Country, kept their carriages and lived in great style and ostentation of life, but since the death of Mrs. Bellasis my Uncle has come into Town, lives quite alone, cannot think of doing any Duty whatsoever, indeed in the main he is not able to do any Duty."

From this ill-expressed but somehow evocative account, William goes on to describe his cousin Helen and her husband Henry Fawcett, admiringly over-estimating the age of their little girl Agnes. Henry Fawcett had been just twice the age of his sixteen-year-old bride, which did not make him very old; he was a Yorkshireman, wealthy, and growing daily wealthier, from the flourishing affairs of Bruce, Fawcett & Co. "The day after my Uncle took me out to Mr. Fawcett's, he lives in the Country about two miles. Mr. Fawcett is a very good looking Man, and Mrs. Fawcett is the same, she is a most graitful girl, both Mr. and Mrs. Fawcett look upon me more like their brother than Cousin; they live in great comfort together, they have an only daughter about the age of four years, a perfect Beauty. My Uncle after two or three days carried me to a large shop, and made me a present of about £30 of Clothes, besides he gave me £12 to keep in my pocket, which I think was a very handsome thing. . . . I cannot give you any account of Bombay, but as much as I experienced it was very pleasant and excessive hot.

"From the 9th of August I set sail for the Cape of Good Hope on board the *Betsey*, commanded by Thomas Megson. I am become an officer and am third on board; our Captain is a most exceeding good man, so are all the officers. All officers in the Country Service dine with the Captain, when the ship is in Port the officers find their own. The *Betsey* is only a small vessal, and indeed not very good, rather the reverse, for soon after our leaving Bombay we had a most violent gale of Wind, which damag'd the Ship very much; we lost in the Gale our Main-top-Mast and sprung our Fore topmast and carried away our Gaff and Foreyard, and worst of all sprung a leak, making 18 inches of water per hour, lost all our Copper and damaged a great quantity of our Cargo, which contain'd Wheat and Rice. Thank God the gale abated, or we surely would have been all lost, but it pleased God it was not to be so; though we were in company with the Homeward bound East Indiamen, they could do us no good at all as long as the gale continued, but after they took from us 200 Bags of Rice, which made us a little better, we have got ourselves a little repaired again but not fit to stand bad weather. Please God I hope we in ten or twelve days will reach the Cape and then we shall make ourselves fit for Sea again. I hope to arrive in Bombay in January 1798, and by that time my Uncle will have got me a good berth on board one of the large China Ships, which will be a great deal better, and likewise one will have a good quantity more pay . . . and liberty to carry private trade . . . but that lays upon one's own carefulness and conduct to save one's own money to buy it with."

The young man then gives particulars of other kinsfolk

in Bombay, Captain George, Emma Brownrigg; and divers north-country friends ("Ensign Hewitson, I believe, is not doing but indifferently"); and he ends with: "Dear Father, I would have you give up and let my brother George have possession, and you and my dear Mother might live happy the rest of your days—and please God if we live we may all meet together again by and by, I have written to my sister Fanny. Please remember me to all my old friends, to Thomas Swinglehurst and all round Dufton Pyke.

"Believe me to be your ever Dutiful Son,

William Bellasis."

The fresh rough lad—Appleby Grammar School hardly taught the graces—with the well-remembered Westmorland burr on his tongue, must have provided a welcome distraction for his uncle in his unhappiness. It must have been the greater disappointment, almost a reopening of the recent wound, when the climate killed William in his first trip as an officer on that fine new ship of Messrs. Bruce, Fawcett's, the *Scaleby Castle*. His hopes, prospects, plans, were all made an end of; and his young body dropped into the sea. . . .

The fate of Charlotte, Anne, and William in this decade had also attended Joseph's young wife, Juliana, and her infant. Perhaps this was the final stroke, impelling him to take up another way of life. After ten years in India, Joseph Harvey Bellasis had not made the fortune at which he aimed, despite some large attempts at speculating in indigo. Promotion in the Company's service was far too slow for his impatient spirit; in the year 1796, moreover, the "double batta" or field allowance pay was abolished, causing such discontent among the Company's long-suffering officers that there was something like a mutiny. Perhaps if Juliana had been still alive, Joseph would not "in a rash moment", as a friend put it, have resigned the Company's service; but he saw immense things being achieved in native service by persons not near so well qualified as himself; and he

determined to find a purchaser for his sword among the
Mahrattas.

It was not only in Mysore that an usurper held rule,
keeping the rightful rajah for a pageant and a show on State
occasions, as did Hyder and Tipu; the like was true of the
Mahratta Empire. In theory, the Emperor Shah Alum at
Delhi was the overlord, the Rajah of Sattara was his vassal,
the Peishwa was the Rajah's subordinate minister, and the
various Mahratta chiefs, including Scindia and Holkar,
were subject to the Peishwa. In practice, this pyramid was
exactly inverted. The Mahrattas had no sooner recovered
from their rout by the Afghans at the terrible battle of
Panipat in 1769, than Mahadoji Scindia and Tukaji Holkar
took and kept the lead among the chiefs. Now adversaries,
now allies, they both built up very fine armies officered by
Europeans, and left immense power to their successors,
Daulat Rao Scindia and Jeswant Rao Holkar. Scindia had
long been master of Delhi, where the unhappy old shadow
Emperor had had his eyes stabbed out by the merciless
freebooter, Gholam Kadir, in 1788.

Determining then upon a new cast of the dice, Joseph set
out to make another life for himself—to find perhaps another
love—in the year before Colonel John was plunged in
tribulation.

John Bellasis had never a thought of another wife. In his
son's time, the Chief Justice's wife was to write in her
Bombay diary: "Here people die one day, and are buried the
next. Their furniture sold the third, and they are forgotten
the fourth. . . . Oh Lord! preserve my husband to me."
Anne Martha was not forgotten; and perhaps it was the
unconscious desire to share her grave, rather than necessity
or ambition, which was to hold John Bellasis so long in
India.

V

THE GLORY OF ARMS

WHEN Joseph Harvey Bellasis rode off to offer his sword to Daulat Rao Scindia in 1796, he was late in the field. All over India, native battalions in private armies stepped to the tap of the drum, wearing fine uniforms, obeying words of command in French and English. For two decades the European *condottiere* of the Free Companies had been working out a story improbably dramatic, black with treachery, bright with blood, and fiery with the most honourable valour.

Before the great De Boigne, the giant from Savoy, with a brain like a Swiss watch, who was to leave that cockpit at his chosen moment with half a million of money to spend in the neighbourhood of Chambéry: before the amazing George Thomas, the unlettered common seaman who nearly conquered the Punjab: there had been many regular corps, or "parties", formed by Europeans. There had been a French party with the Nawab's forces facing Clive at Plassey, and there had been one sent by Dupleix to the Nizam of Hyderabad; these, however, were emissaries of French power; and the sprinkling of European gunners and other deserters always to be found in native service since the days of Albuquerque, had no qualities of leadership. The first professional party of mercenaries to be hired by whoever could pay was probably that formed in 1772 by the infamous Sombre. This fellow was a butcher from Salzburg, of the name of Walter Renard, who seemed unable to dismiss his original trade; for he set up in native service by conducting the massacre of the English at Patna, on behalf of Cassim Ali Khan. Native leaders had refused to take part in this atrocity, and it is said that even the ex-butcher was ever afterwards haunted by the horrid piece of work. He was in any case a black-looking villain with lowering brows, which had obtained for him the nickname under which he operated, and which the natives garbled after custom into "Somru". Sombre's party of two battalions, later augmented, sought little glory; it never lost a gun, but it never gained one either. He cared for more solid rewards, and left lands and lakhs enough behind him when he died, generally cursed, in 1778, and was buried at Agra.

He had held from Delhi the jaghir of Sardhana, with the title of Nawab; a slave-girl of strong character whom he had taken to himself succeeded him, under the name of the Begum Sombre. She took over his estates and his army, increasing its strength, and obtaining European officers whose duties were not easy, for these troops were known to be the most mutinous in India. Even when their pay was not in arrears, they had a habit of clubbing their officers to death; and when it was, they followed an unpleasant custom among these private armies, that of riding their commander on a hot cannon until he paid up. After Pauly, the German first appointed by the Begum, had been trapped and beheaded by a neighbouring rival, three successive Frenchmen were glad to get out of the command with their lives.

It was supposed that their remarkable mistress kept her sway over them by playing Catherine on a small scale in her city of Sardhana, and going to bed with this officer and that, without favouring one above the other. When she broke this prudent rule and married one, tragedy was to result. Remarkable she was indeed. Stories clustered about the Begum Somru: that she buried eight lakhs a year in her gardens, and had once also buried two slave-girls alive, and smoked her hookah on their grave: that she had offenders blown from guns: that she poisoned her stepson. . . . In 1781 she had become a Christian, building a fine Catholic church at Sardhana; but long continued the decorum of purdah, so that her attendants were much shocked, at the time of Lord Lake's Mahratta campaigns, when that genial general came to meet her palki and greeted her with a hearty hug. "It is

the kiss of a padre to his daughter", was her swift explanation; though a figure less ecclesiastic than that of the scarlet-
coated victor of Laswari would be hard to find. The event
of Laswari and Assaye, with the breaking of Scindia's
battalions, spelt the end of the Free Companies; but the
Begum was left enjoying absolute rule, squeezing her ryots
to an extent unknown elsewhere, through the medium of a
Scots bailiff named Dyce, to whom she had married her
daughter. The Company presently intimated that this sort
of thing would not do; the power and extortions of the
Witch of Sardhana, as she was commonly called, were
curbed; but she remained excellent friends with the new
masters of India.

In 1830, the lively young French traveller, Victor Jacque-
minot, visited Sardhana and "had breakfast and dinner with
the old witch, and even kissed her hand gallantly. At dinner
I had the honour of clinking glasses with her like a regular
John Bull. She is an old hussy, quite 100 years old, bent
double and as shrivelled as a dried raisin, a sort of walking
mummy who still conducted all her own business, listening
to two or three secretaries at a time, while dictating to
three more. . . . She was as brave as she was cruel. . . ."
Delighting avidly in power, that solace of age, the woman,
who was in truth about eighty-six years old at that time,
must have felt a stirring of memories, to have had her
jewelled claw kissed by a tall young man . . . there had been
so many tall young men, since the blackavised ruffian who
had raised her from slavery . . . the young husband who had
been hacked to pieces before her eyes, and the towering
invincible Thomas, "George the Conqueror", who had
helped her in her need, and whom she had betrayed. . . .
Often must her fell spirit have hungered for the old days of
the Free Companies, when there was no law in India but
the law of the strongest sword-arm.

One piece of prudence which the Sombre party always
practised under the Begum was never to clash with the

battalions of Benoit De Boigne. Even the wind of De Boigne's name was terrible, not from any repute of cruelty such as made folk shiver at Filoze or Avitabile, but simply from his iron efficiency. Rajahs who heard that he was coming against them would surrender without struggle. He had been Scindia's general since 1784, and made him the paramount power in Hindostan, heartily beating Tukaji Holkar at Lukhari. Big-boned, square-headed, more than six foot in height, De Boigne with his polite, quiet smile and almost prim regard, was nevertheless a fighting-machine. He had been fighting all his life and may be presumed to have liked his vocation; but he did not fight from sheer delight in battle, like the Irishman George Thomas: he fought to make money, of which he was very fond. *Point d'argent, point de Suisse.* The secret behind the success of his battalions was that he did not rely upon haphazard wages from Scindia, but had insisted upon a large jeydad, a grant of territory which he governed himself, and from whence he drew their pay, including wound-money and pensions for the disabled, upon the model of the Company's service. With the Company, he had a fixed rule never to contend. He would fight any number of Englishmen in other parties, or employ any number in his own; but as long as he commanded it, his immense, beautifully disciplined army was neutral in the English-French quarrel.

He had begun in the Sardinian service, changed to the French-Irish Brigade, and then to the Russians; where he was unlucky enough to be taken prisoner by the Turks and sold as a slave, and lucky enough, when redeemed, to hit the favour of the Empress Catherine. With excellent introductions he was sent off to India, decided that the Company's service would be far too slow, was taken up by Warren Hastings, launched at the native courts, and bidden for by Mahadoji Scindia, who knew a good thing when he saw it. His original two battalions—which he called in the old French fashion after the names of cities—were constantly increased, he won victory after victory against vastly superior odds. The hazards of serving Oriental princes were, however, very present to that cool clockwork mind, and he was aware that failure was not more dangerous than too much success. He was at topmost power, and consequently at danger-point, in 1795, when Mahadoji Scindia died and was replaced by his nephew, Daulat Rao Scindia, who was but fifteen and much under the influence of an anti-De Boigne party. Gathering his enormous gains, the soldier from Savoy went home, taking with him the two children borne to him by a fair Persian.

He left his youth and his health in India: but while staying in London he heard a girl of seventeen singing at a concert, and recognised "a voice which must be mine". She was a French aristocrat, daughter of the *émigré* Marquis D'Osmond; and if De Boigne bought her, as he undoubtedly did, it was with every intention of making her happy. The thing would not do; they must separate in a few years' time; but with the most amiable politeness. Annually, Madame la Comtesse—for she obtained a title for her husband when the Bourbons were restored—would quit her Paris *salon* to play hostess at Chambéry. There, orphan-asylums, schools, every kind of charity bore witness to the manner in which M. le Comte Benoit de Boigne spent his Indian lakhs and his declining years. . . . Sometimes he would observe musingly: "My past appears a dream."

The return of the great De Boigne to France had caused some alarm in England, lest he should be lending his matchless skill and experience to Bonaparte's plans for the conquest of India. Even had he not formed this Royalist connection, however, there is no reason to suppose that he would have wavered in his policy of neutrality. His successor with Scindia's army was of a different mind. Before leaving, De Boigne had given young Daulat Rao an excellent piece of advice: not again to put the dangerous power represented by the battalions into a single pair of hands. Of the three brigades, one was based at Poona under the

Frenchman Perron; one at Mutra under his particular rival the Englishman Sutherland; and one at Koil under Pedron, an elderly and unambitious veteran. Their late generalissimo had counselled their being left as separate commands. However, Perron out-hastened Sutherland to Scindia's durbar with gifts, and having indeed some seniority was appointed to succeed De Boigne as Commander-in-Chief and Governor of Hindostan. He immediately increased the number of the battalions to forty, and as ruler of his jeydad, the better part of the Doab—"the French State"—became the most powerful European ever yet known in India. From Kotah in the south to Saharanpur in the north, from Jodhpur in the west to Koil in the east, he was absolute monarch; for his subjection to Scindia must be almost as nominal as Scindia's to the Mahratta Peishwa and the shadow of Delhi. Perron indeed controlled Delhi, and the person of Shah Alam, although he always went through a solemn court farce of "entering into the presence" when he interviewed that wretched prisoner. The annual revenue of his jeydad supplied him with a personal income of at least £150,000. . . . 'Twas considerable promotion for one that had begun life a peasant-lad, peddling kerchiefs. Pierre Cuillier, a sharp and sturdy young fellow, had enlisted, risen to be a sergeant of marines, and found himself off India in a French frigate—with English round-shot whistling past his ears, fired by a certain naval gunner of the name of George Thomas. Each ignorant of the other's existence, in the same year of 1781 both deserted ship into the vast, promising, perilous land of golden fortunes. Taking his nickname, Perron, as a fighting-name, Cuillier had learnt India and learned to soldier there, and had then sought out De Boigne. With the brigades, he at once distinguished himself by tireless relish for duty, and great courage. It was not the common custom for French officers to expose themselves much in battle, unlike the English, who invariably did so—their casualty-lists were surprisingly different. Only at Lukhari had every European officer upon either side been

H

either killed or wounded. Perron, however, soon lost an arm in the field; and his bravery much commended him to De Boigne, who was also accustomed to rely upon his strong plain sense.

But plain sense and peasant shrewdness can grow dizzy when hoisted up too high; they may not be proof against a *folie de grandeur*. Perron began to believe that he might succeed where Dupleix and Lally had failed: he intrigued with the French party at Hyderabad, and with the Jacobins that had been dispatched to Tipu Sahib at Seringapatam; and he sent word to the First Consul that he could deliver India to Revolutionary France. Not to hide his sympathies, he put the brigades into Cap-of-Liberty buttons, and began to apply "French principles" in the matter of promotion. Divers low Frenchmen were suddenly set over everybody's head. "Low they were", writes one superseded English officer, "in every sense of the word. Low in birth, in education, and in principle. Perron's army became a miniature of the French Revolution. Wretches were raised from cooks and barbers to become colonels and brigadiers, and showed into paths to acquire lakhs of rupees." Naturally, every English officer soon detested Perron. It was indeed his aim to get rid of them; they would hinder his plans.

His two principal native enemies, Mahratta chieftains who resented his power, had been eliminated; there remained only, lurking upon his flanks, that fantastic but dangerous figure Jowruj Jung, George the Victorious; or, as he was also called, Ship Sahib.

George Thomas came from some brood in an Irish cabin, possibly descended from a Cromwellian immigrant; he could not read, and when India rang with his name was unable to write it. He was a very handsome fellow, six foot four, with black hair, blue eyes, and broad shoulders. He had been pressed into the navy; and the gunnery which he there learnt was to prove extremely useful, securing a demand for his services among the mountain poligars, the robber tribes of the south. After a year or two with these, and a short stay in the topkhana of the Nizam of Hyderabad, he had taken the road for Sardhana, lured by stories of the Begum Somru. It took him six months' tramping to reach her presence. He found her a woman of forty-two, small, plump, fair, with the remains of beauty in large black eyes, her costly dress "perfect Hindostany", as he puts it, and her conversation "engaging, sensible and spirited". She in her turn saw a ragged knight-errant, as bold and comely as ever wore a sword. Whether she chose to become his mistress in more than one sense is unknown, but certainly she hired his sword.

In his first engagement with the party, against some rebel feudatories of Delhi, Thomas so distinguished himself that his share of the reward was a frontier jaghir, with the duty of keeping out Sikh raiders. When he set forth to govern this, the Begum gave him a little present on parting—a favourite Christian slave named Marie, for a wife. Thomas' little realm had never produced any revenue, owing to the plundering Sikhs; but Thomas had a supreme contempt for Sikhs, maintaining that he could chase any 5,000 of them with 500 Rohilla horse. Putting the notion into practice, he raided the territory of the raiders; and from the sudden prosperity induced by peace and security in his jaghir, sent back a thumping tribute.

But "Ship Sahib", not content with expressing contempt for Sikhs, had unfortunately expressed it freely for Frenchmen—and the Begum's officers, a pretty set of ruffians, were nearly all French. It is idle to inquire why she was so ready to receive their jealous insinuations, or to conjecture some strong emotion—"*Odi et amo*"—pervading the history of her relations with Thomas; the normal suspicion and treachery of any Oriental ruler will be enough to account for her belief that he intended to set up independently—perhaps to dethrone her. She seized his wife and child as hostages. He came whirling back from the borders, snatched them from the guard, and defied her. She sent her entire army to capture him and thrust him into British territory, to begin the world again upon Rs.500.

It was enough for Thomas, as she ought to have known. With it, he armed a few bazaar rascals, and held up one or two of her villages. From the captured brass cooking-pots, he cast four six-pounder guns; and then sold the services of his rapidly augmenting party to one of Scindia's more rebellious chiefs, Appa Khunde Rao, who gave him a wild jaghir from which he himself had never been able to extract tribute. Thomas extracted it. Soon, he acquired two more jaghirs, and then his popular title of George the Victorious. Scindia had sent against the rebel town of Sohawal Garh two crack brigades, under Sutherland and Alan Gardiner; these distinctly looked down their noses at Thomas and his raga-muffins, whom Appa, in a moment of loyalty to his suzerain, had sent to assist them. At a council of war, they decided that the town was impregnable to assault, and must be formally besieged. Thomas alone dissented, and marked his disagreement by going out at dawn and storming it himself; he refused them any share of the plunder.

Not content with wiping the eye of the famous brigades, Thomas went on to win battles in every direction. There is no question that he was made for the life he lived: forced marches, the storm of fortresses, and hand-to-hand combat —often wearing chain-armour and wielding a two-handed sword—were delightful to him; and but for the malice of fate, and one weak place in the fortress of his own per-sonality, George the Conqueror might never have been defeated.

He beat the Begum's party out of his borders, which must have sent her raging up and down behind her purdahs; and he had constantly to foil the treachery of his own jealous employer. Appa was a miserable creature, ever attempting to injure his too-successful captain, and ever sending despair-ing messages, money, and promises of amendment when he found himself in a tight place. Thomas royally forgave him, time and again. He was now able to do as much for the

Begum. In 1793 she had broken her prudent rule and married one of her men, a young Frenchman of good birth, named Le Vasseult. He was not popular in the party, as being the only gentleman; and he soon, with his wife's authority, set about reforming many disorders. The consequence was an immediate mutiny. Le Vasseult and the Begum attempted an evasion, but were overtaken by the mutineers. They had agreed upon suicide in this event. A crying of women from the palki told the young man, who was riding ahead, that his wife had stabbed herself; he snatched at his ready pistol and blew his brains out. He was lucky. The Begum, whose wound was not mortal, was compelled to sit and see his corpse horribly hacked and mistreated. Then she was taken back to Sardhana and publicly pilloried chained to a gun, which she was compelled to ride when it was blistering hot at noon. Meanwhile the mutineers had set up a son of Sombre by another woman. One of the Begum's officers, whether with or without her knowledge, got word of these happenings to Thomas; and Thomas, by some of his incredible forced marches, sprang to the rescue. . . . The Begum's gratitude for her deliverance was to be expressed in continued raids on her deliverer's territory, and a final leaguing with his enemies to bring him down to ruin.

Appa went too far when he summoned Thomas to his durbar, and received him in the midst of a band of villainous Rohillas, whose looks spoke of murder. Thomas grasped and enjoyed the situation at once; although alone, he was fortunately not unarmed; and he bandied Eastern compliment until Appa rose suddenly; then he stuck one pistol in the Mahratta's ribs, levelled the other at the Rohillas, and rejoined his followers outside. Even this episode he was able to forgive his late master, who was a sick man; but thereafter he set up for himself as an independent ruler.

Into a desolate and dispeopled tract of country called Hariana, "The Green Land", rode Jowruj Jung, Sahib

Bahadur, Jehazi Sahib, and took possession of the abandoned stronghold of Hansi. Long and long ago had Hansi been abandoned; 40,000 Mohammedans had once fallen in taking it from the Hindus; but the last enemy to escalade it had been the jungle. When Thomas came to the ancient, red, roofless ruins of the city, a Punjabi legend has it that they were only peopled by one fakir and two lions—this being one of the few parts of India where lions could be found: an appropriate place for the new lord of Hansi. From these rebuilt walls, the man who could not read remade the entire derelict district: set up a code of civil administration and law: apportioned revenue, salaries, pay and pensions for the troops: built courthouses, arsenals, munition factories: and minted his own sikka rupees, with "T" upon one side, and on the obverse "Sikah Sahib. A.H. 1214."

Life, health, population, agriculture and industry immediately flowed into the barren land and the once-dead city. Beneath the strong rule of Ship Sahib, all flourished in safety; while his wild horse and foot went swinging and storming off gaily from time to time, returning with tribute from the Rajahs—Jaipur, Bikanir, Udaipur, Patiala. The Rajah of Patiala's sister had held a fort against Thomas; he said she was "a better man than her brother", and later came chivalrously to her defence. For all his status as a robber-chief, he was, says the free-lance Skinner, "frank, generous and humane. His manners were grave and gentle, and he was courteous to all." Indeed, the big Irishman carried himself like all the knights in Froissart and Malory rolled into one ... that is to say, if one can suppose those paladins occasionally to drink themselves stupid for a week at a time.

So it was; this was the weak place of Ship Sahib Bahadur; and thus would he fall.

At Bahadurgarh, near Delhi, in October, 1801, he met Perron for a parley; with a hostility displayed on Thomas' part, dissembled on that of Perron. Both men were in the thick of great enterprises. Thomas had now ten battalions and a park of artillery; with this he had crossed the Sutlej,

chasing the Sikhs before him, and reduced the Cis-Sutlej
states to agreement and ransom; he was pushing for Lahore,
which he intended to make the capital of his new realm.
Before setting out, he had sent word to the Governor-
General, Lord Wellesley, that it was his intention to conquer
the Punjab, and that he would be glad of the Company's
acquiescence, if not aid. "I have no other design in view
than the glory of my King and country," he stated magnificently, "and do not wish to see my conquests fall to those at
enmity with them." The Company could not meddle, but
must leave him to acquire the Punjab single-handed, which
it really seemed that he might do. Had not Perron suddenly
come trespassing upon his borders, he would have reached
Lahore; as it was, he must fall back on Hansi, fighting an
amazing rearguard action with Sikh horse, and marching
forty miles a day. As for Perron, he had long been summoned south by Scindia, who lay at Koil, headquarters of
the brigades, threatened by Holkar—but he had no mind to
go, for he wished to keep his hand upon Delhi and the
puppet King, all ready to hand over to Napoleon. The
time was coming when he could delay no longer, but must
either obey the summons or declare himself independent.
Thomas must be dealt with first. . . .

At their meeting, which must have been a sight worth
seeing, Perron offered the Irishman Rs.60,000 a month,
with rank and favour in Scindia's service; and Thomas
rejected it with scorn. "Mr. Perron and myself, being subjects of nations in a state of hostility, could not possibly act
together in concert." Had he been subtle enough to tem-
porise, it is quite possible that a rising of Perron's antagon-
ised English officers would have placed him in Perron's
shoes. Scindia must have accepted the accomplished fact, the
conquest of the Punjab then have proved easy, and the most
of India fallen under the Irishman's sway.

Guile was foreign, however, to such a straightforward
fighter; but he was to have one more chance to get the game
in his hand. Since it must be war, and Perron must depart

for Koil, the brigades were left to attack Thomas under the second-in-command, Louis Bourquien. This man was one of the "wretches" promoted on revolutionary principles—he and Perron had married native women who were sisters; he had been a cook, and may possibly have been a good one; but his military incompetence was complete. He began by bungling a plan to cut Thomas off from Hansi, and then attacked him at his other strong post of Georgegarh, with troops wearied from a thirty-hour march—himself remaining in the rear. They collected 4,000 casualties, and the splendid De Boigne guns stuck in the sand with snapped axle-trees. . . . Had Thomas now sallied out, he could have consummated a decisive victory, fresh allies would have joined him, Delhi could have been taken, and Perron defied. But the Irishman had been stricken by the loss of his friend Hopkins, his only European officer, for the hard-fighting Birch and Hearsey were Eurasians; it had hit him so hard that he retired to his tent with a sufficiency of bottles. . . . When he came out again, his chance was gone and his doom was sealed.

Perron had hastily superseded Bourquien by the stout old veteran Pedron; and the troops, hardly recovered from their amazement at not being wiped out, found themselves blockading Georgegarh, while reinforcements flowed in—including the party of the Begum Sombre. Outnumbered by more than ten to one, Thomas determined to cut his way out; hotly pursued, he rode the sixty miles to Hansi in twenty-four hours, on one Persian barb. There he rallied to beat off a storm with all his old fury. The brave Eurasian James Skinner, founder of Skinner's Horse, freely confesses to running from that huge figure with bare tattooed arms, shield, and whirling sword. All would not do, however. Bribery and blackmail—methods at which Bourquien was something of an expert—corrupted a portion of the garrison whose homes were in Scindia's territory, and food began to run short. There was soon nothing for it but a surrender. Though the ex-cook had been boasting of what he would do

to Thomas when he got him, the British officers insisted
that he be accorded proper treatment; and he marched out
with all the honours, wearing his sword. His officers Birch
and Hearsey agreed to join the brigades, as did some of his
men; but more vowed that after serving so glorious a
leader as Ship Sahib, they could serve no other, and would
seek religious retirement.

A camp banquet was prepared, in which all enmity should
be drowned, and his late opponents toasted George Thomas
with heartfelt admiration. It was not, however, shared by
M. Bourquien, who bounced up and insultingly proposed
success to the arms of General Perron. Every British officer
turned down his glass; and Thomas, leaping up, whipped
out his sword with a roar, and chased his enemy out of the
tent. "One Irish sword", he shouted, waving the steel
above his head, "is sufficient for a hundred Frenchmen!"

If he had not been very drunk, he would not have stained
that honourable steel that night by striking at the sentry who
dared to challenge him at the gate of his own Hansi. Next
morning he was overcome with remorse to find that he had
cut off the man's hand, and sent him many rupees. . . .
Under escort, he now left with his family to realise his lakhs,
and proceed down river to Calcutta. To Captain Franklin,
who had charge of him on this long journey, he dictated the
story of his adventures—"with", as that biographer observes, "that energy and spirited animation which distinguished him throughout the scenes of his extraordinary
life". At Benares, he was presented to the Governor-
General, who was there on a tour of inspection. The Marquess Wellesley had every sympathy with a brave, ambitious
man. Together the two Irishmen studied a map of India.
Thomas could not read the lettering, but he understood the
red shading, marking the British dominions. Over the
Punjab he placed his great tattooed sword-hand, saying:
"All this should be red. I could have made all this red with
my own hand." . . .

He never went home to Ireland, for he died of fever at

Bahrampur in August, 1802, at the age of forty-six, and was buried in an unmarked grave. Had any stone been set above his bones, the best epitaph might have been: "One Irish Sword."

The large chances and changes in the life of a free-lance are mirrored in the careers of such men as these; but the daily detail, the actual colour of such a life can best be recaptured from some such book as Sir Henry Lawrence's *Adventures of an Officer in the Punjab.* He wrote of the later period, round about 1830, when the "Old Man of Lahore", the Maharajah Ranjit Singh, was continuing the tradition of employing European adventurers; but India does not change, and conditions in the Punjab at that time were much like conditions elsewhere before the Company's conquests. Moreover, Lawrence chooses for his fictional hero typical exploits belonging to Thomas and others, and gives him what he clearly regards as a typical free-lance name: that of Bellasis.

Into the Maharajah's city the English soldier rides on a fine horse, his tall and handsome person shown off by a rich dress, and several armed attendants following him, with horsekeepers running beside. So rode the knight at adventure in the days of chivalry. The people admire and cheer him, with "*Wah, Feringhi! . . . Shabash* (Well done) . . . *Changa gohda* (Fine horse) . . . *Khub jewan* (Handsome rider)."

He is summoned to the durbar, and brings with him a rich *nazar*, or present. The Maharajah, who has been directing the punishment of some petty thieves, dragged bleeding from the presence with lopped ears and noses, now questions him: "You speak Persian? . . . Can you build a fort? . . . Can you cure a long-standing disease? . . . Can you cast a gun? . . . Can you shoe a horse? . . . Can you mend my watch which has stopped?" Boldly the free-lance states that he can do everything and is ignorant of nothing: that having heard the fame of the King he has come from a far country to offer his services: that the King of Roum, the Shah of

Persia, the Amirs of Sind, have all asked him to join them as a brother, but that he would devote his sword to no one but the lion of the Punjab.

. . . He observes the other European officers, and the Sikh sowars, to be eyeing him with some jealousy; and establishes his footing by beating the leading *chabuk sowar* at a riding contest. The pleased Maharajah instantly makes him a colonel, and gives him a *khilat* of eleven pieces—that is, a formal present comprising a horse and accoutrements, a sword, two shawls, a pearl necklace, a fur pelisse, two pieces of fine muslin, and Rs.1,000; also sending to his lodging a *zifayat*, or banquet of fruit and sweetmeats. Thus he takes his place with Allard and Ventura, with the modest and honourable Court, and the gallows-erecting Avitabile, whose crest should have been a vulture. . . .

The fictional Bellasis then departs for the wild jaghir of Kot Kangra, in subduing and ruling which he encounters violent adventures. Behind him, at the Maharajah's durbar, he leaves a prudent vakil: "Better is a dog in the presence than a brother afar." Reports will thus reach him if treachery against him be meditated, as it inevitably will be. . . . His habit of life is to rise before dawn and breakfast on a crust of bread with a glass of *eau sucrée*; taking a slight repast at mid-morning, and dining on a pilau at sunset. When necessary, he can spend all day in the saddle, living thus with strait temperance. Thirty yards of fine muslin wound about his cap protects him from the sun; but night is his chosen time for long marches. When in residence at Kot Kangra he dispenses justice after the morning crust, deals with correspondence during the noonday retirement, holds another durbar for his followers and tenants afterwards, and gives them: "*Hal Rukhsat ast*: You are dismissed", just before sunset, when he inspects his troops and rides round the farms and villages.

He learns to get at the truth in durbar from persons addressing him flatteringly as Lord of Favour, and Appreciator of Merit; and how to classify information from natives: One man always lies, and must be understood by contraries; one fishes for what you wish to hear, and tries to provide it; one is paid to mislead you, and one hopes that he may be; one knows nothing, but likes to be seen talking to a Feringhee.

A regiment of lancers with their long bamboo spears and ugly little native horses, a regiment of foot—tatterdemalions with matchlocks, and two corps of *Nujibs*—local volunteers of some social standing—are the means by which our adventurer must preserve peace and justice in his district, and extract the revenue: a task thoroughly familiar to Henry Lawrence when he wrote.

He completes his hero's experiences by endowing him with a Rajputni bride, the daughter of a small hill Rajah dispossessed by the Sikhs. This again was typical, for most of the free-lances made native alliances. When these were true marriage, and not casual concubinage, they reached heights of romance. There was the story of the free-lance Alan Gardiner, who while negotiating at a native court saw a wonderful pair of black eyes looking over a screen, and insisted on having the lady produced and married to him. Their loving union endured for forty years, and her blood flows yet in the veins of a titled family. . . . Then there was the story of the house in Surrey with the very high wall. Nobody knew who lived in it, except that it was said to belong to a retired Indian officer who had not been seen to issue from the locked gates these twenty years. One day he died; strangers from the outer world must enter—and were filled with amazement at what they saw. Major H——, it then appeared, had married a lady of Madras named Fyzoo, who had given him two sons, and died in bearing a daughter. He had quitted India carrying with him their embalmed bodies in leaden coffins, and the old *dhai* who had tended them. His sons he had sent away; and he had lived alone for a quarter of a century, with the *dhai* as portress instructed to admit no one, and the two bodies laid out upon a silk bed for all his company. . . .

Lawrence arranges a romantic and tragic love-story for his fictional free-lance and the Lady Mahtab; but neither the name or any other particular of the bride of the real Joseph Bellasis has survived—except that she bore him one daughter. One cannot say if he taught her to play on her wire-stringed *sitar* the air that must have delighted Juliana:

> *How happy we Soldiers, thus destin'd to rove*
> *From danger to glory, from glory to love:*
> *But happier still is the Fair for whose charms*
> *We forego all the danger and glory of Arms . . .*

The story of Joseph Harvey Bellasis—"the brilliant Bellasis"—and his life as a free-lance leader, is a brief one. His biographers dwell upon what he might have done, had not fate been against him. Lewis Ferdinand Smith, his brother-in-arms in Scindia's service, and the author of a detailed contemporary account of the free-lances, thus draws a portrait: "Bellasis possessed all the advantages of undaunted courage, military science, and an excellent education; an elegant person, great activity of body and energy of mind—he was generous, open, candid and affable—an accomplished scholar and a finished Gentleman of fascinating address; but he wanted the intrigue, the assiduity, the duplicity necessary to rise with the native Princes, especially with Umbajee, who has the worst principle of the worst Asiatic."

The peculiar treachery and meanness of Ambaji Anglia, even among his fellows, is everywhere noted: he did his best to sell Thomas on one occasion; and it is satisfactory to find that he was eventually cheated out of a considerable treasure by the joint action of Scindia and Holkar—two wolves suddenly in accord to rob the jackal.

For Scindia, his suzerain, it was Ambaji's duty to provide a certain number of battalions; and the raising of four of these he entrusted in 1796 to Joseph Harvey Bellasis. The four battalions "would have been the finest in Hindostan, if Umbajee's parsimony had not thwarted Bellasis' labours and his genius". However, Bellasis persevered, with his whole heart in the matter, resolved that his party should be the best disciplined, the best uniformed, the most notable for endurance and valour, that the circumstances could possibly admit. . . . We see him—with that "great activity of body and energy of mind"—galloping on an Arab horse under the smiting sun; or riding in a dust-cloud with his cavalry and his marching men, through the long, star-illumined nights. . . . The too-bright moon will suffer him to read the print of his pocket-Caesar; it paints out in white detail here a broken tomb, and here the skull of a kite-picked cow; it sparks off buttons and buckles and the steel heads of the bamboo lances. . . . Under that figure have the European leaders of the Free Companies been mentioned in history: "The steel point to the bamboo lance." Steel, such a leader must be, and truly tempered; that handsome face under the Eastern turban must show the strength of the West, and the reason why, from Alexander to Clive, a handful led by Western men might beat an Asiatic host out of the field. . . . The crust and the sip of water before the stars have set, the meal not taken until all has been disposed, men and beasts fed, every order given, the tented repose upon a string cot, with arms at hand. . . . Jade-green evening, blood-and-gold dawn, unmerciful noon, and dust, dust immeasurable over uncountable kos of that land of Hind which has been beaten by the feet of armies for such centuries past. . . . The villages with well and banyan-tree and tawdry temple—with the salaaming headman and the terrified people, propitiatory with a miserable goat, a miserable bag of millet. The tight hold to be kept of troops with an Oriental tradition of loot and rape. The sharp, swift justice of pie-powder durbar. . . .

The foregathering, then, at headquarters, with other officers, where wine and candlelight make a semblance of civilised company; and where, with that lithe "elegant person" adorned with fine ruffles, our "finished Gentleman" can exercise his "fascinating address". . . . The faces about the board—wild, hard, signed with Indian years, or dark with country blood: coming of every kind of social origin, and denoting every grade of character, from the veteran Sutherland, trained by De Boigne, who was to lead Scindia's forces to victory over Holkar at Indore, to Fidele Filoze, vile mixture of low Neapolitan and sweeper-woman, bribed on that occasion to fire on his own side. . . . The Smith brothers, gallant Irish Brownrigg (Burandree Sahib), James Shepherd (Jamus Sahib), who had worked himself valiantly up from the condition of a servant, Alan Gardiner, of excellent Scots family, the half-bloods, James and Robert Skinner, Maculloch and Mackenzie, Plumet, who was "a Frenchman but a gentleman", and Perron's new promotions who were not—headed by the strutting Bourquien, whom Skinner wrote down "not only a coward but a fool", and Smith judged "as wicked as he was weak". . . .

Despite hot antagonisms, there would be a strong fellow-ship in such gatherings of men who held their lives lightly and were of the same trade. All knew that by the chance of war they might find themselves some day on opposite sides; friends of theirs were in the service of Holkar or of other chiefs whom they must fight. It was a great and deadly chess-game of which they knew each square and every move. In the lees of their wine, they drew familiar fortresses and battles. . . .

Headquarters, for Joseph Bellasis, however, though it might mean wine and singing of old songs, and endless professional talk with his fellow adventurers, must also mean spies and rumours, and dangerous whispers at durbar, the shifting eyes and the grudging hand of Ambaji, con-cessions required at which his pride grew steel-stiff, friendly hints of what he lost by not condescending to cringe suit-ably, much anxiety, and more promises than pay. . . . It must, too, have meant something else, very different—something not spoken about, and decorously hidden behind cere-monial curtains. Two soft arms would go about his neck— not arms like the snow of his native land, arms of gold-brown silk, very young and slender, very loving, very submissive, adorned with many bangles of silver and glass, with the palms of the narrow hands stained red. . . . This girl has been taught to look upon men as infinitely superior to herself: upon the man who shall possess her as a walking god. Has she not reason to give thanks to the other gods that her god is so tall and beautiful, so brave and so gentle, so famous a man of war, and yet so ready to be happy with her in her little world of caresses and sweetmeats, silver gauzes, and new nose-jewels, and the wire-stringed *sitar?* It is all one to her, perhaps, if he has married her by this rite, or that rite, or no rite. In a sense it is all one to him; or why that paper, scrawled with his usual carelessness, leaving all that he owns in India to her and to her child? . . . His goods left in her care, the house where he has placed her, his home; he has that behind him when he must march away again to the dusty routine of warfare in the plains.

More wheeling of cavalry and forming squares of infantry, more mud forts, more battering of a breach, and charging it sword in hand. . . . In August, 1797, Joseph Harvey Bellasis led his battalions to the storming of Larhar: a fort which it had been considered an amazing though costly feat on the part of Popham to have captured, some years before, for it was nearly impregnable without heavy siege artillery. Bellasis, however, succeeded in this most difficult attack—"an assault of uncommon boldness"—and the casualties were bloodily heavy. No congratulations on the news were received from Ambaji, but a message of quite a different character: "Bellasis was ordered with his shattered and fatigued party to march immediately and storm another fort ten coss off, called Gopaulpoor, to leave his dead unburied, and his wounded unattended and unassuaged. These inhuman orders ought only to be issued in the most cruel necessity: such as did not exist in the present case, and Bellasis with the fine feelings of a soldier and with the propriety of a commander, refused to obey the orders, with indignant contempt." Smith's account echoes the spirit in

which most of the other free-lance leaders must have discussed the episode; but Bellasis' refusal to Ambaji—accompanied, we may suppose, with some such message as, that
he would see him damned first—"had been eagerly expected;
and was made a pretext to discharge him and his battalions,
and to plunder his effects".

A thoroughly Mahratta intrigue of this sort had found
the soldier defenceless; nor could the Indian lady behind his
purdahs do anything to hinder the official looting of his
goods. They must go into other territory, and offer his
sword again for sale. A year passed without anything
presenting itself that appeared satisfactory and likely to be
permanent; embarrassments increased upon Joseph Bellasis;
at last Ambaji, who had never found anything equal to him
in the market, and had sudden particular occasion for the
most able men he could get, began again to make approaches.
These, in 1799, were accepted. Bellasis went back to his
own field of action, taking over two battalions to co-operate
with James Shepherd's party.

There was more dissension than usual within the Mahratta
wolf-pack. The young Daulat Rao Scindia had caused a vast
deal of trouble in the matter of the Bhais, the widows of his
uncle, Mahdoji Scindia, for he had shown favour to the
youngest, who was beautiful, at the expense of two elder
ones, who were not. These aggrieved ladies had appealed to
several of the chiefs, who were glad of a chance to rebel, as
they had their own serious grievances against Scindia's evil
favourite, Ghatkay Rao. This man had consolidated his
influence by giving his own lovely daughter in marriage to
his master, and had used it in a general purge and slaughter
of personal enemies. The Bhais had now taken refuge with
the chief Lakwa Dada; and it was against him that Scindia's
troops were to march, with Ambaji in command.

Ambaji, however, sent the battalions under his brother,
and himself tarried at Gwalior, hating Ghatkay Rao as much
as did the insurgents. There were 5,000 horse, three of the
brigades, and a native corps. Lakwa Dada had entrenched

I

himself in the fortress of Sonda, in the Datia State, along with the Datia Rajah and the Bhais; he had 6,000 cavalry, 3,000 local troops, and 200 sepoys commanded by the Irish free-lance Colonel Tone, brother to Wolfe Tone. Moreover, the flanks of this strong place were defended by broken country and several forts, and it was approached by a net-work of hill ravines, through which were only three clear passes, strongly protected. Sonda was going to be the death of many. It was going to be the death of Joseph Bellasis.

The weather for campaigning was good, for it was late December. The engagement opened with some spirited skirmishes; and then Brownrigg brought fifty-two of Scindia's guns into play, with great effect; the rebels had but sixteen. In three columns, the three passes were now attacked: old Colonel Pedron to the right, Shepherd and Bellasis in the centre, and a strong body under Captain Symes upon the left. This last party met with such furious opposition from the Rajah of Datia that it was driven back, badly mauled; and the column opposed to Colonel Tone lost 1,000 killed and wounded, and two European officers. Bellasis and Shepherd made head, for their part, against a fiercely fighting chief named Barar Singh; but, with footing victoriously gained, and his men rushing up behind him, as he waved them on with his sword, the tall Bellasis toppled, with a matchlock bullet through his brains.

. . . Says Smith: "Thus fell poor Bellasis, who was an ornament to society, and an honour to his nation and his profession, who had follies, but whose heart was pure and unsullied, and his sentiments noble and refined." "Thus has this amiable character finished his mortal career," says that correspondent of the *Bengal Telegraph* who characterised the dead man's manners as "inchanting". . . .

Behind the purdahs there must be wailing, rending of gauze veils and black-silk hair; but this is a private grief, nor will the mourner emerge into notice except in a vague contemptuous phrase about a paper attempted to be pro-duced "in favour of a Hindustanee woman and her child";

this second wife is not going to be talked about in the family.

"Let me entreat of you to soften the melancholy news to my ever lov'd, good and venerable parent. . . . If you have any regard for me, lead him into misery as tenderly as you can. . . ." Thus wrote George Bridges Bellasis to Edmund Lodge. When he ended the year of Seringapatam—the most exciting, perilous, and triumphant year of his life—in mourning for his admired elder brother, George Bellasis saw the end of one epoch, the beginning of another. Conquest and expansion, the Wellesleys, and the eventual *Pax Brittanica* lay ahead; the Great Anarchy was over, the day of the Free Companies was done.

VI

THE TIGER'S DEN

WHEN Hyder Ali sat within his tent after the battle of Conjeveram, and the bleeding heads of the English were cast down before him by his chiefs, his son Tipu Sahib affected mercy towards the group of English officers, sickened and horrified, half dead with fatigue and thirst and wounds, who were compelled to witness the scene. Upon several occasions during these campaigns he made much show of succouring the English captives, providing them water and shelter from the sun. It was his policy at the time to appear less barbarous than his father: an easy matter enough.

However, when in November, 1782, he succeeded Hyder upon the musnud at Mysore, it was found that he hated the English even more than his father had done, and campaigned against them more relentlessly; and that the careless cruelty of the foul-mouthed ex-corporal gave way in his successor to something twisted and monstrous and not, in fact, properly human. In the Canarese tongue, "Tipu" means Tiger: an unlucky fact. Whether the black, squat Prince Tiger came to believe himself a beast by any kind of lycanthropy, it was his whim to act out his reign and to order his diversions in strict accordance with his name. Nine cages of tigers were kept in his island capital of Seringapatam; they were his chief executioners, and were also used in the games of the arena, where they were matched against wild buffaloes, or against mounted pikemen. By the end of a day's amusement a dozen or more dead tigers would be lying in the scarlet-slaked dust, and elephants would be goaded in to trample any lingering life out of the beautiful striped carcasses. At these games, also, the Sultan's gladiators would be ordered to fight with the "tiger's claws", a set of steel talons concealed in the hand and drawing fountains of blood at each stroke.

For his throne of state, Tipu had a great gold tiger-head fashioned as a footstool, with eyes and snarling teeth of crystal. His sepoys were clad in a special tiger uniform. He possessed an ingeniously constructed toy which he would spend delighted hours in watching: a life-size mechanical tiger, mauling the prostrate body of an Englishman: when the machinery was wound up, there was a mixed noise of roaring and screaming, and the figure of the man would jerk up its arms as in agony.

He had lighter methods of expressing this last hatred. Upon the blank chunam walls of many of the principal buildings in Seringapatam, he commanded great coloured cartoons to be painted up, representing Englishmen undergoing various obscene and horrible fates; and a buffoon would also attend the bloody games, mounted upon stilts, with whitened face, dressed in the Company's uniform, grotesquely taking snuff or affecting to be drunk.

A sovereign who hated the Company must naturally be courted by the French. Hyder's battalions had been officered by French mercenaries; and although King Louis had slighted Tipu's ambassadors, the Directory took the Sultan to their hearts. General Bonaparte presently sent him the most cordial letters from Egypt, proposing to send him "an innumerable and invincible army" that should drive the English into the sea. The French Admiral Suffrein's conduct in callously handing over his English prisoners, some of them mere children, to the mercies of Tipu was a thing never forgiven or forgotten. Even in the present age, which has revived the torture chamber and the slave battalion, Tipu's dealings with his prisoners are past reporting.

In the narratives of those who survived, something almost worse than the horrors is the utter despair with which the prisoners found themselves overlooked when peace was twice made with the Sultan. In 1792, Lord Cornwallis, the Governor-General himself, lay victoriously outside the walls of Seringapatam, which Tipu only saved by a hasty submission, and by sending his two young sons as hostages. He had been scared enough to commence whitewashing the pictures on the walls, and his Abyssinian stranglers had visited the dungeons of several who could tell too much, while a few were released; but for want of a proper insistence beforehand, the greater part of his victims were left to him when the treaty was concluded. It was to be seven more years before the British broke into his dungeons.

Meanwhile, he continued his tiger's enjoyments, and the pursuit of art, literature, and enlightened progressive politics. He was building a new gold and lacquer palace in his beautiful island capital, with a wing for the 600 women of his own and his father's harem, and all the maimed boys, trained by the nautch people, whom he selected from his prisoners. Of these was "Mr. Randall Cadman", midshipman, twelve years old, who boldly resisted training as a dancing-boy, and effected his escape; also the nine who are related to have shown themselves upon the Sultan's terrace to their captive fellow countrymen, weeping bitterly in their muslins and bangles, and plucking off the turbans of their enforced Mohammedanism. Captured white women were usually allotted to the slaves; one narrative mentions four soldiers' wives given to the abominable Abyssinians.

Every day when Tipu was in Seringapatam, four beautiful Arabian mares, two elephants, and two palanquins were kept in waiting for him outside the palace. He preferred the latter conveyance, being indolent, for all his coarse strength and the breadth of shoulder that made him appear less than his five-foot-nine. In his palanquin he would be carried perhaps to the wide tree-shaded streets at the east of the island, to pay his devotions to his father's tomb in the Red Garden. Hyder's mausoleum was a magnificent square building ascended by many steps, with a door in each side through which the tomb itself was visible, covered in housings of black velvet, and with a large ball of brightly polished steel suspended above it. Great man as that low-born usurper had been, Tipu liked to think himself a greater. After all, his father was a mere horseman who could neither read nor write, while he himself was a scholar, constantly seen with a pen or a book in hand, and ready to inquire into such Western devices as ballooning. His Frenchmen ecstatically praised his learning and enlightenment; and for his part he heartily admired what he heard of the French Revolution: it seemed quite to his taste. When at last Citizen Chapuy came to him with a military mission, he himself put on the red cap and became Citizen Tipu, ordering a salute of 2,000 cannon, 500 rockets, and all the musketry in Seringapatam, while a tree of liberty was planted there. He indeed appeared to imagine this was a kind of ceremony in his own honour; but he was not above taking a hint—it was surely from Citizen Carrier of Nantes that Citizen Tipu copied the idea of martyring the Malabar Christians by causing them to wade out to sea, chained two and two.

His religious zeal must mark another point of superiority to his father. Hyder had cared little about religion, but Tipu was so fervent a Moslem that he missed no occasion to insult, slaughter, or forcibly convert his Hindu subjects. Their sacred cattle he slew in the temples, saying that they made the best beef; and on one occasion tied up a sacred cow elephant to be killed by cuts from his swordsmen. A thousand Hindus in one day were made into Mohammedans; and as the initiatory rite of Islam is nothing so gentle as baptism, this also was a bloody business. According to Hindu sacred law, "He who strikes a Brahmin, even with a straw, shall be whirled about in the Hell named Tamisra for a thousand years". One who should forcibly circumcise a Brahmin, a twice-born of the highest cast, must certainly have this hell in prospect; but meanwhile the wretched Hindus prostrated themselves and suffered in the hell of which their ruler gave them present possession. Such as were reputed rich might expect to be starved in an iron cage, or pinioned to the ground all day with their faces to the sun, until they ransomed themselves with a lakh or two. Such as were recalcitrant might be goaded through the bazaar on an ass, with their lips and noses cut off; or executed by being dragged face down at an elephant's foot. These measures, together with what an English survivor calls "the abject tameness of the Indians" prevented any rising in Mysore.

The European captives were less tame, so they were largely kept in irons; and must be held down by professional strong men while being made into Mohammedans. One officer cut his throat afterwards. The baser sort of common soldiers relieved their feelings by circumcising rats and pie-dogs and running them through the camp to infuriate their captors.

In the eighteenth-century manner of applying cool, flat definitions to everything in the world, however strange or horrible, the English verdict on Tipu was simply that he was a "barbarian" and a "vile tyrant". At the same time he was a very dangerous neighbour for the Company. It was of no use beating him in the field and making fair treaties with him, for he was incapable of keeping treaties, and would rather lie than not. After his sons were restored to him in 1794 there was no hold upon him, and he was clearly crouching for another spring.

Secure in the notion of French assistance, he offered open defiance in '98. Cornwallis was gone, and was coping with the rebellion in Ireland. The magnificent Lord Mornington, soon to be Marquess Wellesley, was come out as Governor-General, and found it instantly necessary to stand upon his defence. The best defence being attack, "with every degree of practicable dispatch", he lost no time in assembling armies in the two Presidencies of Bombay and Madras, and detaching that necessary ally the Nizam of Hyderabad from his French connections. Meanwhile, he made a strong attempt to do the same with Tipu, and settle matters peaceably.

Tipu answered him with mocking civility on gold-dusted paper, but continued to rely on General Bonaparte's promises to come and join in exterminating the English.

All hopes of peace being extinguished, Mornington issued one of his grandly phrased proclamations, and the main army under General Harris began marching towards Mysore in February, 1799. It was joined by the Nizam's army, nominally commanded by Mir Alum, but really by Colonel the Honourable Arthur Wellesley, the Governor's brother: a young man with a big nose and cold blue eyes. At the same time, the much smaller Bombay army began to ascend the Western Ghats; it was commanded by General Stuart, and with him went George Bridges Bellasis, upon his first real campaign. It could be called a form of tiger-hunting.

Although swollen by the usual unavoidable numbers of camp-followers and servants, General Stuart's army was less than 7,000, whereas Colonel Wellesley's horse and foot was about 16,000, and General Harris' some 37,000. Added up, these forces showed a slight superiority to those of Tipu, who had been confidently expecting his 60,000 odd Mysoreans to be joined by an equal number of French. Nelson's victory at the Nile, however, had given Bonaparte check in Egypt, and Tipu must fight this critical, this final combat with his own resources.

It had been expected that he would give battle to the main army when it advanced to within sight of Bangalore, as his horse had been hovering about it, devastating the country; but he was elsewhere employed, and swooped suddenly upon the weakest army: Stuart's. This was advancing through the Rajah of Coorg's territory, who was very much Tipu's enemy, and with reason. Tipu had seized his country and hunted down his people like wild beasts, slain his father, forcibly Mohammedanised himself, and taken two of his sisters. As soon as he had reached man's estate, the young Rajah had escaped and led a resistance-movement so successful that he had soon recaptured the whole of Coorg, and proved a valuable ally to the British in the campaign of 1792. Cornwallis had then insisted upon Tipu's giving up all designs on Coorg. As the frontier lay within forty miles of Seringapatam, it continued a very valuable alliance upon the present occasion.

Upon the 6th of March, when the right brigade of the Bombay army under Colonel Montresor had reached Sedaseer, Tipu fell upon it with nearly 12,000 of his best troops. He counted upon wiping it out, after which he could dispatch Stuart's main force at his leisure, and so maim the English plan that Harris and Wellesley must fall back.

"I will give you a short Account of our Campaign," George Bellasis presently wrote to his friend Lodge. "Our first Action which struck A decisive blow to the late Sultaun's Troops was the sixth March, 1799. We had three Native Regts. in Advance 7 miles in the Coorka Rajah's country an Ally of ours, his Country bordering on the Sultaun's; the Sultaun's Troops were seen Advancing in three Columns by Daylight in the morning about twenty thousand in number"—they must have looked quite that to the dismayed advance guard—"and about 8 in the Morning Action commenced, which lasted till our Regt. had expended all their Ammunition and expected every moment the Enemy to Charge, however with the Artillery they were prevented from that, by our Troops making a false Charge while the Guns were loading, and then falling back—The Enemy finding that our Ammunition was expended surrounded Our Troops completely and began cooking their Dinners!!" In point of fact, the Tiger here discerned room for a little cat-and-mouse play, and plenty of time for his men to refresh themselves before slaughtering the infidel. However, Stuart's main body, George Bellasis with it, were many miles nearer than he had supposed. "At which most fortunate period the Flank Company of H.M. 75th Regt. and the whole of the 77th Regt. (with two *field pieces* under my Command) came upon them, the

Manner in which they were attack'd threw them into the utmost confusion, as they did not conceive there were any Europeans within 20 miles of them."

It was the surprise and "the Manner in which they were attack'd" which did the business. Tipu was driven off by a total force of some 2,000, suffering a loss of almost as many, including many of his chief men. The British losses amounted to twenty-nine killed, ninety-eight wounded, and sixteen missing. The Rajah of Coorg, who was present, wrote glowingly to Lord Mornington: "To describe the battle which General Stuart fought with these two regiments of Europeans, the discipline, valour, strength, and magnanimity of the troops, the courageous attack upon the army of Tipu surpasses all example in this world. In our Shasters and Paranas, the battles fought by Allered and Maharat have been much celebrated, but they are unequal to this battle."

Every man, indeed, had distinguished himself, and George Bellasis, with his guns, especially so; as mentioned in General Stuart's dispatches. It was a cardinal action, quite literally, a hinge on which the whole operation turned. "It is certain that if He had beaten Us on that Day"—observes Bellasis—"Our Army must have fallen back, and the war not have terminated in one Campaign." He continues, "I forgot to Mention one Circumstance that occurred in my Presence on the 6th of March it will serve to give you an Idea of the Mercy any of us might have expected if we had fallen into the Hands of any of that D—d Rascal Tippoos troops—One of the Sultauns Troops was lying on the Road side with his Thigh and both Legs broke, a Man of Mine went up to him to Bayonet him, but finding the State the poor fellow was in, humanely Said, He had got enough, gave him some Water to drink, and was leaving Him, when the infernal Wretch crawl'd to his Musket and fir'd at the very Man that had spar'd his Life and given him relief, the Soldier turn'd back, and in reply to My Orders not to return, he exclaim'd 'He would Obey

Me as his Officer in every other respect, but by G—d he would kill that fellow', he drove the Bayonet so hard through him that it came off the Fusill and he left it sticking in the ground. So much"—comments Captain Bellasis— "for the poor distress'd Natives of India."

Those comfortable persons in Europe, Radicals or pacifists, who believed that the Company was bringing unheard of oppression upon poor distress'd Natives who should be left to live happily under their own peaceable rulers, were always regarded with a certain impatience by the men on the spot. At the same time, if the Christian soldier had been aware that a Moslem who dies in combat with kafirs goes straight to heaven, he might not have wasted his water-bottle, or broken his bayonet.

Tipu's account of this engagement, minuted in his own hand, differed considerably from that of his adversaries. "On Wednesday the 30th or last day of the month Razy, of the Shadeb, 1226 from the birth of Mohammed, corresponding with the 29th of Ramzan, when the moon is not visible, the victorious army having left their baggage at Periapatam, and formed themselves into three divisions, entered the woods of Coorg where the army of the Christians had taken post, and advancing, gave battle, fighting with firelocks and spears, and the whole army of the infidels was routed, some of the Christians taking to flight." He, however, has to add a long list of his officers who "drank the cup of martyrdom".

Some good hard lying, some propaganda of a type perfected at a more civilised place and time, were needed to soothe a raging Tiger, beaten back to Periapatam so badly mauled. He made at once for Seringapatam, and strongly attacked the advance guard of General Harris' army as it reached the village of Malavelly, some 30 miles east of the capital. Here again, although attacking with great force and courage, and with many guns and elephants, he was beaten back with heavy losses.

Meanwhile, no better fortune attended the outnumbering

force which he had sent to attempt once more the annihilation of the little Bombay army, as it emerged from the Coorg jungles. George Bellasis relates this episode with soldierly brevity: "The Next Attack was on our Line, on our March to Seringapatam.—Futty Hyder, the Sultaun's Natural Son with Eight Thousand Horse charg'd, the Charge began upon my 4 12 pounders, I waited till they came within Sixty Yards and then gave them Grape, at which time all the Guns of the Line were open upon them, and they went off in the most cowardly Way I ever saw."

The domes and spires and strong fortifications of Seringapatam were now within sight of the advancing British armies, which effected their junction very neatly by a route which the enemy had not expected, and had consequently not devastated. Their march had hitherto been over "scorched earth" country, and very hard going. "To attempt to describe to you the hardships and fatigues undergone by the Army Prior to the Storm would be impossible", as our soldier observes flatly. But there they were, by the first week in April, disposed along an admirable position fronting the west face of the fort of Seringapatam at about two miles distance. Their intention to attack from the south bank of the sacred river Kaveri was a horrid surprise to Tipu, whose preparations had all supposed an attack from the north bank, as in 1792. With the object of buying time and confusing the issue, he now proposed a conference: he still might save the city, as he had done in '92, by a few lying promises. General Harris replied by a firm ultimatum. After receiving the terms with fury—for they would indeed have rendered him powerless for further harm—the Tiger took another look at the closing trap, and sent some more civil proposals of negotiation. Harris gave him twenty-four hours in which to submit.

Prostrated in the Grand Mosque, Tipu now prayed fervently for deliverance from this strait. What was more, he, the true-believer, even had recourse to the temples which he had desecrated. It was possible that mantras, many mantras, might save him: it was possible that the many-armed Siva, and the black-faced Kali, with protruded tongue, dancing on the dead, might forgive him the blood of the cattle shed at their door-sills: the Brahmins were heavily bribed to make intercession. The sorcerers also were called in, to read the sand and the ink-pool, to throw the magic sticks, and to calculate the stars. All was without avail: every one of them foresaw nothing but calamities impending over Seringapatam and the person of the Sultan.

At these omens, Tipu sank into a kind of sullen stupor. The time of grace expired, there were clear indications that the enemy intended attacking at a quite unexpected point, but he would take no order in the matter.

Thousands of workmen had been employed in opening new embrasures on the south face of the fort: but it now appeared that the British would attempt the north-west angle, opposite to which the bed of the Kaveri was bare rock, and the water wading-shallow. Beside the battery on the south bank, General Stuart's guns, Bellasis with them, had crossed to the north bank, joining to render the enfilade perfect, and the defence of the curtains impossible. They had already silenced the fort guns, and dislodged the besieged from their last exterior entrenchment.

On the 2nd of May, the pioneers began a 60-yard breach to the south of the bastion in the north-west angle; by the next day it was reported practicable, and the assault was fixed for the 4th. There was one man in the camp with a special claim to lead it: he had begged to do so: General David Baird, who had passed the better part of four hellish years in Seringapatam as Hyder's prisoner.

Before daybreak, 4,376 men took their appointed stations in the trench, and lay upon their arms while the sun grew high. They had moved invisibly in the dark; but they were not to attack until half-past one.

When the attack took place, it acted as a complete surprise, for the defenders had not expected the maddest of

Englishmen to charge the breach under the fury of an Indian noon. The Sultan was actually at meat, and his troops taking their noonday rest.

General Baird must have had a good deal to think about while watching the hands of his watch. His experiences in Seringapatam had not been such as a man forgets. The Sultan had kept the captive officers chained two and two. Baird's old mother had made a dry Scots jest on hearing the story later—"God help the man that was chained to oor Davie!" Now it must be: God help the man that should meet our Davie sword in hand, on his return into Seringapatam. The expression on that plain Scottish face should have been worth seeing, as the General leapt out of the trench, brandishing his sword above his head, and shouted, in the fashion of his day: "Come, my brave fellows, follow me, and prove yourselves worthy the name of British soldiers!"

Two columns of troops at once rushed for the breach, across the bed of the river. In six minutes, a forlorn hope gained its summit and planted the colours there. These were in the hand of a Sergeant Graham, who by that act entitled himself to a commission. "Three cheers for Lieutenant Graham!" he cried as he mounted the breach. "Damn them, I'll show them the British flag!" The charging troops were cheering his gallantry, when he was shot through the heart.

Once on the ramparts, the two columns wheeled off right and left, to force their way to a meeting-point on the eastern face. So dismayed were the defenders that many threw themselves down to death in the rocky bed of the river; and the only strong resistance encountered was along the northern rampart, where it seems to have been led by Tipu in person, his marksmen picking off most of the British officers. Hand-to-hand fighting of the most desperate kind ensued, as Colonel Wellesley's heavy reinforcements came up: the primitive struggle of body against body, stabbing and smiting and trampling, upon a pile of corpses, some in scarlet and crossbelts, some in silks and mail, with round shields strapped on dead arms. When the right column of the attackers completed the pincers movement, however, it became a mere butchery, a slaughter that went on until the victors' arms were tired.

As soon as all the ramparts were occupied, and all fire silenced, General Baird sent a flag of truce to the palace, offering to the Sultan and his household a choice between surrender and protection, or instant death. Two of Tipu's younger sons received the flag, and swore that their father was not there. Baird was not disposed to believe this; he set a guard about the zenana in which he suspected the Sultan to be lurking; and questioned the killadar in command, somewhat ungently. The man said that his master lay wounded in a gateway on the north face. The battle, the search of the palace and of the prisons, and the dispatch of the young princes to the commander-in-chief, had taken so long that night had come down, as it does in the East, like the clapping of a box-lid. It was by torchlight that Tipu must be sought in the shambles that was Seringapatam.

His horse was found shot, and then his palanquin, beneath which a slave had concealed himself, and so saved his life: for of the hundreds of dead piled about him in the gateway, numbers had died of suffocation or being trampled underfoot. The slave pointed out his master's body among these many, and the killadar identified it. By the glare of the torches, the English officers crowded to behold the ogre, the bogy-man, as he lay in a coat of rich crimson damask ornamented with green silk, and a green velvet turban with flaps of crimson silk and a wrought-gold nasal. His coarse dark face was fixed in its last expression of fury and despair, and there was a bullet through his head—fired, it is said, by a common soldier who coveted his jewelled sword-belt.

The picked guard of his followers, that favourite possession, the woman "past all description fair", the horse and the palanquin, might seem to indicate that Tipu had counted upon escaping through that gateway, a small one, while his troops held back the enemy. He had been in as sore a strait ten years before, when he had attacked the Rajah of Travancore, only to be repulsed with the loss of his jewels, his turban, and almost of his life. But this time, the omens were fulfilled. As one singes the whiskers of a dead tiger, his enemies cut locks of his hair with their swords; George Bellasis took one, and with it a blood-stained shawl. Then the body was borne off in the palanquin to the palace.

At least eight thousand persons had been killed— Bellasis put the "shocking Slaughter" at ten thousand —"and if one might judge by the Appearances as many More Wounded, that were in the most distress'd Situation". The cries of the wounded, and the wailing of the women, and the terrible noises made by the Sultan's tigers, which could smell blood, but had not been fed, made the night hellish indeed; while in a city which spilt over with gold and jewels, it was impossible to stop a burst of plundering. For four-and-twenty hours the conquerors ranged among corpses and treasure.

Tipu had always sworn that none of his European prisoners should live to be rescued, and he had arranged some hasty murders just before the assault. When General Baird went to the dungeons which he had once known too well, the sight of what had been done, and the state of the survivors, threw him into such transports of fury that he was almost ready to put every one of Tipu's officials to the sword. When he had collected himself into a correct soldierly conduct, he had a hard job restraining his indignant men from a palace massacre.

As for Citizen Chapuy and his Frenchmen, who were to have been the forerunners of invincible hosts, and from whose counsel and ability so much had been hoped, their tricolour flags and cap-of-liberty buttons were not seen in the fighting. They had not fired a shot, but had locked themselves up until they could ask and obtain quarter. They proved to be a poor lot, their appearance being described as mean, demoralised, and debauched.

K

Next evening, the body of Tipu Sultan Bahadur, second and last of the usurpers of Mysore, was carried with Mohammedan ceremonial and European military honours to the Lal Bagh, the great mausoleum of Hyder. The worst storm within memory came on at the same time. Thunderstorms are not uncommon in those parts, but this was one which passed into history. The Europeans said that it was due to the heavy cannonading; the natives said that it was due to the anger of the gods. Amid amazing thunder, people were struck dead by lightning, right and left. George Bellasis had a brother officer killed, and he himself was knocked insensible, while several of his servants, horses, and dogs perished at his side.

Torrents of rain washed the blood off Seringapatam, now that Tipu troubled the earth no more; and in the morning, the Governor-General's brother, that brisk young Colonel with the big beak nose and the frosty glance, came to take over as Commandant. Poor Davie Baird, who had taken the city, was astounded at his supersession; perhaps it was felt that he would not easily administer that place with impartiality, perhaps it was merely a case of Governor's brother; at all events, this young Wellesley proved very efficient. In a matter of hours, disorders were suppressed, the dead were cleared away, the bazaar people flocked back to their huckstering, the city's life flowed into normal channels. But every British soldier was able to gamble with gold coins as big and heavy as greengrocer's weights; and Tipu's dazzling throne, surmounted by the jewelled peacock, and with the tiger footstool, had vanished in fragments hither and yon.

"I shall send Charlotte a Ring made of the Gold from Tippoo's Throne," wrote George Bellasis to his fond friends the Lodges, brother and sister. "I took it off myself, it is as pure as can be." Also—"I have a Lock of the Sultaun's Hair, that probably may be as great a Curiousity as one of Buonoparte's Teeth, and a few other Articles which I'll send you."

Her younger sister, Eliza, shows as a spoilt beauty, lively, wilful, witty, following every vagary, saying and doing just what comes into her head, with a royal confidence that no one dare oppose her. If she ever set up her liveliness to rival Esther's sentiment, who could then foresee in what that rivalry would culminate?

As for the next sister, Lucy, she was painted in 1795 by Thompson, a pupil of Opie, who blurted out a proposal before he had finished the portrait. Lucy rejected him, more gently than the haughty Eliza would have done, but the painter departed straightway, taking the unfinished canvas with him. Twenty-five years later, when Lucy was a wife with a grown son, she recognised Thompson passing in a London street, and sent her son to fetch him. The painter burst into tears, and taking them to his house, restored the uncompleted portrait. He had always kept it, like an object of religious adoration, hung in a special recess with a curtain before it.

Perhaps Lucy—Lucy who took the wheel of her husband's ship, running down the Straits of Sunda, with an enemy brig pursuing, and roundshot falling close—was the most beautiful of the sisters; for in her the family spirit and sensibility were forged into courage and devotion; but of them all, Hannah was to have the most golden good luck, and Ann was to cause the blackest disaster.

Like the five daughters of Mr. Bennet, the seven daughters of Mr. King were handicapped by having very little fortune; the dower of each was something like that "one thousand pounds in the four per cents" with which Mr. Collins so generously promised not to reproach his bride; but to balance this came their lucky connection with India: in that market, a girl's face was her sufficient fortune. There was a family friend, a rich Mr. Holmes, retired from India, and whether from his introduction or not, the eldest of the sisters was early wedded to a Bengal civilian named Morris.

The next eldest, Esther, was thereupon invited out to her: and so it was that she came to marry "the handsomest man in India". George Bellasis was an old acquaintance; at many an Assembly, in his Portsmouth days, had he led out Miss Esther King; and no doubt such envious neighbours as thought the beauty languid and affected, whispered that she had journeyed all the way to India in especial pursuit of the handsome George.

Elizabeth and Lucy were duly dispatched in 1796. They sailed upon an American ship, the *Harriett*, of Richmond; probably for the good reason that the United States was then neutral in the war between England and France, and her shipping in no danger from enemy action. On board was a young master mariner named Thomas Kent, late second officer on an Indiaman, who had thriven so well in the Company's service as to set up for himself. He was now accompanying a cargo to Calcutta; and when he got there, would buy and captain a ship of his own for the highly profitable country trade. His prospects were thus excellent, and he was in a fair way to make a large fortune quickly. Eliza King was rather impulsive than calculating, but it was not imprudent of her to look favourably on Tom Kent's wooing, when he fell rapidly and deeply in love with her.

It is not known whether they had met before; but he came from her own part of the world, having a home at Frimley, where lived his somewhat formidable widowed mother: a very tall, strong old lady, who, one day finding a tramper in the kitchen frightening her maids, seized the fellow by the collar, ran him down the garden path, and sped him with a kick.

If Captain Kent took after his mother, he was an upstanding young sailor; one pictures him as the quiet type, most likely to be captivated by Eliza's lively rattle; and he is described as being exceptionally frank, trusting, and generous-hearted.

When the ship was got no further than Madeira upon her six months' voyage, the British Vice-Consul there married

Elizabeth King to Thomas Kent, with Miss Lucy King among the witnesses. Thereafter, the voyage was a prolonged honeymoon for the young couple, and the less tedious for Lucy, dreaming hopefully on deck in the tropical moonlight of her own coming fortune. The normal perils of their situation would have been enough to prevent boredom in any passenger with imagination: those hazards of shipwreck and barbarian captivity which had occurred to Mrs. Fay, and the unabated activities of the Geria pirates in the Bay of Bengal, who would not care what flag their victims flew. Ships that flew the British flag now had to contend not only with French but with Dutch privateers, for England had been a year at war with the Dutch, as well as three years at war with France. In these eastern seas, the French had been doing particularly well. The notorious Surcouff, of the *Confiance*, had wrought amazing damage to British shipping: two million pounds' worth had been lost in one year.

But this ill fortune had a golden lining, for by consequence freight rates were so high that captains grew rich in a couple of voyages, and would have done twice as well had it not been for the corresponding high rate of insurance. Allured by the profit, and undismayed by the peril, Captain Kent, having disposed of his cargo to advantage, lost no time in buying a suitable ship at Calcutta, and renaming her the *Eliza*.

Meanwhile, Lucy, lodging with them, obtained a husband almost as soon as she had landed. The romance of a long sea-voyage and the sight of her sister's happiness had probably predisposed her to like a sailor; so, before any wealthy civilian or high-ranking redcoat could get a chance at her, she was swept up by the headlong devotion of Captain Robert Eastwick, owner—at only twenty-four years old—of the good ship *Endeavour*, and a former fellow officer of Kent's on board the *Barwell*, where, as he records, the officers were "one and all gentlemen by education and family". He was a fair, square-built young man with sea-blue eyes, whose open and courageous disposition was written in his handsome face. He had already experienced more adventures than most persons thrice his age, and was to experience very many more before he died, an old blind man, well on into the new century—a thick bookful of adventures, in fact, when they came to be written down.

He was married to Lucy on December the 17th, the witnesses being persons very eminent in Calcutta—Sir J. Cox, and Messrs. A. and F. Vansittart. The stern-cabin of the *Endeavour* was most elegantly fitted up for the bride; and they set forth on their first voyage together. The strangest scenes unfolded themselves before Lucy's lovely, wondering eyes. It was probably the happiest time of her life, even though it was not all a matter of gliding through tropical waters full of flying fish.

They were riding at anchor off Old Croee, with half the crew engaged on shore, when a squall blew up and drove them out to sea, with tattered sails, into the predatory path of two Dutch privateers, which still dogged them after a night during which they had hoped to give them the slip. Lucy was on deck at dawn, watching with a glass, as the prospect of captivity at Batavia came nearer and nearer. The Dutchmen were crowding all canvas, and soon were close enough to send shots fountaining into the sea near the quarry. On board *Endeavour* the depleted crew strove frantically to replace the split sails. Eastwick looked aloft with despair—he dared not leave the wheel. At this moment Lucy, tumbled and wet with spray, proposed herself to replace him. It had been a favourite play of theirs for her to take a trick in smooth weather. Now she clung to the spokes, Eastwick, blessing her, sprung aloft, a new foresail was bent on swiftly, and they suddenly began to draw away from their pursuers. As the Dutchman sank at last beneath the horizon, the whole crew raised a cheer for the Captain's wife. For so saving the valuable cargo of pepper, Government rewarded Eastwick with five hundred dollars and a new anchor and cable.

After another adventure with two French frigates, which *Endeavour* contrived to distance in a squall, sheerly by daring sailing—during which half the sails were blown away, the masts nearly went, and Lucy stayed on deck all the time, holding to a rope, and prodigiously enjoying it all—it can hardly be wondered at if young Captain Eastwick should feel that his precious bride would be safer ashore. Nor is it wonderful that Lucy disliked leaving her elegant stern-cabin, and these breathless hazards in her husband's company, for a safe house ashore—even for a very neat and pretty little place at Entally, with a large garden.

But as 1798 came in, she had baby-clothes to sew; and Robert must take her miniature to sea as a substitute. In April, at Madras, he was asked to give a passage up to Calcutta to Lord Mornington's brother "the Hon. Col. Wesley". This officer struck Captain Eastwick very favourably, as an active, sociable personality. He seemed also a great admirer of beauty, and was for ever walking the decks with the second mate's pretty wife, who was aboard. By way of showing him something superior, Eastwick plucked the miniature from his breast. It was received with an exclamation of delighted incredulity—"Surely she is not so handsome as this!" Whether as the possessor of so charming a wife, or upon his own merits, Colonel Wellesley took a decided fancy to Captain Eastwick, cemented by the efforts which that seaman made to get him up to Calcutta by a given day, in order to save his monthly allowance. *Endeavour* was obliged to anchor at Diamond Harbour, the tide being against them; and Eastwick organised a boat to take his friend as far as Fultah, and Gammage's tavern; there they must get another, but the only one available was "a *paunchway*, a common native river craft; and squatting in this, the future conqueror of Waterloo proceeded to the Presidency".

In 1814, with Waterloo still in the future, but a victory banquet in full swing at the Guildhall, the Duke recognised his old friend Eastwick, and called down the table to him to know if he were still "cutting sticks with a wooden hatchet?" However cabalistic this phrase might be to the other diners, it recalled old times for both of them; for it was the Captain's usual shipboard phrase for rallying idlers among the crew: "Come, what are you all about there—cutting sticks with a wooden hatchet?"

Victory banquets and dukedoms were far enough away in '98, when young Wellesley had still to win his spurs, and the armies that should menace Tipu were just beginning to be assembled. The Colonel had intended to proceed on that campaign in the *Endeavour*, but the French having practically blockaded the coast, it was thought safer that he should go with his regiment in the Company's armed ship *Earl Fitzwilliam*. They had a shocking voyage, and it was upon this occasion that Wellesley sent off that fervent dispatch about victualling, saying that he conceived it "very inconsistent with the principles of the Christian religion to give people bad water"—and to "give us a bottle of good rum by way of muster, and fill the casks with the worst I ever saw".

Robert Eastwick was temporarily uninterested in the movements of armies: his wife had borne him a daughter. However, all profit being now doubly welcome to him, he must be pleased with a Government contract to deliver bullocks to the Bombay Army at Calicut. Conversely, what befell him at the beginning of '99 must be the more terrible. So crippling had insurance premiums now grown, owing to the French tyranny of the seas, that most captains preferred to sail without insuring, and trust their own skill. Eastwick did this with a valuable cargo, and was captured by the *La Forte* in Balasore Roads, near the Juggernaut Pagoda. She then took the *Mornington*, commanded by a friend of his, giving him a companion in misfortune. It was misfortune indeed. Both captains were utterly ruined, and prisoner to boot. It was some relief to exchange disgusted comments on the appearance of a ship devoted to Liberty and Equality: where the forecastle hands ate and played cards on the quarterdeck, and the officers were low fellows in open check shirts, indistinguishable from the men.

But the *La Forte*'s turn was coming; British sea disasters were avenged by her capture, after a hammering action, by His Majesty's Ship *La Sybille*. She was brought to Calcutta, among the cheers of excited crowds; but the victorious captain—a son of the great Captain Cook—lay dying aboard the *Sybille*, aged twenty-seven. The Company gave him a splendid monument, which may be seen in Westminster Abbey near that of General Wolfe.

Robert Eastwick was seeking consolation in Lucy's arms. For a young man of his professional standing, a fresh start was not difficult. He soon obtained a small brig, the *Harington*, upon credit; and it was a good omen that he arrived in her off Fort St. George, Madras, at the beginning of June, just in time to witness public rejoicing at the reception of Tipu's standard and the captured tricolours. Victory was in the air, and a new chapter opening for everybody.

A couple of profitable voyages, to Persia and to Penang, shortly filled the Eastwick coffers again; but the Captain now thought it well to sell the *Harington*, that he might buy a ship more suitable to convey his wife and child to Bombay. For Lucy's health had weakened after her confinement; she was feeling the climate; she desired very strongly to see her sisters again, and three of them were now in Bombay.

Esther Bellasis had not returned alone from Europe, but had brought with her the next batch of beauties, Hannah and Ann. "Three such women are not often seen in one house," wrote the admiring Leah, when they paid their farewell visit to Dr. Bellasis before sailing; "there is not half an inch between them. Miss Ann, the youngest, is the tallest, she is five-foot-seven."

Being youngest and tallest was all that Miss Ann had in common with Miss Lydia Bennet; the trouble she was to bring upon her family arose from no fault in her own character.

Esther was now verging on thirty, and had been some five years married; her sisters were ten years younger. If she were a little faded, a little languid, if the freshness of England had been bleached out of her cheeks, she can only have shown by contrast how brightly it bloomed in Hannah and Ann, as they stepped ashore at Bombay, all expectant of conquest; and all unconscious that Ann carried with her death and an uncommon measure of calamity.

Bombay in 1800, on the threshold of its new importance, between the fall of Tipu and the conquest of the whole Mahratta empire, had already acquired that atmosphere as of an English county town which has been remarked in it. Its looks were not perhaps greatly altered since Charlotte Bellasis had come there to marry and die in '84; or even since the bad old days when John Bellasis had brought his romantic ambitions there in '69; but European society had increased, and continued to pride itself on being very gentlemanly. No swindling adventurers, or flashy Nabobs, troubled Bombay; nobody lost £40,000 at cards to anybody else—and not for the reason that they had it not to lose. The Parsees were perhaps the wealthiest persons there—Lord Valentia said that they "owned Bombay"; but the European merchants prospered richly, particularly the two great houses of Bruce, Fawcett and Co., and Smith, Forbes and Co. There was a degree of rivalry between these, their supporters and dependants. Henry Fawcett and Charles Forbes occupied various official positions in the settlement, and ranked, of course, at the top of its hierarchy as Senior Merchants. In that useful publication *The Bombay Kalendar and Register* ("Printed for the Proprietors by Moroba Damotherjee, No. 7 Forbes Street") Forbes appears as a magistrate, as the treasurer of the Literary Society, as a major of Fencibles, and in a number of other characters. He was a man born to make a large figure in a wider world than that of Bombay.

As there was a brand-new Mrs. Forbes—late Miss Stewart—in the "Alphabetical List of the Ladies in Bombay" at the back of the *Register*, Ann King, even if she read it through to ascertain her chances of obtaining a good match, can hardly have thought that Mr. Forbes would be important to her destiny. But with brightening eyes, the sisters must have skimmed down the list of officers, both of His Majesty's and the Honourable Company's troops, serving under the Presidency. Of the King's troops, there were detachments from four regiments—one being that 86th in which Jane Austen's favourite brother Henry had considered obtaining a commission recently. With such a quantity of military officers, not to mention the officers of the Company's Marine, and those of such of the squadron of King's ships—five seventy-fours among them —as happened to be in the harbour, there could be no lack of gaiety.

There was indeed no lack. Such an entertainment as a wild-beast fight between leopard and boar, though characteristic of country manners, would hardly appeal to the ladies; more especially as when this was tried in 1800 the leopard got loose; but no young lady was yet too refined to giggle at the farce of *Miss in Her Teens and the Padlock*, presented by amateurs at the theatre; and there were the races at Byculla, excursions to view the ruins of Bijapur, where artillery officers could make merry over the antique dragon-shaped cannon with jewelled ear-rings, and picnics to Elephanta, a favourite goal for gay water-parties with music. There were, of course, dinners and balls without end. The *Bombay Courier* reported:

"On Thursday last, Major-General Bellasis gave an elegant entertainment to his friends at Randall lodge; on which occasion the extensive and beautiful gardens of this Mansion were displayed and illuminated in a style of varied magnificence which reflected the highest credit upon the taste and fancy of the projector. Notice having unexpectedly circulated that Masks would be admitted on this evening, those who could prepare themselves on the short notice which was afforded to their option, appeared in Masks accordingly

—and though the characters were few, yet most of them were well supported; and they all contributed much to the gaiety of the evening.

"No character was ever better supported than that of the well known and faithful Syrang at this Presidency named Peirbhoy; it was completely hit off in all its bearings. An Irish Blackguard enlivened the Company with many excellent National Songs, as excellently delivered; A Gipsey and a Fortune Teller exposed the books of fate as adepts in the art; a weary Pilgrim pursued her lonely way, and forcibly pourtrayed the effects of a tedious pilgrimage. A gentleman as a boarding-school Miss supported the character with much spirit. An unfortunate politician was mistaken for a farmer, and though primed with the balance of power, could give no account of his crops of Wheat and Barley. Some highly finished old Men and Women mingled among the crowd; and upon the whole so much good humour and vivacity was evinced, and the novelty of the scene gave so much satisfaction that we trust it will prove only a prelude to other similar entertainments, at which Masks should be generally encouraged—the company did not separate till four the following morning."

From the fine gardens of Randall Lodge, and the eminence of Malabar Hill above it, one saw the whole of Bombay, from the flat foreground of parrot-green paddy-fields to the amazing skyline of the Ghats beyond the harbour—standing up bluely in funnels and peaks and high table-land. In front of these the islands hunched themselves out of the water: Elephanta, Butcher's Island, Hog Island, Gibbet Island, Caranjah; and tiny ships rode between the islands and the town. This appeared a sea of low white buildings with red roofs—the "bangala" or "bunglo", so strange to English eyes, with a few buildings of greater pretension, such as the Adawlat, or Courthouse, on the outskirts: beyond which the prospect shaded away to the left into the countryside at Mazagon. That way also, toward the Breach Water, lay the shooting butts and the race-course. To the right, an

immense coconut wood shut out a view of the fort and the
landing piers, but another fairy forest of miniature masts rose
distantly behind it to indicate all the shipping. Here and
there about the whole scene, the stiff shafts and tousled
heads of coconut palms stuck up like hatpins; and little
round trees were planted along the bold right angles of
Bellasis Road, leading from the town to Malabar Hill.
This road had been made by the General upon his return
from Europe in '93, to aid the refugees from the great
famine in Surat.

George Bridges Bellasis must maintain a modest establishment as compared to his uncle; but it was also a garden-
house out of town. It would, of course, be one-storied:
with glass windows, green venetians, and a twenty-foot
veranda, opening with low, graceful arches upon the
garden, where the formally planned paths would be of small
sea-shells, a surface found discouraging to snakes. The
roses, tuberoses, and jasmine would only blossom by means
of the ceaseless drawing of water from the well with a
buffalo-wheel, and the muddy distribution of it by many
Mallias. Some fifty other servants must also be kept; and no
doubt but this ran away with the rupees. The increased
expense caused by the advent of three ladies must make it
impossible to continue out of debt—not, perhaps, to the
shroff, but to one or two of the friends to whom Captain
Bellasis was so readily liberal at their own moments of need.
Like most men constitutionally incapable of managing
money, he was often talking about it, and attempting
shrewd calculations as to prospects and possibilities. He
wrote at this time to Edmund Lodge: "I am in A Snug way
as Commissary of Stores at Bombay, it enables me to live
without incurring any Debt, but this at my time of Life is
terrible as I can never return to Old England till I am
upwards of Fifty if I should live so long." This, he added,
he hardly dared expect, with his contemporaries dying of
liver complaint all round him, and his own robust health
shaken by a year of strenuous campaigning. Can Lodge

inform him what are his prospects of soon receiving a legacy from his rich godfather, Mr. Bridges? Or would that gentleman be likely to afford him substantial present help? "I think myself he will do A little towards curtailing my time of Transportation to this Country, for such it certainly is." Such it certainly might seem to him at despondent moments; but if he had known what the next year held for him, he would not have used that phrase.

Freedom from debt might fly before the advent of his wife and her two lovely young sisters: but so must despondency. They were a honey-pot attraction for the liveliest society in the place. The regular burra khana was not more entertaining at Bombay than at any other place where all had their nicely calculated positions in the parallel hierarchies, civilian and military, and might rely upon sitting next to the same person who had partnered them on the last such occasion, and facing the same regulation round of beef, turkey, and ham; while the gentlemen sweltered in silver lace and prodigious cravats, envying the ladies' muslins. Such formality was not much observed in the hospitable house of George and Esther Bellasis; they preferred bright little dinner-parties with impromptu balls, casual droppings-in to breakfast after the morning ride, excursions here and there; in all which the Miss Kings, as new beauties, temporarily queened it.

Miss Hannah King had no time to get tired of her brother-in-law's house: within a matter of weeks, even days, of her arrival she was sought in marriage by Lieutenant-Colonel Robert Gordon, Adjutant-General, and Member of the Military Board. This officer had so handsome an income as to be quite indifferent to his bride's lack of fortune, and delighted to bestow upon her cashmeres and jewels, and dozens of snow-cobweb muslin gowns inwoven with gold bees. Thus, as Mrs. Gordon, the lovely Hannah became mistress of a fine large house in the Fort, in Nesbit Lane, and began a delightful new life of elegant profusion and expensive pleasure, which caused a pretty constant town buzz of

admiration or disapproval. Both were provoked by such
items as the Gordons' new courtyard: for one of the relics
of Portuguese manners in Bombay was the habit of paving a
courtyard with elaborate patterns in black-and-white or
coloured pebbles: and the Gordons would have theirs contrived in semi-precious stones—malachite, onyx, serpentine,
and the like.

Very soon they gave a great ball, to which everybody in
Bombay who could procure an invitation was happy to
come. It had been arranged to coincide with the arrival of
the Eastwicks. Captain Eastwick was come with Lucy and
her little girl in his new ship; and there was a very pleasant
family reunion. They stayed with the Gordons; and Eastwick, dining and wining with the handsome Bellasis,
exchanged his own adventures for tales of Seringapatam.
Meanwhile the four beautiful sisters spent the greater part
of each day in one another's company; had not Eliza Kent
now returned to Europe, there would have been five of
them.

It must have been one of those happy times which come
seldom, and are rather frightening while they last. There
was indeed something a little frightening about both the
Gordon and the Bellasis households—particularly the latter,
with so much less money to back it, for the Deputy-
Commissary's pay was only about £1,200 a year, and he had
not yet had time to profit from many trading ventures. The
pitch was too high, the pace was too rapid, there was too
much fiddling and feasting, too much laughter to last.
Esther Bellasis, very sensitive and not very strong, must
surely feel an occasional breath of uneasiness. . . .

Meanwhile, the object was to find a husband for the only
beauty left unmarried: for the youngest and the tallest, Miss
Ann King. It did not seem that this would be difficult; but
perhaps the young lady herself was not easy to suit. Middle-
aged civilians or veteran officers with fortunes handsomer
than their persons might seem dreadfully yellow old fogrums

L

to her youthful eyes; she perhaps longed after a lover who should be young and comely. Bombay gossip wondered as the weeks went on that nobody made a winning bid for her charms: was it true that Captain Moncrieff had made an offer? and what was this about young Mitchell—was he indeed paying attentions? if so, were they serious? Could anything be allowed to come of them? . . . As time went on, the name of Mitchell was heard more and more in connection with that of Miss Ann King.

Arthur Forbes Mitchell was a young man of two-and-twenty with a small estate in Scotland. He was a Company's Writer, and fourth partner in Smith, Forbes & Co., being kin to the head of the house. At nineteen he had managed a post of much responsibility in Malabar with such credit and success that he was regarded as being very promising. His career with the house was marked out before him, and it was confidently expected that if he applied himself to business for the next ten or twenty years he would be a rich man. It was perhaps rather too much to expect that he should not also have some eye to pleasure. His personality emerges pretty clearly from the events to be related. One feels that there was something pleasing about it, if only the ingenuousness of youth. Those making excuse for him, when excuse was badly needed and nearly impossible, must rest their defence upon his youth: "He was young and inexperienced. Fate was against him, or undoubtedly reflection would have brought him soon to other behaviour." It was all that could be said: that, and his own last admission: "it was all, all my own doing."

The poor young fool must have been good-looking; and a personable figure and well-cut features probably combined with Scots reticence to give the impression that his character was more maturely formed than it actually was. There are some persons whose society is pleasant because they are in some way admirable: dashing and genial, like handsome George Bellasis: or lovely to look upon, like his wife and her sisters. There are others, again, who please by admiring.

Of these, Mitchell was surely one. He had known and admired George Bellasis since first coming to Bombay, and had testified his admiration by pressing a loan upon him when he was short of cash. As soon as Ann King joined the Bellasis household, this faculty found full exercise. It was less admiration than adoration that the young Scot displayed as he dangled dumbly after the tall beauty.

Ann, it appears, was touched and pleased. This was the youngest, the most personable of her wooers; and the devotion with which he followed her, apparently without hope that she could favour him, must appeal to all her girlish romance. No matter that he was not rich—that might come in time. She was ready to say Yes, straightway—if he would only ask her. But he did not ask her. He continued to lead her out at balls, hand her to table, attend her at races and picnics, and sit with his eyes fixed upon her, to the observation of all the world; but he said no open word of love. In February, sitting by her side at breakfast, he suddenly blurted out the offer of a present—"a Lady's Work Box being inlaid with Ivory and Sandalwood". Ann accepted it, with all the delicate encouragement she was able to express; but when she afterwards told her "sister Bellasis", Esther pointed out that she could not possibly accept a present from a gentleman who had not made his declaration. George was deputed to reject the work-box. Perhaps there was some hope that this might cause young Mr. Mitchell to declare himself; but it did not; and George was not going to press him. If he thought fit to propose, no doubt he would do so; and anyhow, Ann might make a much better match. Esther might agree with this, but at the same time she must be anxious about talk being caused, about more eligible suitors being driven away, about Ann's own feelings and whether she would make herself unhappy if the young man did not soon speak.

Arthur Mitchell had excellent reasons for not speaking— or one excellent reason: the vehement disapproval of his

relative and senior partner, Mr. Charles Forbes, upon whom
his present comforts and future prospects in great measure
depended. Charles Forbes appears in this story in a light
strangely opposite to his recorded character. A man whose
qualities of justice, honesty, kindness of heart, and clear-
thinking were admitted even by those opposed to him, he
was so much trusted by the natives as to be probably the
only person in India able to persuade Indian bankers to
provide money during the crisis of 1803, and thus to pay
for the campaign that resulted in Assaye. Years after he
had left India, they subscribed £9,000 to set up a statue in
his honour; and large sums of his great fortune were spent
helping the natives, particularly in seeing that the inhabitants
of Bombay should get pure drinking-water. He came of an
ancient family, and had enough Scots romance to make the
revival of the family baronetcy, attainted after Culloden,
a main object. Twenty years after we meet him here, he was
distinguishing himself in Parliament, and that with no fixed
unthinking notions, Whig or Tory: he supported, for
instance, not only Catholic Emancipation, but the wild idea
of female suffrage. . . . However, in 1801, he undoubtedly
behaved with a lack of discretion, a blind, insensitive arro-
gance, that led to the worst consequences. He was young to
be in a position of such authority, being still short of thirty;
he had a very strong will which he was used to see prevail;
and he had generations of hot-tempered, feuding High-
landers behind him.

Beside being his taskmaster at business, Mr. Forbes also
expected to see a good deal of young Mitchell after office
hours, although he did not live in the Forbes household but
shared a bungalow on the Esplanade with another young
man, one Jonathan Michie—not, it would seem, of out-
standing character—who was a lieutenant in the Bombay
Marine, assistant to the storekeeper. There were in Bombay
no such temptations to expensive dissipation as might easily
ruin a young bachelor in Calcutta—gambling hells, costly
wenches, and systematic hard drinking: but it was still

perfectly possible for such a one to make a disastrous fool
of himself in some other fashion: as for instance by an
imprudent marriage. Charles Forbes was fixed that his
promising junior partner should not so commit himself: it
would not be proper for him to marry these many years to
come, and he should then marry a lady with a competent
fortune. It was the era of *Sense and Sensibility*, of *Pride and
Prejudice*, when rich people in authority expected to dictate
the matrimonial choice of relatives and dependants, and
were extremely angry when their benevolent plans were
thwarted.

The common gossip concerning young Mitchell's infatua-
tion for Miss Ann King appears to have come slowly to the
ears of Mr. Forbes. He was not by way of observing it
himself, as he did not visit Captain Bellasis. There is no
telling why there was ill-will between the households, but
there was always a good deal of ill-will going about Bombay,
which was known as a quarrelsome Presidency. It was not
wonderful that a small society cooped up together in that
climate, at that date—that is to say, without ice, quinine, or
trips to the Hills—should stew up many mutual enmities
among the fever and prickly heat. There was enmity
between the two European trading houses: to some extent,
between the Scots and the English: between soldier and
civilian. Under the soldier Malcolm's governorship, this
latter issue was to be expressed by him as being a struggle
between "honest fellows with glittering sabres", and
"quibbling quill-driving lawyers". Whatever the combination of motives, Charles Forbes chose to dislike, without
personal acquaintance, the household of George Bridges
Bellasis; and to be very much annoyed and alarmed when
he found that young Mitchell continued to frequent it
despite his wishes. Some busy person—probably the
attorney Cumberlege, stigmatised in a letter as "a creature
of the House of Forbes"—now came to him with the information that Mitchell was daily expected to offer for Miss
Ann King: and Forbes angrily summoned his young partner

for interrogation. His anger could not be pleasant to face; he was a man of fine presence and, even so young, of resolute and commanding manner. Mitchell shrank before him and, trembling, denied everything: he had no serious intentions towards Miss King: he was not the least attached to her: he would be more guarded in future. Charles Forbes believed him, and was appeased.

Not the less did he feel his subordinate in danger of being "drawn in". These were dangerous people, with their frivolous round of balls and drinking parties; and as for the King young women, they had all come to India as "speculation misses". It seemed clear that Miss Ann King, on the catch for a husband, had marked promising Arthur Mitchell for her victim, and that her relatives would by every means abet her. Mr. Forbes glowered upon the situation watchfully.

His busy friend Mr. Joseph Cumberlege also kept an eye on it as well as he might. Mitchell had introduced him to George Bellasis, and he had since, as he afterwards stated, "declined several" of that hospitable gentleman's invitations, but in public parties he might watch Miss Ann and see what possibility there was of her cajoling a proposal out of young Arthur. He had already warned Arthur of the danger of frequenting her company, even though he might have no intentions; but the lad had turned it off as a joke. Towards the end of April, in a large party returning by water at nightfall from viewing the caves of Elephanta, Cumberlege edged up to Captain Bellasis who was standing by the mast, and asked him impertinently enough whether or when he expected Mr. Mitchell to offer to his sister-in-law. Bellasis probably glanced down from his tall height, wondering whether to kick the attorney or bid him go to blazes and mind his business; but finally gave one of his great laughs and said that he didn't think Mitchell would marry Ann if she went down on her knees to him. This satirical picture of a reigning toast in desperate straits did not appeal to Mr. Cumberlege's sense of humour, for he had none. He, in fact, "did not suppose it to be spoken ironically".

To be quizzed in connection with a reigning toast must have flattered young Mitchell; but he continued to protest, to such friends as Cumberlege, as to his chief, that he had no intentions in that direction, and that he could not be made to propose to Miss King, however often they danced together. To his intimate associates, especially to his house-mate Jonathan Michie, he told another tale, and freely confessed that he did love the girl consumedly, but that nothing, alas, could come of it. None of his confidants seems to have had the sense to tell him that not only prudence but an honourable regard for the girl's possible feelings, her reputation and prospects, ought therefore to keep him out of her company. With the natural egotism of youth, it probably did not occur to him to think of anybody's feelings but his own.

These were very much engaged. One can suppose the day-dreams in which he would indulge: of how this lovely creature might be his if Fortune somehow smiled on them: if the Montague-and-Capulet situation between the two business houses were relaxed: if Mr. Forbes relented and said, "Bless ye, my children!" if—oh, most tempting impossibility!—if he himself could but summon up courage enough to rely on his own exertions, and bid Smith, Forbes and Co. go hang! Meanwhile he could not forgo the sight of her, and must still haunt her side, delighting and tormenting himself; scowling when she favoured another, yet obstinately dumb when she turned encouraging glances in his own direction. As long as he kept his mouth shut, as long as he made no declaration, he was safe. . . .

Stewing in this muddle of desire and alarm, vanity and frustration, the young man was hardly equipped to notice that Ann was building up a romantic response to his silent devotion, and was anxiously awaiting the declaration that did not come. He could not see that he had already made a

great fault in honour, and was in the way to make a far
worse one. He did not reflect that a man who is walking
one way and looking another is almost bound to meet with
an accident; or that resolutions of prudence would hardly
prevent disaster if one should step into a gunpowder store
with a naked light.

Towards disaster the situation now rapidly advanced.

VIII

A NOISE ABOUT HONOUR

UPON Tuesday, April 28th, 1801, a dinner-party, to be followed by dancing, was given at the Bellasis bungalow, and Arthur Mitchell was there, sitting opposite to Ann. Several persons afterwards testified that the company did not sit long or drink deep, but rose earlier than usual, the fiddles being come for the dance: moreover, that young Mitchell was not pressed to drink, and seemed perfectly sober: and that after dancing with Miss King he placed two chairs in order to sit apart with her.

Mr. Forbes, according to his subsequent evidence, had elicited quite a different account of the evening from the wretched Arthur: that the company sat unusually late at table: that he was made by his host and hostess to drink a vast deal of wine and beer: that when the fiddles struck up and the set was formed, there was more wine upon the sideboard, to which he was perpetually pressed, until he yielded, saying, "Since I must get tipsy, I may as well get tipsy at once!": that when he seated himself beside Ann King he was in "a state of stupefaction", and not at all aware of what he was saying.

There is no doubt that Mitchell told Charles Forbes what he wanted to hear, and that Forbes implicitly believed it; but there appears no reason why anybody else should do so. Ann King was not in a state of stupefaction, and her account of this and the subsequent incidents is clear and detailed. The standard of after-dinner sobriety in 1801 was not a high one: dancing, the real and vigorous dancing of that day, and in India, was surely appallingly thirsty work: of course the young man must have breathed an odour of wine when he sat down beside the girl at about ten o'clock; and he may have drunk enough to banish his usual ignominious caution. But it may have been her mere proximity, bare-bosomed in cobweb muslins, that caused him to blurt out a clumsy, jealous inquiry as to whether it were true that she was going to marry a Captain Moncrieff.

No, said Ann King, she was not going to marry Captain Moncrieff. The hard-breathing youth exclaimed that he was very glad of it; and when—enlarging her eyes over her waving fan, as we may fancy—she inquired why, he replied "that he had long wished to marry her himself, which she must have expected from his attentions". Miss King at once, probably dropping her lovely eyelashes, modestly inquired if he had yet spoken to her sister or her brother Bellasis. In the same moment young Mitchell must have become aware of what he had done—that which he had been taking miserable precautions to avoid for months. He said hurriedly that he had not approached her relatives, and begged that she would not mention it to them that evening. He would see Bellasis next day at his office—or write to him.

With this he took a hasty leave, going away before supper in the company of a naval officer friend, Lieutenant Bryan; and probably completely sobered by finding that he had actually taken the plunge.

Ann kept her secret that night, and all the next day, Wednesday, waiting impatiently for the declining of the sun and her brother-in-law's homecoming. He came, as handsome and jovial and ready for his dinner as usual; but when she met him with the anxious inquiry as to whether he had seen Mr. Mitchell, he said with surprise that he had not. An explanation ensued; and Bellasis was therefore prepared to receive upon the next day, Thursday, a somewhat incoherent note from young Mitchell. Its muddled apologies must after-wards be seen as a half-hearted but desperate attempt to back out of the affair; but Bellasis had no notion of this—he took it that Mitchell was apologising for not having made his proposal in due form to Ann's guardian relatives.

A messenger was dispatched for Ann and Esther; when

their palanquins arrived the note was discussed, and it was resolved that Arthur Mitchell should be interviewed forthwith. The ladies adjourned to the house of the Fawcett cousins; and Mitchell was summoned to the Commissary's office. In what a tormentingly divided frame of mind he came may well be supposed; but the moment he crossed the threshold he found his mind made up, for Captain Bellasis received him kindly as a brother, congratulated him with back-slapping, and said that it would have been better, certainly, had he been first applied to, but that it was of no consequence. Thus committed and thus emboldened, Mitchell freely confessed that he had long wished to marry Miss Ann. . . . He must do his best to forget Mr. Forbes, and let himself be happy.

Ann and her sister were happy enough, when George repaired to them in Helen Fawcett's drawing-room and told them that all was settled. That night Ann could retire beneath her mosquito-net, fluttered with felicitations, and confident of seeing her lover next morning.

Nor was she disappointed. He appeared at seven o'clock on Friday, the 1st of May. The passages that followed, precious to the eager girl, look particularly cruel transferred to an affidavit and prefixed with "this deponent now saith". Ann, then, came to greet him upon the veranda, and he hastened up to her, caught her by both hands, "and in the most affectionate manner kissed her face". For this kiss he must have thirsted long enough and perhaps she too; he was enjoying the moment with complete recklessness, committing himself now as deep as he could plunge. "He was in very high spirits, and said that if anything was to break in on his expected happiness he should go mad."

He went on to say that he feared objections from his partners to his marriage; and "with much earnestness added: 'Damn them—what have they to do with me—I will not consult any of them—the 31st of July is at hand, and if they disapprove of my marriage with you I will resign the part

I have in the House, and trust alone to the Company's service, and three or four hundred a year that I can always draw from Home'." It was a brave defiance—if it could have been maintained.

Ann, doubting nothing, led her lover within to her sister; he sat down between them, and they had some talk before breakfast. Arthur Mitchell wanted to know if Ann liked his bungalow on the Esplanade, which she had once seen when some trade goods were brought there for sale. She told him that she would be satisfied with any house he thought proper, but that this house would be very pleasant as being near Colonel Gordon and her sister Hannah. "I hope we shall be as happy as Gordon and his wife," observed Mitchell. "We have a fairer chance, as we have taken a longer time to study each other's disposition, and, of course, know each other better."

He then took her hand, also that of Esther Bellasis, and pressing them warmly, said what a pity it was that Mrs. Forbes did not visit them: that it would be pleasanter after marriage if they were on a friendly footing: that Mrs. Forbes was a pleasant woman and he liked her very much. In his exalted and rosy state at the moment, love and reunion all round seemed even probable, no doubt.

Turning to his means of supporting a wife, he said that if they did not live in so dashing a style as the Gordons, they need not be less happy. Ann answered, "I care not, Mr. Mitchell, so we live as comfortably as my brother and sister Bellasis, and you know pretty well what their monthly allowance is, they have very little money." To be sure, £1,200 a year in the hands of George Bridges Bellasis might amount to very little; but it was certainly a good deal more than Arthur Mitchell could command. He said boldly, "As for money, we shall not want for that. I only wish, now matters are gone so far, to have the happy day fixed as soon as possible."

A couple of guests had meanwhile arrived for breakfast, Mr. Luke Ashburner, the Sheriff, and Lieutenant Johnstone, of H.M.S. *Suffolk*. These gentlemen drew a quick conclusion from the significant smiles of their host and hostess, from the sight of the young man talking excitedly apart with Miss Ann, and from the gallantry with which he armed her to table. After breakfast, too, the young couple retired into the veranda in an unmistakable way. It was clear enough that all was settled.

Young Mitchell now expressed great regret to the girl that he had not been invited to Mr. Nesbit's dance that evening, saying, "You will all be dancing happily, and I shall be at home miserable." To this, Ann said, "Come with us, and I will make my brother Bellasis apologise to Mr. Nesbit for bringing you." Mitchell declined, saying that he was angry at not being asked when his friend Bryan had been asked in his presence at the Bellasis party on Tuesday. He then led to the subject of house furnishing; and he and Ann were deep enough in domestic plans when they were interrupted by the doubtless deliberately loud step and warning cough of Captain Bellasis, come to say that his curricle was at the door and that he would give Mitchell a cast into town.

Promising that he would call next morning, the young man took his leave, and another kiss. Bellasis we can see pursing his handsome mouth with a smile and a whistle, while he raised a black eyebrow and strode away to make a diversion with his syces. He anticipated a pleasant drive. Ann had given him one agreeable message to her lover: that, confiding in his kindness, she would require no settlements.

The friends of Miss King were now licensed to rejoice; a shower of congratulatory chits began immediately. Ann must have been in glowing beauty at the Nesbit ball that night. Like another happy young lady, we can suppose that "she bounded higher, flew farther down the middle, and was in a continual course of smiles".

But while the fiddles sang for her, Arthur Forbes Mitchell was, even as he had prophesied, very miserable;

and with the best of reason. He had been having a little interview with Mr. Charles Forbes.

Unquestionably Mr. Forbes had some financial hold and some assumed authority over his young partner; but the real reason for Arthur's terrified lies and evasions when taken to task by his senior must surely be that of a strong nature's ascendancy over a very weak one. After all, it was not so long since Arthur had been a schoolboy, cringing from the dominie's rod. It was all very well for him to damn and defy his partner's opposition at a safe distance, pot-valiant with lovely Ann's smiles and kisses—it was quite another matter when questioned and brow-beaten, hectored at and commanded by a thundercloud Forbes who could be a terrible enemy.

Forbes was determined that all this nonsense must finally cease. There is excuse for him, for it is plain that Mitchell never dared tell him about the irrevocably committing visit of Friday morning. As far as the angry merchant was concerned, all that the young man had done was to get himself talked about by dangling after this confounded girl, and then, while in liquor, to blurt out an incautious compliment that had been twisted into a proposal. Seeing the Bellasis family through a black veil of prejudice, Mr. Forbes was convinced that they had manœuvred the foolish youth into this position, ignored his attempts to retreat, and would spread news of the engagement all over Bombay, if the victim could not be rescued in time. He therefore put his foot down, with stern threats and orders. By the time he left, young Mitchell was abjectly promising to do his will.

This young man had not behaved well; he had, in fact, behaved very ill—but he was certainly paying, in having his recklessly joyous morning followed by such a night. Left alone with his house-mate, Jonathan Michie, in whom there was no strength or counsel, he can be pictured as gulping brandy-pani, groaning, perhaps weeping, head upon arms, like a schoolboy after a beating; and lying sleep-forsaken, seeing Ann lost for ever, and himself as unutterably base and idiotically weak.

All this had marked his white young face when he faltered into the office of Captain Bellasis on Saturday morning. To use that officer's own words: "He was met by me with open Arms, telling him Ann was very well and desired her Love to him. I was then struck at his appearance, and more so at his conversation, as he began by calling himself a Scoundrel and other opprobrious names." The scene acts itself clearly: the loud, happy greeting, checked at the looks of the tormented young man, as he, grinding his sweating palms together, called himself cur, villain, rascal. At the first stammering sentence which involved the name of Forbes, George Bellasis went off like one of his own cannon: he struck the desk, he roared. Hurcarus and chobdars and palanquin men, waiting his pleasure in distant verandas, quailed and called upon the gods. Before the blazing passion of his usually easy friend, Mitchell cringed also. Bellasis shouted at him to get out. If he had anything to say, by God, he must put it down in black and white.

Mitchell went, poor shuttlecock, to the office of his senior partner; for it is pretty plain that the letter which he presently sent was written from that gentleman's dictation.

"Dear Bellasis—From what has passed between us this Morning you are not a Stranger to the subject of this letter, and I hope therefore that you will survey the matter coolly, and blame alone my rash Conduct. I then tried to explain to you the difficulty I laboured under, but you seemed unable to hear me. I wonder not at this, and can only rely on your more maturely considering the matter—Were I any longer to impose on your Friendship, without candidly Laying my Circumstances before you, I should only add to the folly I have already been guilty of; and I now therefore tell you Candidly that my Circumstances in Life are much below what you have no doubt ever conceived them, and at present I have not a Rupee I can call my own, beyond what I am indebted to my Friends for.

"My Property at Home is burdened with heavy Debts, for the Payment of which I have agreed to its being made over, besides a provision for a large Family—under these impressions would it be proper for me to disguise, I have already done it too long, and for which I have suffered many an anxious hour. The Conversation which took place the other night at your house was on my part highly improper, as I have already expressed to you, though then very Sincere, the Note I wrote you was meant in extenuation of it, and although then I felt how wrong I had acted, I hoped things would not have taken the turn they have.

"From what I have said you will observe that everything I have depends on my Friends, and the sentiments of the most particular of them I made you acquainted with this morning. Could I then permit myself to involve another in misery, and one for whom I have felt so much. After I have thus fully stated my Circumstances I must leave you to make what remarks you think they deserve, in hopes that however Wrong I may have acted, you will acquit me of any disrespect to you or any part of your Family.

"I am your unhappy Friend, Arthur Forbes Mitchell."

It will be seen that this letter made absolutely no mention of the clinching events of Friday; pretty positive proof that Forbes was standing over the lad while he penned every line, quite ignorant of how far the affair had really gone. Had it only gone as far as he supposed, this would have been, to put it mildly, an unsatisfactory letter. No doubt Forbes had contemptuously told his junior that when these harpies were persuaded that he had no money they would loose him readily enough; but granted that a man's bile should so blind him to consideration of the feelings and reputation of the poor young Ann, Mr. Forbes, as a man of the world, should have been awake to another point: he should have realised to what mortal danger he exposed Arthur Mitchell by making him pen that letter.

The wretched performance ranked with that—also dictated by an interested party—in which Willoughby jilted

Marianne Dashwood: "A letter which instead of bringing with his desire of release any professions of regret, acknowledged no breach of faith . . . a letter of which every line was an insult." True, it hardly proclaimed its writer "deep in hardened villainy", and the whine at the end—"your unhappy Friend"—must even have roused compassion in the generous breast of George Bellasis, when the first gust of his wrath was past.

Wrath there was. The distress of Ann and of her three sisters gathered round her, the fainting-fits and tears, could not be viewed by their menfolk and friends without a good deal of swearing about the proper deserts of young Mr. Mitchell; but it was too serious a situation for mere anger. Soberly, Bellasis showed the letter to several officers. They had but one opinion as to what must be done.

Even now, however, he proceeded in a cautious and considerate manner. It was not the fire-eating Colonel Gordon whom he dispatched to the bungalow on the Esplanade that night, it was Captain Byne, paymaster of the 86th, a steady young man, the support of a widowed mother and two sisters, and especially known in the regiment for having successfully composed an affair of honour before.

It was between eight and nine o'clock when Byne arrived. Mitchell and his friend Jonathan Michie were sitting at their wine, after an unpleasant little dinner-party—for Charles Forbes had been gloweringly present, and still sat keeping an eye on the now sullenly desperate young man.

Captain Byne was shown in by the salaaming servant, a courtesy of bows and greetings passed, wine was proffered, of which the visitor drank a glass. He then said in a low tone, "Mitchell, I wish to speak with you, if you please."

The wretched youth led the way to an adjoining bungalow which was used as a bedroom; and in two or three minutes returned, saying, "As we expected, Byne is come with a challenge. Michie, go and speak with him as my friend."

M

Jonathan Michie, although inexperienced in such matters, knew what to say: his friend, anticipating this visit, had told him that no adjustment was possible—that he had offended beyond apology. Captain Byne for his part thought that all this was very melancholy and deplorable: surely it could be adjusted? Supposing now that Mr. Mitchell admitted his ill-behaviour to those whom he had injured, and privately made them submissive apologies, while at the same time it was given out to the world that Miss King had refused his proposal? . . . Michie said no word in favour of this expedient; but Byne insisted upon going off to Colonel Gordon, to see what he thought of its practicability.

In his absence Michie went back to the wine, over which his principal was sitting with a fixed face, and whence he was presently summoned by Byne's return to the other apartment. Colonel Gordon had given his opinion that such an arrangement was not possible, as all Bombay knew the actual state of the case, visits of congratulation having been paid for two days.

Nothing further could be done, and Mitchell made no move to avoid the issue, but was clearly determined on going through with it. As was said afterward: "The greatness of his offence was the impetus urging him to his own destruction. There was no pacific step he could take, no apology . . . nothing but a fiery trial could appease the tumult in his mind."

It is to be hoped that Charles Forbes was satisfied, for he was certainly the architect of the situation. All that he could now do for the lad whom he had driven up to this point was to purvey him a good surgeon, and upon this errand he stalked away.

What kind of night was passed by Arthur Mitchell may be supposed; nor could George Bellasis be very much happier to be taking the field against a friend greatly younger than himself, and plainly wretched and ashamed—one also to whom he had money obligations. The position was invidious, but there was no choice. Even as a civilian he must have avenged Ann; as a soldier, he could have been court martialled for cowardice had he not thus ritually broken the law.

So dawned Sunday, the 3rd of May, 1801, the stars retiring as the lovely Indian early morning, before the sun begins to flame so monstrously, turned from pearl grey to innocent blue above the island of Bombay; and the sea, reflecting it, surged and muttered all along the white beaches. At between five and six o'clock, the hour of the early ride, certain gentlemen set out for the artillery butts by the race-course, not far from the Windmill and the Breach water.

Captain Bellasis rode a handsome horse, Captain Byne and Colonel Gordon drove in a curricle. Byne had with him a case of "satisfaction pistols" belonging to his principal. Young Michie had agreed that Mitchell should make use of one of these, as he had none of his own, and there were no good ones to be obtained in the shops. On the road they passed the palanquin containing Dr. Baird, the surgeon from the hospital, who had been applied to by Mr. Forbes upon the previous night, just after he had been knocked up by Colonel Gordon upon the same errand.

Forbes had parted with his young friend on the Esplanade, and was not coming to the ground. Instead, he rode off to the house of his brother-in-law, Major Stewart, who lived on the Breach Road, and whose back veranda commanded a good view of the place of meeting. He took with him a spyglass, and invited Stewart out of his bed to watch the scene.

Arthur Mitchell drove to the ground with his second. It is not probable that much conversation passed between them, but one thing Mitchell did say: that he would not attempt returning his opponent's fire: it was his fixed intention to stand and be shot at.

When Dr. Baird got out of his palanquin, with a grim case of surgical instruments, he spoke both with Colonel Gordon and with Michie, who was all to pieces with agitation, whatever might be the case with his principal. They then moved out of sight beyond the artillery butt, and the doctor waited.

Mr. Charles Forbes, on his distant veranda, trained his spyglass on the group of Europeans, little and bright, with their ethereal early morning shadows long beside them. Arthur Mitchell was wearing "a blew jacket", which he removed. Captain Bellasis had apparently done likewise with his scarlet, for both stood all in white, though Byne and Gordon showed the military colour.

Byne was engaged with the pistols, powder-flask, and ball, making the tremulous Michie do his share of the loading. He then held the pistols behind his back, and gave him the choice of hands. Michie chose the right-hand pistol. In regard to the distance, he agreed to twelve paces; they stepped it. Asked how they should fire, he said that he was too much a novice to know. Byne said, "He conceived the injured and aggrieved person ought to have the first fire", and Michie agreed to it, adding that his principal admitted as much. Byne then asked him to convey to his principal a question from Captain Bellasis: "Was anything in Miss King's conduct the cause of Mr. Mitchell breaking his engagement?" The answer was, "No, certainly not." Bellasis desired a second question: "Was his own conduct, or that of any part of his family the cause?" Mitchell answered: "Ye were not to blame. It was all, all my own doing."

There have been worse last words.

The antagonists now took their ground. Mitchell cocked his pistol, leant forward, and presented at Bellasis—then, remembering his resolution, dropped his pistol-hand. Bellasis fired. Mitchell fell, shot through the heart.

At the sound of the shot, and a beckoning signal from Gordon, Dr. Baird ran round the butt, attended by a bearer with his instruments. One glance at the prostrate figure told him that they would not be needed; he rose as soon as he had stooped.

"Oh, Doctor, is there no hope?" cried Jonathan Michie, completely unmanned, and clung to him, almost falling.

At the same time, George Bellasis cast off his hat and twined his hands in his hair; then turning, he threw his arms about his brother-in-law's shoulders, crying out: "Oh, God, Gordon, what have I done? I did not think I should have killed him."

Voiceless puppets, the little coloured figures gesticulated in the round of Mr. Forbes' spyglass. It is certain that he had no thought of having set them jigging; that he was not the least disposed to echo the last despairing words of the slain lad. On the contrary, he burnt with the most righteous wrath, and rode into the town lusting for vengeance. Before the day was out, he cast all his powerful influence into causing the arrest of Bellasis and Byne upon a charge of murder.

It is recorded that "the news that Mitchell had been killed by Bellasis in a duel came upon Bombay like a thunderclap".

It was twenty years since the tight-lipped little Governor-General himself, the great, the powerful Warren Hastings, had gone out with the unpleasant Mr. Francis and winged his enemy; but for nearly another half-century the great ones of the earth were to set an example of arbitrament by pistol, and be followed with more or less impunity by meaner persons. In these first years of the dawning century it was understood that should an affair of honour result fatally the survivor had best keep out of the way, as he might have to stand trial; but that if he were tried, nothing would come of it. Typical was an item in a Calcutta paper: "On Monday last came on the trial of Mr. A. for killing Mr. G. in a duel. The trial lasted till near five o'clock in the afternoon, when the Jury retired for a short time, and brought in their verdict *Not Guilty*. Mr. G. was a very respectable man, very able in his profession, and is much regretted by all who had the pleasure of his acquaintance."

However, the Bellasis-Mitchell duel was altogether

exceptional. From one circumstance and another it raised a furious storm. The animosity and the power of Forbes and his friends were both great. Bellasis and Byne not only suffered arrest and confinement for two anxious months in Fort George: they must also be aware of the ever-mounting passion and prejudice which threatened their chance of a fair trial.

The Quarterly Sessions of Oyer and Terminer and of Gaol Delivery began upon Tuesday, July 14th, before the Recorder, Sir William Syer, his associate judges, Robert Henshaw, who was Mayor of Bombay, and three Aldermen. The Grand Jury—twenty-three leading citizens—were addressed by the Recorder "in an eloquent and impressive Speech, upon the nature of the various Bills which were to be brought before them, and explaining the Law thereon, particularly upon the subject of *Duelling*". . . . For everybody knew that a few unimportant cases of murder and rape among the natives amounted to nothing—and indeed no bills were found—whereas this business of the Bellasis-Mitchell duel had swelled into something very big indeed.

During the past weeks Bombay had been halved into two vehement parties, with roughly the lawyers and merchants upon one side, the armed forces upon the other—another case of "quibbling quill-drivers" and "glittering sabres"—while the furnace of the hot weather boiled the whole thing up. The Forbes party were much the more vocal: their version of events soon pervaded the place like the malarial mist which brooded under the toddy trees in the morning; their gossip buzzed and stung like the evening mosquitoes. The life of young Mitchell, it would seem, had been sacrificed to a fire-eating bully who had covered his own bad conduct by deliberately killing his victim . . . there had been something very fishy about the pistols both belonging to Bellasis . . . Mitchell had been given no chance for his life . . . he had been shot unarmed, or before he could fire, or before he was ready. . . . This last idea was most persistent; it was to pass into one of those indestructible legends against which fact and reason have no power: and in after years to swell into a muddled but damaging notion that this Bellasis had shot an unarmed enemy alighting from a palanquin.

When the Court assembled in robes and wigs which, considering the weather, were enough to make judges and advocates drop dead upon the spot, every person there must have heard the rumours in which the town was stewing; and any notion that they might not have affected the Recorder was dispelled after his address to the Grand Jury.

On the next day, the 15th, the Court again met at ten o'clock, and a True Bill was returned against Lieutenant George Bridges Bellasis—indicted in his substantive rank —and Captain Charles William Byne for the Murder of Mr. Arthur Andrew Forbes Mitchell. No Bill was found against Lieutenant Jonathan Michie, of the Bombay Marine, and the Court rejected a motion from the Crown advocate, Mr. Dowdeswell, that Michie should be put to the bar and have his case disposed of straightway, so that he might presently give evidence. Lieutenant Bellasis and Captain Byne were therefore put to the bar, and being arraigned, pleaded *Not Guilty*.

George Bellasis in all probability looked haggard enough, and unfamiliar to those used to seeing him flushed and jovial over the wine; but his very tall, very handsome person, which appeared to such advantage in regimentals, was certainly held with the uprightness of a soldier, and all the pride of one who felt that he had acted as an honourable gentleman, and with irreproachable correctness, whatever his anxieties. These were terrible enough. Apart from his own situation—and he must have felt the breath of mortal hostility as it were on the back of his neck—his wife had collapsed under the strain, and was lying very seriously ill.

By his side, his particular friend and fierce partisan, Lieut. Kemp, scowled upon the opposition; his advocate, James Morley, glanced reassurance; the inoffensive Byne sought the encouraging looks of his comrades. The courtroom was packed with military officers, the whole garrison seemed come: no doubt with a few exceptions such as General John Bellasis, whose sympathy with his nephew was undissembled, but who could hardly appear openly in his support. In a temperature like that of hell, but slightly modified by dampened kus-kus tatties, the red coats and the black robes sweated and glowered.

The first clash came over the choosing of the Petty Jury. In so small a community it was hard to pick jurymen who should be of neither party. There were eight peremptory challenges on the part of the prisoners, and three on the part of the Crown; and it ended as being entirely composed, but for one shopkeeper, of ships' captains and mates.

Mr. Dowdeswell opened the prosecution with a telling speech to these seamen, and he then called Charles Forbes. That eminent citizen—who was to be sworn in as a Justice at the end of the Sessions—told his story, one may suppose, in what denunciatory Scots tones. He described how the challenge was brought in his presence, how "by the assistance of a spying-glass," he watched the meeting, and saw young Mitchell lie dead; and how, seeing Bellasis later crossing the Esplanade with Byne and Colonel Gordon, and a quantity of servants and baggage, he applied to Mr. Carnac to take them up.

Cross-examined: He had never said he would be glad to take away the life of Lieutenant Bellasis, or blow his brains out. Never sent his hamals to the hamals of Colonel Gordon to discover evidence against Lieutenant Bellasis— once sent a horse-keeper to Colonel Gordon's to see if Lieutenant Bellasis was there.

As to the cause of dispute, he gave his version of his young friend's entanglement and effort to free himself, with the story that he had been "in a state of stupefaction" on the night of the party.

Mr. Morley had before him some neatly written foolscap: Ann King's sworn deposition, taken as Lieutenant Bellasis could by no means allow her to be distressed by a personal appearance in Court. It covered the passages between her and her lover in the greatest detail, and put quite another complexion on the matter.

Mr. Forbes must have been shaken at hearing the incidents of the Friday breakfast: he must have been near realising that the dead young man had lied to him pretty heartily; but it is most probable that he put any such realisation behind him straightway, and continued to hug his righteous wrath and puissant enmity. He concluded his evidence with the admission that he was much against the marriage, and had warned Mitchell against it months previously.

Dr. Baird was then called and gave vivid details of the duel, the death of Mitchell and the agitation of his opponent. Many must look in the face of the prisoner at the bar, and surely it would whiten and twitch at the recollection . . . *"Oh God, Gordon, what have I done?"* . . . The doctor described the wound: the ball had broken a rib, passed through the base of the heart, and come out an inch lower. He had given that evidence to the coroner.

Minor witnesses followed: Major Stewart with more spyglass evidence; Mitchell's friend Lieutenant Bryan, whose observations were rather in favour of the Defence, for he persisted that Mitchell was quite sober on the night of the proposal.

The first Defence witness was William Nesbit, Esq., as important a citizen as Mr. Forbes: he deposed that he had been at the Bellasis dinner-party, sitting next to Miss King and opposite Arthur Mitchell: Mitchell did not drink much, and was not pressed to do so. Sheriff Luke Ashburner next spoke of the Friday breakfast: had seen Mitchell lead Miss King to table and take her into the veranda afterward: had no doubt that they were engaged. Mr. Joseph Cumberlege, a hostile witness, spoke to the conversation in the boat returning from Elephanta, and to Bellasis acknowledging the engagement to him upon the Thursday. Then came a

Dr. James, who had been introduced to the ladies at the
February races and had observed when driving back to
town with Mitchell that "Miss King was a devilish fine
girl"—and found him to agree heartily. Was aware of the
report about them, but—added the doctor gallantly—would
have said this anyhow. Captain Malcolm had made a call
of congratulation upon the Saturday: had been told the
news by Colonel Coleman.

It grew late; the retracement of the pitiful, tragic, or
merely silly details of the affair had taken all day, allowing
for intervals of refreshment, and everybody must have
been exhausted by the time the accused were called upon to
speak. Byne stood up and said a very few words to the
jury; but Bellasis had prepared a speech, and this he now
read, in his clear, loud, military voice, here and there wavering with emotion.

"Gentlemen of the Jury: Though I will not long detain
you, it is my wish before you retire to submit a few general
observations to your consideration. It is my unhappiness,
in the protection of an injured and insulted young woman,
who is not only my relation but under my especial care and
guardianship, to stand here in the face of a whole community
charged with a crime at which human nature cannot but
shudder.

"Under such a circumstance, I am sure you will not
disregard the incentives which called me forth, as the
champion of a sister's wounded and insulted feelings, nor
view me in the sanguinary light of an assassin or a murderer;
for I persuade myself it has been clearly manifested that on
my part every opening was given to prevent an hostile
determination. But the unfortunate young gentleman
feigned to see no other mode of adjustment, than to carry
matters to their very extremity. It is you, Gentlemen, who
are to determine whether the observance of such a conduct
in him did not plainly evince his own ideas of the magnitude
of his aggression, and whether the greatness of his offence

was not the impetus urging him to his own destruction. There was no pacific step he could take, no apology to me nor my Sister, nothing but a fiery trial could appease the tumult in his mind.

"Let me beseech you to recollect that on the fatal ground he admitted that no part of my sister's nor of my conduct was the cause of his dishonourable secession. It was his last words—'*Ye were not to blame. It was all, all my own doing*'. As to the letter which has been given in evidence, I submit that so far from its being any extenuation of his conduct, that I consider it as adding insult to insult. It seems more intended to prevent a prosecution for the breach of a promise of marriage, than any exculpation of his offence. These are the premises I would wish you to carry in your remembrance.

"I am sure I need not remind a Jury so well informed that there are rules in refined and polished society that operate *so* imperatively as even to supersede the written Law. And although the Jurisprudence of our Country (for essentially wise purposes) ordains that every person who shall occasion the death of another in a Duel *shall* be capitally arraigned, you must yet be sensible that even in cases of less atrocity than the present, the legislators themselves have not made their own written law the rule of their conduct. Those laws, the pride, the boast, of Englishmen, do yet humanely leave all alleviating circumstances to the conscientious breasts of the Jury.

"Surely then the vindication of a beloved sister's wounded feelings is entitled to some degree of alleviating compassion. Some of you Gentlemen may have sisters. Judge me as ye would be judged! Not forgetting that being a Man, I am subject to all the calamities of Man!"

It was now nine o'clock at night, and lamps shone on the mopped wet faces, white with fatigue, or red with pulls at the claret-jug during the last adjournment. Perhaps the Recorder had been so refreshing himself, for he wept during his summing-up. The official account published in the Bombay paper says that he "summed up the whole of the Proceedings with his usual perspicuity and accuracy, and delivered his Charge to the Jury in a manner which reflected the highest credit upon his abilities and impartiality".

It would be interesting to know the writer's standard of impartiality. Sir William Syer made no secret of his opinion of this "awful" case, this "awful" crime; although he was to reserve his full and free expression of it until the time came to deliver sentence. As it was, sobs interrupted his utterance. He spoke earnestly of King George as of the Fountain of Mercy; he movingly made the prayer for God to guide the jury on their judgment.

It was midnight before the jury retired. Captain Barfoot of the *Nottingham*, and his mate Mr. Ramage, Captain Isaacke of the *Skelton Castle*, Captain Wakefield of the *Henry Addington*, and all the others, took until half past one o'clock in the morning to decide upon a verdict of Guilty, with a Recommendation to Mercy.

Had it not been for the Recorder's charge, they would certainly have returned the usual Not Guilty verdict. As it was, they clearly intended that no penalty should follow. To place this beyond dispute—they perhaps had been rendered uneasy by the spectacle of the prisoners removed in close custody to await judgment upon the following Monday—they composed a letter to the Recorder during the ensuing day, stating that their Recommendation to Mercy really meant a recommendation to immediate pardon and release.

At the same time, the greater part of them signed a special plea for Captain Byne, which had originated with the officers of the 86th, and had actually been signed by the prosecuting counsel: it pointed out his excellent character, his former success in averting a duel, and his attempt to avert this one.

Everybody was no doubt glad of a rest during Thursday; and on Friday, Lieutenant Jonathan Michie was brought to the bar and arraigned for aiding and abetting. No evidence being offered, he was discharged by proclamation.

It was a long while since Bombay had spent such a week-end of report, dispute, and suspense; and on Monday the 20th, at ten o'clock, the courthouse was thronged with even more officers than before. Scarlet, with gold and silver lace on high collars, swords and sashes, were bright before the eyes of the Recorder, as he looked upon them with lowered brows and pursed lips.

Lieutenant Bellasis and Captain Byne were put to the bar, and being asked in the usual form what they had to say why Sentence of Death should not be passed upon them, they severally addressed the Court in a few words, throwing themselves upon its mercy.

Now came the Recorder's moment, for which he had throughout been waiting. He "addressed the Prisoners in a long and very affecting speech, wherein he recapitulated the leading circumstances of the Melancholy case, and took Occasion to Admonish the Audience, addressing himself *in particular to Military men* to take warning from the unfortunate example before them, of the danger of flying in the face of the Laws, and actuated by *false notions of honour*, seeking the Lives of their fellow creatures or risking their Own, by that most barbarous practice of *Duelling*—a practice in direct Opposition to the Laws of God and Man, and Consequently highly *dishonourable*".

Not content with this, Sir William Syer proceeded to give his opinion that young Mr. Mitchell had not been allowed a fair chance for his life, and had been given no time to fire. He ended with a further insult to the man who stood with compressed but quivering lips before him. How terrible was the fate of the young man who had fallen—cried the Recorder, affecting himself almost to sobbing again, as he spoke of the light suddenly darkened and the life struck out of one so young and hopeful—but if the case of he who fell was shocking, how much worse was the case of the survivor! The one had lost his life, but the other had lost not only his position and income—"he had lost—he had lost—the honour he made so much noise about!"

Certainly he must have been heard with a breathless attention, though with sensible fury and dismay, by the greater part of his auditory; and the stifling silence could only deepen as he went on to say that in consideration of the jury having recommended the prisoners to mercy, the Court had determined to avail themselves of the late gracious Act of His Majesty enabling the Courts in India to award Sentence of Transportation instead of Execution, and further that from some favourable circumstances which had appeared upon the trial affecting the case of Captain Byne, as well as a representation which had just been put into his hand from the officers of the 86th Regiment, the Court would be induced to recommend him to His Majesty for pardon; but that the case of Lieutenant Bellasis appeared in a very different point of view, and he must not expect the smallest remission of his punishment.

After an impressive pause, the Recorder concluded: "It therefore only remains for me to pronounce the Sentence of the Law as the Court have determined to apply it, which is: That you, George Bridges Bellasis, shall be transported to the Eastern coast of New South Wales, for the term of fourteen years; and that you, Charles William Byne, shall be transported to the same place for the term of seven years."

IX

AFTER THE VERDICT

"TO Mr. William Bridges of Wallington House, Croydon, Surrey.—Bombay, 26th July, 1801.
"My much respected Friend.

"The untoward Situation in which I'm thrown, not by any bad Action of my own induces me indeed obliges me to call on you for that assistance I know from experience your humanity never withholds from the Unfortunate.

"It has been my Misfortune in the protection of an injur'd Sisters wounded feelings, to fall a victim to A Sentence of the Law, namely fourteen years Banishment to New South Wales—Under the presence of Woe that I at present feel, pardon me if I do not express myself as correctly as I could wish—The short and melancholy fact is as follows—Mr. Mitchell a Young Man a Friend of mine paid his Addresses to my Wife's Sister Miss Ann King who was living with me, and gain'd her Affections and finally propos'd Marriage to Her which was accepted by the young Lady, and every circumstance settl'd but the day of Marriage; for dissembl'd reasons, Mr. Mitchell retracted his Engagements, without once making an Apology to the Young Lady, Myself or any of my Family—I consulted my Friends how I was to act, when there was but One Opinion, that I must either call on Mr. Mitchell, or have a Court Martial, my Honor induc'd me to follow the former line of Conduct—Unfortunate was the result, poor Mitchell fell the first shot from Me—Unhappy as I am at the Event, I have still the consolation of having preserv'd my own Honor, as well as A belov'd Sisters—In what light would you Sir have view'd Me, if I had return'd to England and solicited your Assistance after having been turn'd out of the Army here for Cowardice—I have now to solicit your kind Assistance in behalf of the Gentleman who will deliver this to you, Mr. Nash with whom you will see I have been for some Years concern'd, and should ultimately have made a Fortune, but those prospects are now vanish'd, and my good Friend, you will see by a Letter I inclose, will lose much more than He can afford, unless you Sir in your kindness for me will repay him, and in such Case Mr. Nash will supply me with Articles for Sale on Commission at the Place I am destin'd to—My Situation is truly deplorable, and that of A belov'd and Amiable Wife, whose Affection for Me is unbounded, and must now if my Friends do not assist us share poverty with me in all its Horrors—You I know Sir will feel our situation and I trust add to our Comforts, by enabling us to have the common Comforts of Life, Luxuries I never wanted, I would not have appli'd to you if I had not lost this Service, together with it nearly twelve Hundred per Year, and being now reduced to Beggary, but now pardon me Sir in requesting you will pity my poor Wife's and my Misfortunes and give us such assistance as you shall think proper, and We will ever remember You with the greatest Affection and Gratitude—The whole Army have sign'd Letters to the Governor of Port Jackson in my Favour, likewise the Inhabitants of this Place—I must now conclude with wishing you all Earthly Happiness in which my Dear Wife unites—I am Dear and respected Sir your Affectionate and Sincere and unfortunate Godson,

George Bridges Bellasis."

If the condemned man here wrote something wildly, even with more dashes and fewer commas than usual, it might well be excused; especially as Esther Bellasis had been passing from raving hysterics to swooning passivity, while the doctors talked of danger either to her life or her reason.

Besides the eighty officers who had signed the letter to the Governor of Port Jackson praying for the obtainment of a pardon for Bellasis, a half-dozen of his special intimacy had signed in addition a testimonial to his honourable character and to his "being esteemed a good-tempered pleasant companion". His immediate superior, the Commissary of Stores, certified him a good officer, obliging and good-tempered: "I have never known or heard that he was quarrelsome, and from all that has come to my knowledge of the affair for which he now suffers the sentence of the Law, I think the line of conduct he adopted was unavoidable, and as polished society is at present organised that every member of it having unmarried sisters or daughters or other Females under his protection is liable to similar misfortune."

"The verdict of a timid Jury alarm'd by the heavy Charge given by the Judge," was the phrase of Colonel John. Writing news of the King beauties to an English friend, he mentioned first the happiness of Hannah with Colonel Gordon, continuing: "It is grievous to me to add the very widely different and most unexpected hard fate which has befallen her charming sister Miss Ann on the eve of Marriage. . . . My Nephew has by one of those points of Honor which any man might unfortunately be led into, fallen a victim. He acted as every person must have done, so unfortunately circumstanced."

"All the persons here who are unconnected with Mr. Mitchell commiserate Bellasis' fate," wrote the lawyer, James Morley, sending a full account of the matter to his client's father at Basildon.

But by the time the packet of heavy news reached England, six months later, it was Leah who must open and suppress it; for old Dr. Bellasis lay upon his death-bed. Of a letter to the same effect from George Hutchins Bellasis, she read only the passages recounting that young man's safe arrival in Bombay; and the dying man said feebly, "I am glad my good brother has got his sons with him. I hope he is quite happy now." . . . It was plain that he was thinking of his own sons, of the death of Joseph. . . . Oh, no, no; certainly he must not hear what had happened to George. Leah summoned all her considerable self-command;

but surely her frightened thoughts must have flown away
from the pillow by which she watched to wonder what,
now, six months after the verdict, was happening to that
gallant, heedless figure, and to the very beautiful woman
who had walked triumphant in the garden below the
window of the death-chamber. . . . It was cold, still weather
in the ending of January, and the stiller for being a Sunday.
The sexton was waiting to break the silence with nine
strokes on the passing bell. At the foot of the lawn, the
river talked with a low voice on its journey to the sea: the
river beside which the tall sons had spent their youth; the
sea which they had crossed to go so far and far away. . . .
Leah brought up her two children to the side of the four-
poster: she held up her baby, the Benjamin, little Edward:
and the old man blessed his other son. A few hours later,
supported on her arm, with his eyes on her fair, comforting
face, he died.

It had troubled him that his youngest son would not be
able to remember him; but the elder child, his dear little
Anna Maria, was now four years old: and upon her memory
he endeavoured to print some recollection by leaving
directions that she was to follow his body to the grave,
holding a long black ribbon attached to the coffin. Important in her black frock, the little girl trotted, clutching her
ribbon, after the eight poor men of the parish who bore the
coffin, cascading crape from new hats given for the occasion;
while the servants followed in their mourning. Rimey tears
from the black yews damped the Doctor's Walk, so strongly
associated with the tall, black, stately figure in the powdered
wig that surely there must arise a village tale of haunting.
The black rooks opened their beaks with hoarse and mourn-
ful cries. They would have built their nests and reared
their next broods, and the roses would be dropping before
word of this burial reached to the other side of the world.

Far away in space and time, in Bombay during the rains,
where life was lived as in the steam of a boiling kettle, the

ruined family, six months back, had been preparing to embark for New Holland. Esther, sick or well, was going with her husband. Ann, at first, was eagerly fixed upon accompanying them, to atone, by nursing her sister, for being the prime cause of all. From this, however, she was presently persuaded; and when her sister and brother-in-law sailed, she remained behind in the Gordon household to await another fate—as it proved, a greatly happier one.

During the weeks before the sailing, while Esther was being preserved from the alternatives attending too great sensibility—death or madness, and while signatures and subscriptions were being gathered for her husband, the poisonous rumours of unfairness in the duel did not die down: they grew worse. This indeed was to be expected. What had happened to George Bellasis was such a particularly cruel thing to follow a mere compliance with the ordinary rules of honour, that his enemies must endeavour to prove he had broken those rules and thus suffered justly.

Against this intangible bogy of slander, Lieutenant Kemp rushed to do battle for his friend: announcing bluntly that the Recorder had been biased by the lies of common report, and must be induced to reconsider the evidence. His raised voice added to the noise which the case was beginning to make all over British India. "For God's sake!" pleaded Bellasis, as soon as his attention could be distracted from Esther: "Kemp, you will ruin me!" But Lieutenant Kemp, pointing out that this was impossible, and that he had nothing to lose, continued to clamour for justice after the ship which bore his friend had departed to an infamous destination. Pressingly, he invited Jonathan Michie to deny the groundless report of the duel's unfairness. He called on that young gentleman, in the company of a brother-officer named Lovell, with a paper of five categorical questions, to which he extracted answers: all going to prove the fair and honourable conduct of the meeting: proving also what rumours were afloat, for one question and answer dealt with whether Mitchell had or had not been shot down unarmed.

Having given his answers, however, Michie dug in his heels and refused his signature. Kemp, therefore, in the presence of witnesses, told the Naval Lieutenant loudly that he was no gentleman and needed a sound horsewhipping. Young Michie, who had probably seen enough of duelling to last him a lifetime, did not contest the proposition. Lieutenant Kemp was in full regimentals: he now suddenly whipped out his sword and forced the hilt into Michie's reluctant hands: arming himself then with his friend Lovell's sword, he flashed it on guard and bade the other fight. Lieutenant Michie did not want to fight: he dropped Kemp's sword with a clatter, like a hot poker, and hurried away to a lawyer. Next Session came on the case of "The King at the Suit of Jonathan Michie *v.* Edward Thomas Kemp and J. Williamson Lovell, for Assault and Provoking to fight a Duel."

This was just the sort of move on the part of the "glittering sabre" party which George Bellasis had been anxiously desirous to avoid: the painful efforts in his letter to his godfather to prove that he had not acted on impulse, the testimonials to his peaceable nature, had all been designed to clear him of military fire-eating. Kemp, however, if he could not have Michie's blood, asked nothing better than to drag the whole thing out in open court again. The wretched Mitchell, he proclaimed, had been given a perfectly equal chance. "Those who systematically behave ill to women, to the defenceless, are systematically cowards. Mitchell was not so bad as this—he was young and inexperienced. Fate was against him, or undoubtedly reflection would have brought him soon to other behaviour—unhappy those who had any concern in bringing him to danger." It may be supposed how Mr. Forbes liked the reflection. As for Lieutenant Michie—"Whose friends have endeavoured to frighten me into an apology by threats ranging from loss of my staff appointment, to the common jail"—he, however

Forbes might be deceived, had been in Mitchell's confidence all along, and knew, moreover, that the meeting had been perfectly regular—knew it, and declined to avow it. "He bears a commission, a sword is part of his full dress, he should know what a sword is, he has no right as an officer to express any fear whatever on being shown a sword"— and he had covered his bad behaviour by refuge in legalities. Here Lieutenant Kemp had some hard things to say about ungentlemanly lawyers. He then quoted Blackstone upon judicial impartiality, and announced that he would proceed against the Recorder in Parliament, with the assistance of "Every gentleman in Bombay, without he will give up the society of the fair sex, for should he undertake the charge of a lady, though even only the honour of her arm for a walk in the fresh air, if he dares resent ungentlemanly behaviour to her, which from the new doctrines may grow very rife to ladies, he is liable to transportation, and an insult for making a noise about honour".

The soldier was hurriedly found guilty, but no penalty seems to have followed; and meanwhile James Morley, the lawyer, was attempting something in his different way, arranging for the original trial to be published "in reply to a general demand in India, Egypt, and the United Kingdom". So far was this now a *cause célèbre*, so far had rung the echoes of what many Presidency officials no doubt called, in their native tongue, this "collie-shangie". The *Bombay Gazette* offered copies of the trial for sale at the *Gazette* office, also to be obtained from G. G. Richardson, Esq., at Madras, Mr. Francis Green at Surat, Mr. Akers at Calicut, and Mr. Sam Greenway at the *India Gazette* office, Calcutta. However, the Government suddenly panicked, deciding that the thing would not look well in print: they forced the *Gazette* to retract it and state that it had been "compiled under the influence of individual prejudice." . . . The Editor said to Morley, "My poverty but not my will consents"; and Morley sent all the documents, with a protest, to the Hon. Jonathan Duncan, the Governor in Council.

While all this was going on in India, strings were being pulled in London; but though George Bellasis must know it and found his hopes upon it, it can hardly have medicined the desolation of his feelings when he arrived with his stricken wife at Port Jackson.

Port Jackson was not a pleasant place, whatever the magnificent view of Sydney Cove, the beauty of the orange trees, the strange birds and foliage, the wooded inlets glassing themselves in the blue water. The smallest observation upon landing would disclose the place for what it was, the common jakes for all the vileness of a realm. Pinchgut Island spoke of the starvation by which refractory transports could be tamed; the Provost Marshal's lash fell bloodily at the triangles; hemp was cheap and plenty. Fifteen Irishmen had just been hanged for trying to make a break beyond the Blue Mountains. These were political prisoners, "croppies" from the late rebellion; and if George Bellasis had wished to lighten his lot by contrast, he might have considered the case of the Irish gentlemen among them: Counsellor Sutton, Dr. McCullom, Mr. Brannan, late High Sheriff of Wexford, Mr. Lysight, who had forfeited an estate of £2,000 a-year, General Holt. These, some of them sick, were being used to carry cargo ashore through the surf. General Holt, a handsome old man, was to be seen staggering up the beach, dressed in a fine blue coat with a black velvet collar, bowed under a sack of sugar. . . . But it is poor consolation for a person suffering under injustice and hardship that others are more unjustly treated and worse used than he. The thick atmosphere of cruelty and horror, of crime and of tormented innocency which hung over that land at that time, could hardly have been lifted for George Bellasis by his knowing the particular ingredients of it. His life had come to a dead stand. The finger and thumb of Fate had lifted him out of all that he had loved and transferred him to all that he must loathe. When he looked at Esther, his only link with the past, she appeared like a ghost, fading more faintly every day; for she did not rally, and the nervous disorder occasioned by shock now kept her on her couch, she could not walk. Social temptations were few; but if Bellasis dined with the Governor, or attended the coarse comedies that were got up at the theatre, he must go alone.

Perhaps not many stared at the handsome haunted-looking officer and wondered about the details of his story. There were so many faces marked with strange happenings; folk kept their own counsel; there can be small curiosity in Hell. . . . When Bellasis' brother-in-law, Eastwick, brought a cargo to Port Jackson about this time, he was accosted in Mr. Lord's store by a delicately lovely young woman, servant-maid to the Judge's wife, who asked earnestly if he had encountered in India a certain well-born young officer. She explained the reason for her interest: she was this officer's sister. She had been taken shoplifting in London—"a species of madness"—tried and transported in a false name, unknown to her family, who had given her up for dead. She wished that she were. . . .

By an odd coincidence of name, the Governor to whom George Bellasis' letters of recommendation were addressed was Governor King; and he, a worthy ex-Navy man, who had been one of Phillips' officers, was very ready to help. In the *General Standing Orders of New South Wales*—the first book ever to be printed in the Colony—occurred the passage: "Mr. George Bridges Bellasis is appointed to act as Colonial artillery officer. January 16, 1802." Later in the year: "H.E. the Governor has been pleased to appoint Mr. George Bridges Bellasis to a Colonial Commission as Lieutenant of Artillery, and to rank as such in the Colony, being charged with the inspection and direction of the batteries and cannon in this settlement, and also as Commandant of the Governor's Body Guard of Cavalry."

Despite this exalted situation, time must have worn away desperately hard with the banished man, living from mail to mail, and penning endless letters to all those friends,

inconceivably distant, who might be supposed to assist
him. At last, on May 23rd, 1803, he was enabled to scribble
rather incoherently: "My Dear Lodge—

"This letter will I trust be delivered to you by a Friend of
Mine, Lt. Inglis, R.N. who can give you any information
relative to my unfortunate situation in this Country—I have
pestered you so much and often with my Miseries that I will
now only make a request to you that you will wait on that
respectable and worthy gentleman Mr. Bridges. Pray thank
him in the most polite manner possible for the steps he has
taken in endeavouring to restore a person overwhelm'd
with all of the earthly Calamities—My Mind is so agitated
I can scarcely connect two Ideas—Governor King assures
me I shall shortly be able to quit this vile Country, with what
pleasure I shall fly to Mr. Bridges and my other Friends to
thank them for their Interference, I shall leave your feeling
Heart to conceive—Ingratitude my Dear Friend forms no
part of the composition of George Bridges Bellasis."

Then came out the official announcement that the friends
in England had been successful in their efforts: "June 5,
1803. Sydney Cove. The Royal Standard having been
hoisted for the first time in this territory, on the anniversary
of H.M.'s birth, His Excellency is pleased to extend the
Royal Grace and free pardon to Colonial Lieutenant of
Artillery and Engineer George Bridges Bellasis. By command of His Excellency. W. M. Chapman, Secretary."

The longest three months of exile must have been those
which now elapsed, for it was not possible to take ship for
England before September. The Bellasis' departure was
then advertised in the local paper; and when spring was
coming among the queer foliage of the upside-down-
country, George Bellasis could stand on deck while the
sails filled to carry him for ever out of the most beautiful,
and to him the most hateful, harbour in the world.

For the better part of three years, life had been painfully
marking time for him; he perhaps expected that it had been

standing still for others, and was shocked, as the long absent commonly are, to find great changes. The actual sight of his father's tomb must be one shock, and the meeting with a half-sister and brother never seen before, but old enough to talk with, another; but there was a further change: Leah, his "amiable and excellent" stepmother, was married again, and that at the age of forty, to a bridegroom twelve years her junior.

It seemed that the Rev. Joseph Maude's reluctance to take a Westmorland curacy depended not wholly on climatic reasons. That fair, even-featured, gentle face which had been part of his life since it belonged to a sedate girl of seventeen and he was a staring little boy of five, had exerted a magnetic pull. It had changed very little in the years during which he had been curate to her husband, in the months during which the old man had moved slowly toward death, and they two had faced one another alone across the hearth. Often she had mildly rallied him upon his silence, his low spirits, his insensibility to the charms of divers young ladies; but in those last months at least she must have understood what he was feeling. Decorously and in order, the widow retired to an old house in Reading, shed her weeds, prepared the Maude family to approve by letter, and on the 8th of August, 1804, was there married to young Joseph Maude. Two of his brothers, her one-time pupils, attended; but not Anna Maria, the warmth of whose female friendship had perhaps been cooled by her own recent marriage.

It was thus a wedding-visit which George paid to his stepmother in September, when he passed through Reading on his way to Bath. It was hoped—and he was loudly sanguine about it—that Bath might do something for Esther. He would not openly acknowledge what everyone else could see, that she was broken beyond mending, that she was marked for death. He now carried her about in his arms, for she was light as a skeleton, and the death's-head began to shape itself clearly under her once-lovely face; she was to be the second casualty from that early-morning pistol-shot more than three years back.

Before another year was out, there was no denying it. Communication between them must have grown, as it were, fainter and more muffled daily, as she withdrew further from the living world. Her husband, vigorously alive, must have found the sight of her a perpetual secret torment, with the knowledge that the world was blaming him for her fate. He had anxieties enough. All his efforts to procure a reinstatement in India were being blocked by Forbes opposition, for old John Forbes was powerful in Leadenhall Street. "To bear revenge in the mind for so long a period"— exclaimed Henry Fawcett in England to John Bellasis, at Bombay—"is the characteristic of a Bedouin Arab and not an Englishman." He might have reflected that it is also the characteristic of a Highland Scot. Meanwhile George's financial situation grew, throughout 1804, 1805, and 1806, first bad, and then worse, and then desperate. No doubt such a tangle of calamities wearied the patience of his friends, no doubt many liked to believe the worst of him—that his imprudence was criminal. There seems to have been a breach with "that respectable and worthy gentleman Mr. Bridges". One person, however, beside the staunchly attached Lodges, was his champion throughout: his sister-in-law, Mrs. Kent. Of her he later wrote: "Had it not been for her kind attentions to me, I should never have supported myself under my great afflictions in England, when I was penniless nearly, and forsaken by those on whose friendship I had a claim. She only was kind and Affectionate towards Me, and as my Miseries encreased if possible her kindness was greater—I retrospect with Enthusiasm on her conduct."

Eliza Kent, always the most alive of the seven beautiful sisters, must have appeared startlingly vital beside the couch of Esther. She had joined them upon landing, and travelled with them. When Bellasis came into the sickroom, stooping his tallness, moderating his stride, and lowering his strong voice as best he might—what a relief to leave that shaded stillness presently, that Eliza might support his spirits by her singing and playing and jesting! If the sick woman heard the music, and her husband's loud, clear laugh, was she more desolate, or more thankful that he could be consoled? Who knows what girlhood history there was of early rivalry for his notice, by the Berkshire riverside? . . . It was there that she left them finally, for she died at Sonning-on-Thames, on the 12th September, 1805, at the age of thirty-six. "I think it a fortunate circumstance, all things considered, that it has pleased God to release Mrs. G. B. Bellasis from all her troubles," commented General John.

They laid the ashes of the beauty in the box-shaped family tomb at Puttenham; her father had been buried there while she was at Botany Bay. Within the church, a tablet —"A Tribute of Affectionate Regard"—was set up "by her Husband Capt. George Bridges Bellasis of the Honourable East India Company's Service, Bombay Artillery, who will ever lament with unfeigned Sorrow the loss of so much human Perfection."

It is a pretty phrase, with the smoothness and also the coldness of the marble.

Mrs. Kent at once carried off her "brother Bellasis" to the home at Frimley which she shared with her somewhat formidable but genial old mother-in-law. Captain Kent does not seem to have been in the picture. He must then have been at Madras, exchanging the *Eliza* for a far more ambitious ship, the splendid *Malabar*, in which he hoped to make a final fortune for himself and his lovely wife: happily without prevoyance of the disaster to be brought on by his too-trusting nature. One night in harbour, being laden for her first voyage to England, the grand new ship was to go roaring up in flames, caused by the fall of a rum-cask into the hold, and a seaman's naked candle: and it would presently appear that the London firm—Kent's own cousins—whom he had trusted to effect the insurance, had done nothing about it, confident that he would not inquire after the fat premium.

When a simple man loses his faith in life, as well as his whole fortune, perhaps something may break in him, as it broke in Esther, that May morning in Bombay; suffice it, that Tom Kent would not long survive his ruin, and that within a measurable distance of time, Eliza would be a widow.

Meanwhile, she devoted her energies to delivering George Bellasis from a widower's gloom. In a letter to Lodge in December, he says that she is playing the piano, and singing her favourite song *Rosa*, as he writes; adding, in response to some gallant aspiration of Lodge's to kiss the lady's fair right hand: "My Sister's Kiss Fist has taken my pen"—Eliza's smaller feminine handwriting goes on: "We have this moment some fine Whitings sent from Portsmouth, and at the fire a fine piece of roast beef—and you not here or coming to partake with us this homely fare—I tell you what, my friend, be upon your guard that instead of saluting my fair hand, it does not salute your ears when we meet on Wednesday or any day—My brother Bellasis has made me as saucy as himself." A battledore and shuttlecock game of nonsense was kept up between herself and the two Lodges; she was never tired of teasing Edmund about his Heraldic character, demanding that he supply her with Arms, complete with Supporters and all other trimmings. "A very charming amiable woman, but with too much candour for this world. I never in my life met with a creature (particularly of the *feminine gender*) with so natural a character and so compleatly without disguise or cunning, which in my opinion gives a charm and grace to all she says and does": that was Charlotte Lodge's verdict to George, understanding that to him she could not praise the charming Eliza too much.

For the lookers-on must clearly have discerned what feelings were at the root of Eliza's "kind attentions", and George's "enthusiasm". Esther dead, Tom Kent living, and the law against marrying a Deceased Wife's Sister, stood in the way of their development. None of these were hopeless obstacles, for people—including one of Jane Austen's brothers, and Maria Edgeworth's father—did marry their deceased wife's sisters; but it would appear upon the face of it that here could be nothing but friendship, to be revelled in while the gentleman was in England, and fervently "retrospected" upon when he sailed away.

This he at last was free to do by the end of 1806.

During the years when George Bridges Bellasis had been travailing in exile, very much had been happening in India: he had missed all the rattling victories of Arthur Wellesley and Lord Lake: Assaye, Argaum, Delhi, Laswari. All gloriously, His Excellency the Most Noble the Marquess Wellesley—"the Akbar of the Company's Dynasty"—had paced in proud isolation in his palace at Calcutta, "like a Royal Tiger", revelling in a vision of peace imposed and extended by conquest. But the Directors would have been glad to cancel those expensive victories. They were not *"Gloriae percupidas"*: they did not want glory, they wanted dividends. Moreover, Parliament had long placed upon the statute book the statement that "To pursue schemes of conquest and extension of dominion in India are measures repugnant to the wish, the honour, and the policy of this nation." A retrograde movement being earnestly called for, it was desired to find a Governor-General that would carry this out. The obvious choice seemed to be Charles, Marquess Cornwallis.

Cornwallis had never quite ceased to regret that he had not returned to India in 1797 for a second term of office, instead of staying to suppress the '98 rebellion in Ireland, with as much justice and mercy as could be fetched into that witches' cauldron. His first administration, the Permanent Settlement, the victorious campaign against Tipu, had left him with immense prestige and gained him his Marquisate, together with a statue representing him as a laurelled Roman hero in armour and toga: the sculptor having had some difficulty in minimising that "great belly" about which my lord was used to jest. The good old General needed no more laurels; but he had been serving his country all his life, and considered that he could do it service by returning to Calcutta, although he thought he was committing even "a desperate act, to embark for India at the age of sixty-six". He, in fact, knew that it could be a death-sentence: as indeed it proved.

In August, 1803, just before George Bellasis got quit of Botany Bay, war had been declared against the Mahratta chief, Daulat Rao Scindia—technically on behalf of the two overlords against whom he had rebelled, the puppet Peshwa, and the puppet Emperor at Delhi—and had run through a litany of victories to a period of peaceful negotiation. Suddenly then, in April, 1804, the other rebel chieftain, Jeswant Rao Holkar, who had held aloof, had rushed into war, and, supported by the disbanded troops of the defeated had—assisted by appalling bad luck and bad management on the part of the English—wiped out an army under Colonel Monson, and had got the best of several other encounters. This had spirited up Scindia to back out of his engagements, to assume a threatening attitude, and to hold the British resident, Mr. Jenkins, humiliatingly a prisoner. An ultimatum was eventually sent by Lord Lake; but Scindia had not done anything about it, when the new Governor-General arrived in 1805, announcing: "It is my earnest desire, if it should be possible, to put an end to this most unprofitable and ruinous warfare." His errand was, in fact, to give way, to draw back, to eat humble pie all round —particularly that provided by the faithless barbarian, Daulat Rao Scindia. Lake acted quickly, extricated Jenkins, and let Cornwallis, his old comrade-in-arms, understand how strongly he disapproved of the grovelling concessions which were proposed.

Cornwallis, still thinking of the achievements of twenty years back—for his Permanent Settlement of land-tenure in Bengal, though finding small favour with modern historians, seemed to him a far finer thing than his triumph over Tipu—could not understand that conditions had changed:

that it was impossible to cram the genie back into the bottle:
that for good or ill, England was being saddled with India,
and must go forward because she could not go back.
Cornwallis desired to go back; he was bent upon reversing,
even in trifles, the Wellesley policy; and the scene of his
arrival at Calcutta, as recorded by the graceless and entertaining diarist, Mr. William Hickey, is very funny indeed:
"Lord Cornwallis upon landing looked surprised and
vexed at the amazing cavalcade that was drawn up . . . he
said, 'What, what! What is all this, Robinson, hey?' Mr. R.
answered, 'My Lord, the Marquess Wellesley has sent his
equipages and attendants as a mark of respect, and to accom-
pany your Lordship to the Government House.' To this
Lord Cornwallis replied, 'Too civil, too civil by half. Too
many people, I don't want them, I don't want one of them.
I have not yet lost the use of my legs, Robinson, hey?
Thank God, I can walk, walk very well, don't want a score
carriages to convey me a quarter of a mile' . . . and he
accordingly did walk." On the stairs of Government
House, the bulky old veteran, in his determined simplicity,
and strong resemblance to his master and friend, the King,
was met and embraced by the other Marquess, "the glorious
little man", the magnificent imperious Wellesley; and the
two dissimilar noblemen mounted hand-in-hand to the
banqueting-hall, where the band was playing martial airs.
Cornwallis blurted bluff compliments: "Upon my word,
Wellesley, you have shown much taste here. . . . It is very
handsome, very handsome indeed, Wellesley."

It was not his own taste, and he told his friends his private
opinion of it; losing no time in dropping all the former
Governor's ceremony of address, "Excellency" and "Most
Noble"; and in contrast to Wellesley's coach-and-six, with
dragoons and outriders, drove himself in a phaeton with a
pair of steady old horses. To his only son, he wrote home:
"I sit down at 9, with two or three officers of my family, to
some fruit and a biscuit, and go to bed soon after the clock
strikes 10. I don't think the greatest *sap* at Eton can lead a

duller life than this!" His table talk is reported to have been
confined to: "Pass the wine", and: "Fie, fie, sir! How can
you omit to put the cork in the bottle before you pass it?"
But for all this prose, there had been one passage of youthful
poetry in the life of Charles Cornwallis; and as the event of
it was to connect his descendants, in an unforeseen manner,
with those of General John Bellasis, it is worth retracing here.

The hot weather and the monsoon of 1805 did Cornwallis
no good; and he was badly worried by the unpopularity of
his policy. He began a toilsome peace-making journey to the
upper provinces; and by the time he arrived at Buxar in
September, he was plainly very ill. He, however, would not
halt, and continued to voyage up the Ganges: presently
reading in the faces of his attendants that they knew him to
be dying. Up the broad sacred river swam the Governor-
General's budgerows, passing the burning-ghats, with their
death-fires, death-garlands, death-chant: while the black
stick-and-rag remnants of those whose ashes had been committed to holy Gunga floated out, interesting the croco-
diles. India passed by, temples and palaces, ruins and mud
villages, seemingly as limitless as the staring sky; but the
eyes of the dying man must be misted with darkness, and to
his ears, grown suddenly dull, the sounds of that alien land—
cries of the rowers, the bellow of a conch from temple
steps, the beasts of the jungle—would come like noises in a
dream. So he continued, to and fro over the edge of
consciousness, until they carried him ashore at Ghazipur to
draw his last breath, upon October 5th. And during those
last ten days of voyaging, must not time have flowed back,
like Gunga, for the dying man? Surely my Lord must have
traversed again the years of his honourable life, and thought
less of the battles and triumphs than of the brief space when
he had been happy with a lovely young wife.

Forty years back, at the court of the young George III,
they had all been young together. At that innocent dull
court, in full reaction against the licentious past, he had been
the King's aide-de-camp, especial friend, and somewhat

RANDALL LODGE, BOMBAY

As painted by Major John Brownrigg Bellasis about 1845.

JEMIMA JONES

LORD CORNWALLIS

plainer double; and he had fallen in love with an exquisite young creature, full of the new grace of "sensibility": seventeen years old, like Miss Burney's *Evelina*—"with timid air and blushing grace". Jemima Tullekens Jones was the daughter of a Guards officer, descended from Cromwell's regicide Jones—but not choosing to boast of that at Court; her mother was the granddaughter of one of William of Orange's Dutch officers. She had one brother, who changed his name to Skelton in order to inherit an ancient property in Cumberland, left to him under romantic circumstances. Jemima changed her name in 1768; her adoration of Cornwallis, and his of her, had formed a perfect idyll for Court contemplation. They were allowed to go away into Suffolk and be happy together at lonely Culford Park; and they had more years of felicity than is allowed to many mortals, before the great concerns of kings and nations broke up their home, as the plough drives over a lark's nest. There were two children in the nursery, a daughter, and the long-hoped-for little heir, when the American Colonies broke into armed rebellion.

Cornwallis was one of the many who sympathised with the colonists' cause; but he was a general now, and it was his duty to go to America and engage in that unnecessary war which was to be so unnecessarily lost. The delicate countess could not be carried to battlefields in the wilderness, but she became ill with grief at the prospect of parting, and even went on her knees to the King, to keep her husband at home. All would not do; she must rise to the occasion, and manage a dignity in her misery. . . . A contemporary puts Lady Cornwallis' farewell into verse:

> *So heaven ordains, love must to duty yield,*
> *Britannia calls Cornwallis to the field; . . .*
> *Yet go, my only life, where glory leads,*
> *Astonish Europe with thy warlike deeds;*
> *When you return, with crowns of laurel drest,*
> *You'll find a thorn deep-rooted in my breast. . . .*

o

The laurels were earned; Cornwallis achieved many and striking victories; it was almost wholly due to the bungling of others that he must surrender at Yorktown in October, '81, almost upon the anniversary of the Saratoga capitulation of General Burgoyne in '77. But Jemima had not lived to hear of victory or disaster; she had been buried at Culford in 1779, with a slip of thorn planted over her heart, to symbolise the grief that had killed her.

She left a little girl of ten, and a boy not yet five. Charles Cornwallis never took a second wife to be a mother to them, or to share his future honours. The letters between him and his motherless boy make touching reading: but there are some which never got into the published Cornwallis correspondence: letters with many mentions of "Papa" written by the little Viscount Brome to his Jones grandmother, to be preserved, through the involvements of destiny, in the Bellasis family. For Jemima's brother, Arnoldus Jones-Skelton, had several children; and the youngest son, Daniel, would one day marry his daughter Fanny to the grandson of General John Bellasis. To Fanny and to her descendants would fall the letters, penned with a labouring quill from nursery and schoolroom. There is one dated "October 13th, 1781"—just before Little Charles's seventh birthday; which was also the date of his father's capitulation at Yorktown. It is ironical to read the boy's prattle against such a setting.

"My Dear Grandmama I am very much obliged to you, for your kind letter. Carolina has left me, but I am a very good Boy, I had a little Dog at Culford, but it is sent to Brome to be Nursed up till I go a Shooting, for it is a Pointer. I am to have a pair of Boots because I do my Book well. . . . I have wrote three letters to my Papa I have had two from my Papa . . ."

These artless missives, and their slightly more studied successors from Eton, were to be put away with quantities of letters from the sons of Arnoldus, who were all assisted by the patronage of their uncle the Marquess, and later of their cousin, to serve their country in Army or Navy. One was at Assaye; one was killed at sea; and Captain Daniel Jones-Skelton, after serving in the Peninsula in the Horse Artillery, would live well on into the peaceful reign of Victoria, settled at Dover and keeping a Journal; and would one day be consulted by the daughters of the second Marquess—who married a daughter of the match-making Duchess of Gordon, and had no son—as to his recollections of his Aunt Jemima. He did, he said, very well recollect the tale that she died of a broken heart—and about the thorn-tree that grew from her grave. . . .

To the statue of Cornwallis the Hindus would make Pujah, worship with offerings; and every little pinafored Miss who recited her Mangnall's questions would gabble out how that Charles Cornwallis "eminently shone as the patriot, warrior, and man. The great services rendered by him to his sovereign and native country will be long recorded in the historic page." . . . But perhaps in 1805, dying in the hot desolation of a strange land, the old warrior thought less of the fame he might leave behind him than of the wife that had preceded him, five-and-twenty years before —and of the thorn-tree grave at Culford that he must have hoped to share. . . .

The news of Cornwallis' death, and the necessity for the appointment of yet another Governor-General, reached England in 1806, while the struggle for the reinstatement of George Bellasis was still proceeding. It was a real struggle. The aid of every powerful friend was enlisted, but the victory was properly due to Henry Fawcett, who since his return to England in 1803 had been of the utmost service to his father-in-law at the Court of Directors. General John had been determined to see his nephew righted, and must have read with great satisfaction Fawcett's report: "We have at last got George Bridges Bellasis's business settled, but not without a warm fight against the Forbes and old mother Warden. A Sable Adversary has been in the lists against us, but completely failed, and all their infamous reports so completely refuted that their future representations can never be deemed worthy of credit. . . . I have some idea that John Forbes has committed himself so far as to render himself liable to an action for damages. On this point it will be for George's consideration after consulting lawyers how far such process may be prudent. I should like to see him pay for the trouble I have had."

George's tardy reinstatement came through dated as from December of that year: he was free to return to an India in which the power of the Company had grown immensely, despite the late dose of appeasement: and where there would be full employment for his sword. General Bellasis, being now in the Chief Command at Bombay, would be able to issue a directive forbidding all further mention of the duel, and could also arrange that his nephew should be posted not to Bombay but to Poona.

Ann King, spring of the late tragedy, was now well married to a Captain Joseph Watson, of the Company's service; and the one remaining King sister, Amelia, last to be shipped out, had secured George Waddell, Collector of Baroach. Both were returning to England, and the General wrote rejoicing in their fortunes. He liked happy endings. Here, with George's business settled, was a happy ending and a new beginning all round.

George sailed, sped by that jolly spinster Charlotte Lodge with the adjuration: "Get all that you can with honesty and humanity—and come home soon!"

X

GLITTERING SABRES AND GALLOPER GUNS

LORD LAKE delighted in galloper guns: one more reason why it was a pity that George Bridges Bellasis should have missed serving in the victorious campaigns of a general with whom he would have agreed so well in so many respects. Certainly this Commander-in-Chief was the kind of man to be popular with his officers. As a young Guards captain, he had fought at Minden alongside Charles Cornwallis; he was then a dandy, one of a set who would go into battle exquisitely ruffled and powdered, protesting that they must arrange "to leave a genteel corpse". Hard and distinguished service in America and Ireland had brought him to the appointment of Commander-in-Chief India in 1800, at the age of fifty-six; and in January, 1801, he had landed at Calcutta, accompanied by his son, Captain George Lake, as A.D.C.; and by four charming daughters, Amabel, Eliza, Fanny, and Anne. He was a strong believer in attack, and his personal courage may be measured from the fact that his idea of agreeable light recreation was to ride out and shoot tigers with a pistol. The native troops considered him a perfect "Lord of War". Although his dispatches were vividly expressed, he was not exactly an intellectual personality: indeed, one of his sayings has been remembered: "Damn your writing—mind your fighting"; but for persons of spirit, even when they belonged to Malcolm's despised "quill-drivers", he had a hearty regard. When that rising young "political" Charles Metcalfe—one day to be Acting Governor-General—insisted on joining the terrible storming of Dig, Lake ever after referred to the civilian delightedly as "my little stormer".

It was the victory over Tipu which rendered the Mahratta War of 1803 inevitable, for when the British took over Mysore and Hyderabad, after the fall of Seringapatam, they also took over the troublesome relations of those states with the Mahrattas: who, being accustomed to live by preying upon their neighbours, had always some arrears of *Chaut* to demand. Lord Wellesley had begun by seeking an alliance with their nominal head, the Peishwa Baji Rao II—son of Ragobah—one of the more unpleasant of the scoundrels then in charge of Mahratta affairs: "a more abandon'd worthless fellow never existed," was the opinion of George Bridges Bellasis, in the field against him on a future occasion. The death of Nana Furnavis, he who had been keeping the Mahratta Empire together for so many years, in March, 1800, had left a scene of complete confusion—that confusion amid which Joseph Bellasis had perished; the Peishwa, Scindia and his uncle's widows, Holkar and a number of other participants, were engaged in the most complicated strife. More particularly, Jeswant Rao Holkar, the terrible, the One-eyed, was endeavouring to hunt down his lord the Peishwa, who had executed Etoji Holkar, his brother, by having him dragged at an elephant's foot, while watching the spectacle from his palace window. It was not long since Scindia and the brigades had thoroughly defeated Holkar at Indore; but so complete had been his recovery, that he now retorted with the defeat at Poona, where Scindia was attempting to protect the Peishwa. Baji Rao fled to the British, and had no choice but to sign, from his refuge at Bassein, the treaty which made him their subsidiary ally. He signed it because he must; and had, of course, no intention of keeping it. Arthur Wellesley replaced him in his palace at Poona with brisk efficiency and some extraordinary forced marches. Holkar had plundered the place and fallen back to Malwa. Scindia had made alliance with the Berar Rajah, and desired a general Mahratta confederacy against the British.

Lord Wellesley asked nothing better. During the cold weather of 1802, Lake's army trained at Canauj, having a very pleasant time. The nights were as cold as winter nights in India can be: glass doors were fitted to the tents, and also brick chimneys, to provide an English fireside, about which the officers might sit with their wives and families. Plenty of excellent wine flowed in the Mess, "from the exhilarating shiraz of Persia to the ruby carbonelle and humble port"; the regimental band played tunes appropriate to every toast, and one was always drunk standing: "No heel-taps, gentlemen! General Baird and the heroes of Seringapatam!" A sparkling social life centred about the pretty persons of the Misses Amabel, Eliza, Fanny, and Anne; and General Lake and his son became deservedly popular for such pleasant tricks as the secretly purchasing a grey-haired lieutenant's promotion, of which he had been hopeless. They also pistolled a good many tigers. At Poona that "mean-looking fellow" the Peishwa received British officers; and juniors taken unawares by the ceremony then used of removing their boots, were embarrassed by holes in their socks. At Calcutta, Lord Wellesley paced among his worshipping young secretaries—those picked Eton lads who called themselves "the Howe boys", after the victor of the Glorious First of June; he expected not only to settle finally with the Mahratta wolf-pack, but to "break the neck of the French power": the 40,000 trained men of the brigades under Perron in the Doab weighed upon his mind.

War came in 1803, with the formal withdrawal in August of Colonel Collins, the Resident at Scindia's court. At the same time Lord Wellesley offered employment and a pension to every British officer in Scindia's service, and nearly every British officer accepted it. In Holkar's camp, Vickers, Dodd, and Ryan, for their refusal to take the field against their countrymen, had their heads struck off and paraded upon spears, while a crier proclaimed that thus would Jeswant Rao Holkar do to all the English.

The armies of Lake and Wellesley marched, undaunted by the fact that their entire strength could not amount to more than 55,000; while the forces opposed to them numbered at least 290,000. . . . And indeed the campaign was literally all over by Christmas: in four months, four great battles had been fought, eight fortresses besieged and captured, several provinces subdued—and De Boigne's famous and once-invincible brigades annihilated. In the south, General Wellesley captured Ahmadnagar on August 11th, and won the battle of Assaye on September 23rd—throwing 5,000 men against a force four times as great; the Mahrattas could not stand against the bayonet, and the brigades, with their fine Frenchified uniforms, were but "dressed for the sacrifice". Meanwhile, on August 29th, General Lake had attacked Perron's headquarters at Koil, and his almost impregnable arsenal-fortress of Alighur. From Skinner we get a glimpse of Perron, routed in the first skirmish, galloping for Agra "in confusion, and without his hat". He had furiously sacked such of his British officers as had not already departed, including Skinner: who now hailed him with an offer to help him make a stand. "Ah, *non*, M. Skinner," cried the Frenchman, "I no trust—I no trust!" "Then you may go to the devil!" roared Skinner after him. Perron had some reason for general distrust. Scindia had superseded him by Ambaji Anglia—and Bourquien, whom he himself had raised from the mud, had been the first to turn against him: going so far as to incite his cavalry ressaldars to murder him. . . . Perron knew when the game was up: he applied to the English for a safe-conduct, and took his large treasure and his copper-coloured family back to France, and a very cool reception from Bonaparte.

His late subordinate, Pedron, that "stout elderly man in a green jacket with gold lace and epaulets", would have surrendered Alighur, if his men would have suffered it, but they would not, and fought to the death. "British valour never shone more conspicuous", said Lake of the storming. Delhi was the next objective and there Bourquien, rallying the brigades, was defeated. Lake had a couple of horses killed under him, and personally led the decisive bayonet charge. The possession of Delhi still meant much; the blind old Mogul, seated miserably under his tattered canopy, was pleased to be put on a larger allowance of rice, and bestowed upon Lake the title of Sword of the State, Hero of the Land, Lord of the Age, and Victorious in War. Agra was then taken, together with twenty-two lakhs of treasure; and then, upon November 1st, the brigades made their last stand at Laswari. Upon that bloody field, they died with honour, to the number of 7,000; so tainting the air that the British camp had to be shifted.

Lord Wellesley received with particular satisfaction the news that French hopes of India had again been destroyed. "The foundations of our empire in Asia are now laid in the tranquillity of surrounding nations, and in the happiness and welfare of the people of India. . . . My public duty is discharged to the satisfaction of my conscience by the prosperous establishment of a system of policy which promises to improve the general condition of the people of India, and to unite the principal native states in the bond of peace under the protection of the British power." Thus wrote my Lord Marquess after the victories; rejoicings in London, and the ennoblement of General Lake succeeded; but less than half-heartedly upon the part of the Directors. They were to dispatch Cornwallis with his humble pie, just as Holkar broke up the peace negotiations. Then came Lord Lake's summer campaign, in a great horror of heat, so that strong young soldiers withered like paper in the fire, and dropped dead; and then the monsoon disaster of the Mokundra Pass, when Holkar's cavalry loomed up through the drowning rains, and broke Monson's detachment to pieces. . . . At the storming of Dig, on Christmas Eve, the five companies that had deserted from Monson during his retreat were found drawn up at the gate in full uniform, with ordered arms, crying, "Englishmen, pray do not kill us!"— but the order was to give no quarter. Holkar had caused his nautch girls to dance about the severed heads of Monson's men. . . . Losses were heavy at Dig; and Lake, who was far better at a charge than a siege, was now to sustain serious reverses before Bhurtpore. With the departure of Wellesley, the coming and the death of Cornwallis, the war fizzled out. *Ek-chasm-ud-daula* ("The One-Eyed") was glad enough to come to terms, and so was Scindia.

Unfortunately, the new retrograde policy left all the Company's allies at the mercy of the Mahrattas, unsuccoured. From then onward, the wolf-pack, with the wild crowds of Pathans and Pindaris attached to them, were to harass the country more savagely than ever before. The Pindaris were something new in frightfulness; they would strip a village of the last anklet, and fill the well up with women and children. The policy of neutrality by no means secured peace in the land; and there was plenty of work for a soldier awaiting George Bridges Bellasis, despite his having missed the recent campaigns, when he returned to India early in 1807, at the same time as the new Governor-General, Lord Minto.

"It is impossible to describe what I have endured since I have seen you—I retrospect on it with astonishment—I am now once more restored to that society I was so cruelly and *Illegally* separated from." That is pretty well all that George Bridges Bellasis has to say about it, in writing to his cousin and namesake George Hutchins Bellasis; he is not going to "retrospect" more than he can help. He had rather dwell on present and future, as in a letter to Lodge, of June, '07: "I am now in command of the British Artillery at Poonah protecting the Peishwar of this country against Holkar, who is making great preparations to make another little fighting business, after the rains are over, which will be in about three months, when I imagine some of us may have a broken Head, however that is better than a broken Heart, which I fear may be my end. . . ." Strictures from friends upon the imprudence which had left him with no savings and many debts when disaster struck, had come home to the reinstated man, though his good resolves were still mingled with a certain impatient scorn of businesslike habits: "Out of my present pay I shall be able to remit to England about £200 per annum, but on getting a staff appointment at least £100 a month, so you see I yet have hopes of seeing you all again in *a few* years with a handsome Independence. I shall be satisfied, if I can carry certain points, with £1,000 a year, and retire into the Country and cultivate a little farm, and I trust to a better account than you and old Thatcher did at Carshalton, though I don't believe we are either of us (thank God) much calculated for Trade, as you know there are certain things which Trade allows of that Gentlemen may be a little averse to—Rely my Dear Friend on what I now tell you, that I shall never suffer any person whatever to induce me to do an extravagant thing. I shall never deviate from a line of conduct that must be most pleasing to my Friends, and ultimately ensure me the society of those that will ever be most dear to me—I do not keep even a horse, and have as few servants as I can possibly avoid, I have only nine, which for this country is very few indeed—When I was here before I had upwards of Fifty and really use for them."

In reply to this earnest letter, Edmund Lodge made that jest about driving a pig backward across Salisbury Plain. Charlotte confided to Mrs. Kent her belief that George would never reform—and was somewhat dismayed to have her words straightway reported to him. She might have realised that there was a correspondence between George and Eliza. . . . However, there were no bones broken. She sends him her "maternal affection—if I were some twenty years younger, I would say Love"; and hopes "to retain my gaiety and good spirits to receive you". He promises to send her a parrot: "Tell my dear Friend Charlotte I have not forgot her Commissions, the Bird I have now in my possession, but as He came from our Barracks his Education is not the most Refined, He is a terrible low bred Fellow, and if he *only* *swore* I would send Him, but he is too bad for a Gentleman's House, and I must return Him, as the least noise even Conversation causes such a terrible volley of Blasphemy etc.

from Him that it is quite damnable. I fear he must go to the Devil, instead of England."

Some bird, if not this low-bred one, was dispatched, for Charlotte presently states that her beautiful parrot is flourishing; adding playfully: "If you could send me a husband it would be very agreeable and I should be most grateful—I should not like to have him *black*—brown if you please—I am not particular as to his age, but I must make a point of his having *a good sound liver*, and plenty of money."

Bellasis' familiar, loud, ringing laugh sounds in the letter about the parrot; and his eager determination to save, his expectations of getting a staff post through his uncle's influence, all add up to a new and youthful spring of plans for the future. If he must begin life again at forty, he intended to do so completely. . . . He was not to distinguish himself against Holkar in any "little fighting business", for Jeswant Rao was drinking himself into a state of savage imbecility: the exertion of poisoning two near relations at this time finally overset his reason, and he was to linger helplessly for another two or three years, while his favourite mistress mismanaged the realm. As to the staff appointment, the Commander of the Forces at Bombay would no longer be able to help his nephew: John Bellasis died very suddenly, after a manner to be related, in February, 1808.

This event was a shock to everyone, and must have sharply dismayed George Bridges Bellasis, who had now no friend in power in India, to help him catch up the wasted years taken out of his career by the business of the fatal duel. Promotion and prosperity had become especially precious to him; for he was about to marry again.

In London, on a January day of 1809, foggy airs were obscuring the flat bricks of the new-built houses in Somers Town and Bloomsbury, and a post-chaise was waiting outside a house in Union Street. Captain Robert Eastwick, among a great bustle of servants with wraps and portmanteaus, emerged with his sister-in-law Eliza Kent upon

his arm, and handed her into the chaise. We may suppose
Eastwick, having mounted up after her, to be thrusting his
head and shoulders into the raw air as long as the last
flutterings of Lucy's handkerchief were to be seen behind
him. Lucy must have been looking a good deal paler and
thinner than the girl who had taken the wheel in the Straits
of Sunda more than ten years ago. Many things had happened to the Eastwicks since then. The trouble in Bombay
in 1801—the breakdown of her sister Esther, the ordeal of
the trial—had so affected Lucy that she must return to
England at once, aboard the *Skelton Castle*: the master of
which, Captain Isaac, had been one of the jury. Eastwick
must stay to finish making a modest fortune; but by 1805,
he was able to leave £20,000 in the hands of a Parsee merchant in Calcutta, and join his wife in London. Their
Nabob friend, Mr. Hunter, now offered the Eastwicks a
house near his country home, Bewley Hall in Worcester-
shire; and they accordingly travelled down there with him,
eight wagon-loads of their goods following, and entered the
village in three carriages, with six horseback servants, and
all the bells ringing. 'Twas very like the happy ending of
some novel of the period.

Life, however, does not conform to Minerva Press
standards; this prosperous happiness lasted for only one
year during which the Eastwicks' first son was born; and
then news came that the Parsee merchant had failed, and the
fortune was all to make again. Back to sea went Robert
Eastwick, in the *Anna* to the River Plate, only to find that
Buenos Aires, recently taken by Sir Home Popham, had
just been retaken by the Spaniards, and that General Whitelock was unable to retake it. Eastwick returned without
much profit from this scene of defeat; and Whitelock
returned to be court martialled. Lord Lake of Delhi and
Laswari sat upon the court martial, and by refusing to wear
his greatcoat in a London February, although so recently
returned from India, caught his death of cold. The Prince
Regent came and wept over his pillow; and better men

sorrowed for a brave and generous-hearted soldier. As for Robert Eastwick, he found his little boy dying of whooping-cough, and Lucy hysterically hating Bewley after the child had been buried under their pew in the church. He brought her to London, refused a splendid command in order to stay with her, and when she was comforted by another child in her arms, also a boy, set forth again for India. Eliza Kent —long enough widowed to have cast her weeds—was going to the Gordons at Bombay; Lucy wished Eastwick to take charge of her.

It was not going to be an easy charge. They had started in ample time, but it was necessary to stop in Howland Street while Mrs. Kent said good-bye to her sister Ann Watson. The two beautiful creatures chattered and embraced, and ordered in refreshments, at such length that the short day grew alarmingly into afternoon. The brother-in-law repeatedly got out his watch, and finally pointed out that they must cross Hounslow Heath, and had far better do so before dusk. This amused Eliza exceedingly. "What, Eastwick, are you afraid!" she rallied him. As, however, she had upon her person a hundred guineas, and several hundred pounds' worth of jewels, he was not amused; and when they changed horses at the Hounslow inn—sure enough, not until dusk—he was dismayed to hear the postboy cautioned by the landlord, in a low voice: "Mind—be civil!" It might seem a natural admonition, but it too obviously meant civil surrender to a highwayman, lest the post-horses should be shot. Such an incident had happened only the week before; and the capricious Mrs. Kent now grew very nervous; when a traveller came riding up across the darkening heath, Eastwick found himself encumbered with a clinging, screaming sister-in-law; so that it was well it proved a false alarm. They got to Frimley that night, stayed with old Mrs. Kent, and presently pushed on for Portsmouth and the Indiaman *Neptune*.

The *Neptune* was one of the Company's largest ships, and she sailed together with the *Addington*, which was nearly wrecked at the outset by striking on Bognor rocks in a storm. To make up for this, when the great ships were two days out in calm weather, they hove to and gave one another dances, to which the passengers were conveyed in boats: a risky business which caused Captain Eastwick and other experienced persons to shake their heads, but which Mrs. Kent thoroughly enjoyed. She must have enjoyed the voyage altogether, despite the desperate storm off Madagascar, with balls of fire, and lightning striking the foremast. She was the beauty of the ship, and at least one gentleman proposed to her, Colonel Backhouse, of the Company's service. But she was not going to marry Colonel Backhouse. . . .

Eastwick handed her over to the Gordons, and took a command at Madras, the *Ganges*, conveying to England Lord Minto's dispatches about the Madras mutiny, and racing the account of Sir John Barlow, Governor of Madras, who was anxious to get his word in first. The mutiny, a widespread disturbance among the Company's officers, like that of '96, had been very serious; and Barlow's pigheadedness had made the worst of it. Possibly everybody was a bit on edge; officers had been sleeping with pistols under their pillows since the Vellore incident in '06: that alarming sepoy mutiny due to a new turban which looked too like a Christian hat; made more alarming by Tipu's son, Futteh Hyder, having been settled at Vellore, and suddenly unfurling the Tiger flag at one stage of the proceedings.

None of these troubles appears to have touched George Bellasis at Poona, with his galloper guns. He had other things to think about. Early in the following year, he wrote to Edmund Lodge: "And now my good fellow for a little information that perhaps may not astonish you much but which I think must give you pleasure—I am married to Mrs. Kent, this took place on the fourth of January, 1810, at Bombay, and I am now commanding the Artillery in the finest Country in the world, Guzurat. If I thought it necessary or even pleasant to you to read a long letter saying

how happy we are, I could write for hours and still find
endearing epithets for my dear wife. I shall only simply say
—We are happy."

For all the rest of his life, his almost adoring love for Eliza
continued to be thus expressed.

The Pindari and Mahratta wars which began in 1817, and
for which all available British forces were mustered, did not
succeed to any state of peace. The ignominious policy of
neutrality imposed by the Directors had led to very shocking results, directly negativing Wellesley's large vision of
the *Pax Britannica*. Not only was there bloody chaos beyond
the Company's borders, there was large-scale marauding
across them, making constant defensive measures necessary.
It had also been necessary to undertake campaigns against
the forts of brigand chiefs in Bundelkhand and in George
Thomas' late realm of Hariana. A small but full-scale war,
moreover, had been thrust upon Lord Moira in 1814, the
year after he had succeeded Lord Minto as Governor-
General; it was with the little hill-men, the Ghurkas of
Nepal, who had been encouraged by notions of the Company's weakness; and its most satisfactory result was to turn
Lord Moira into the Marquess of Hastings. The Ghurka
war, however, had little to do with campaigners in the dusty
plains; and the emerging power of Ranjit Singh in the North
had almost as little. George Bellasis had gone from Poona
with his galloper guns, storming forts with Colonel Walker
in Malwah; he had then commanded the Artillery at Surat,
and then gone into the Deccan with Colonel Montresor. . . .
He writes of the difficulty of breaching mud walls twenty-
seven feet thick: of a four months' separation from his wife:
of "expecting to distinguish or perhaps extinguish" himself
in the storming. This fort, however, surrendered: "they
were afraid, which at all events you must allow is a sufficient
reason for not fighting, and gave in to our terms, which you
may depend on it were hard enough. . . ."

"We are unwilling to incur the risk of a general war for

GEORGE HUTCHINS BELLASIS
(1778–1822)
aged 20.

JOHN BROWNRIGG BELLASIS
(1806–1873)
As a cadet, Bombay Army, aged 17.

THE ROADS, ST. HELENA

Drawn by George Hutchins Bellasis and published by him in "Views of St. Helena," 1815.

the uncertain purpose of extirpating the Pindarries" had been the cold fiat from London in 1815; although Hastings, upon arrival, and Minto before him, had insisted that this was a necessary measure. If Hastings had not been an old boon-companion of the Prince Regent and able to use his influence, the misery of Central India might have continued even longer. There were two sets of Pindaris, those subject to Holkar, and those subject to Scindia; and at the end of the rains every Pindari *durra*, or company, was accustomed to ride forth on a *lukbar*, a plundering expedition; they carried no baggage, and lived upon the land. They wore wadded cotton coats of proof, rode very fast, cleverly-trained horses, and were armed with swords, matchlocks, and seventeen-foot spears; their women rode with them, handling these weapons equally well, and proving even more merciless. At an alarm of approaching Pindaris, the wretched country people would flee into the nearest fort, driving their cattle with them. If they were not quick enough, or the fort not strong enough, every imaginable horror occurred. In March, 1816, a durra which got as far as Masulipatam spent eight days moving about at the rate of thirty or forty miles a day, and a commission of investigation found that during this time 182 persons had been slain, 505 wounded, and 3,033 tortured. A favourite and ingenious torture was to tie a bag of hot ashes over a man's mouth and nose, and thump his back, he would be eager to give up his valuables, under this treatment; later, he would die slowly of the effect on the lungs. The numbers of the Pindaris were vastly on the increase, also their boldness; where they had been formerly used to blot out villages, they now aspired to the sack of cities, and they were penetrating more and more into British territory.

In October, 1817, the Governor-General took the field in person, having wrung sanction out of the Directors. A great army was gathered together and thrown in an encircling loop about the robbers' haunts. Scindia dared not interfere. Holkar's chiefs, however, engaged the British, and were

P

heartily beaten by Sir John Malcolm at Mahidpur. Other of
the Mahrattas broke out, more particularly the Peishwa,
who under a plausible mask had been intriguing madly
against the Company; and two years' brisk hostilities were
begun. Fighting the generally loathed "Pins" was quite to
the taste of the British soldier, but was not exactly a pleasure
excursion, although the storming of a Mahratta fort meant
good plunder, and did not mean finding all the women with
their throats cut, as in a Rajput fort—a superfluous piece of
ceremony, for the Company's troops, white or sepoy, were
known not to rape. Malcolm commanded at the taking of
Asseerghur the impregnable, towering 1,500 feet out of the
plain: "None but the hawk or the lark ever saw inside
Asseerghur", said the proverb: but Malcolm's men succeeded in "Planting Old England's banner in the place of
glory", as they put it, despite the guns and mortars, the
great stones and trees that came hurtling down, the stink-
pots and blazing bales of straw, the hedgehog bristle of
spears. . . . A taken town, with pie-dogs howling in the
streets, and the ditch full of puffy corpses, was no pleasant
sight, to be sure; even though a private soldier could hide
from the prize-agent as many as 500 gold mohurs, concealed
in his shako. A young fellow would soon learn to think
more of the mohurs than of the corpses, and to listen to the
advice of veterans: never pass a man supposed dead without
putting your bayonet through him—the fallen Mahratta
gunners at Assaye had sprung to life and manned their guns
again; get as close as possible to a rocket or a shell, and lie
flat; take notice that wounds by iron balls turn yellowish and
are bad to heal. . . . As for the big, noisy Sir John Malcolm,
who had charged the batteries at Mahidpur like a subaltern,
he kept his officers in a roar with his wit; he had a favourite
story over the wine at mess, of how he had been asked to
breakfast by a Colonel of Artillery at Bombay, and had found
nobody to receive him, and the laden breakfast-table veiled
with a cloth: hungry after his ride, he had lifted this for a
peep, and found his host laid out there coldly, having died

overnight: an anecdote which always caused a deal of laughter.

Sir John Malcolm was to receive the surrender of the Peishwa, after the Pindaris were finally broken and scattered, and their chief appropriately eaten by a tiger. Baji Rao II, last Peishwa of the Mahrattas, like many worthless persons, had a good deal of plausible charm, and had got along very well with the Hon. Mountstuart Elphinstone, the Resident at Poona, who was well aware that he could not be trusted half an inch. Immersed in classical literature and the putting together of a valuable library in the handsome Residency with the terraced gardens above the river, Elphinstone yet kept cool watch upon the Peishwa's brothel of a court, and the intrigues that seethed about it. The contingent of Company's troops, nominally under the Peishwa's authority, drilled and paraded in their lines, conscious of the vastly outnumbering host of Mahrattas that could be whistled up from his jaghirdars, if things came to a clash. They very nearly did so when Baji Rao and his favourite Trimbukji murdered an ambassador from Berar whose safety had been guaranteed by the English; Elphinstone compelled the surrender of Trimbukji, who was imprisoned at Tannah, escaped, headed an insurgent army which was pretty openly encouraged by his old master, and then was chased away by the Company's troops, while Baji Rao was compelled to sign a far more rigorous treaty. Nobody doubted that he would break it if he could; and indeed he did so a couple of months afterwards.

Under pretence of wishing to take full part in the Pindari war, the Peishwa had spent September and October of 1817 collecting troops from all quarters. As they crowded into Poona they were encamped so as to enclose the British cantonments on the north-east of the city; and Elphinstone, though loath to precipitate matters, must order the British brigade to remove to the nearby village of Kirkee, a strategic point, meanwhile sending for reinforcements from Seroor and from General Smith's army operating in the north. Things then happened rapidly; the Mahratta army formed up, the Peishwa joined it outside the city, and Mr. Elphinstone and his suite had barely time to hurry across the river and join the troops at Kirkee when the Residency was blazing behind them, with all its valuable books and papers.

This was on the 5th of November, and hostilities at once began again, the Mahrattas keeping their distance and cannonading, but suffering many casualties before nightfall. They, however, consoled themselves by murdering and mutilating the native women left in the cantonments, and cutting the throats of two British officers who were prisoners. Before the British reinforcements came up, Baji Rao, who had always an earnest concern for his own skin, had taken sudden fright; and Smith found nothing to attack but empty tents. He instantly set forth in pursuit of the flying Mahrattas, accompanied by George Bellasis, who had been taking part in the battle, and was commanding the Horse and Foot Artillery. This was the start of a long hunt, all across the Deccan, as Bellasis described to his friend the Herald, adding: "Now you will abuse us poor Devils for speaking so lightly of running down Kings; but a more abandon'd worthless fellow never existed than that said Peishwa. Poor Mrs. Bellasis was within a mile of the action on the 5th of November, and behav'd nobly, but her situation was a most critical one, for had the Peishwa been victorious Her life would certainly have been taken, and if they had not been the greatest Cowards under the Heavens they must have beaten us with the greatest Ease." It was long before General Smith came within sound of Baji Rao's kettledrums, he had fled with such admirable address: only standing, upon New Year's Day, 1818, when heavily re-inforced, to attempt overcoming a British battalion at Korigaon—taunting his commanders from a distant hilltop with their non-success. At last, however, the hunt drew to a close, the Peishwa must give in and submit to the terms of Sir John Malcolm: deposition, and a very liberal pension,

£90,000 a year. It was considered that Malcolm had acted with his usual extravagance, about this pension; and perhaps if it had not been so large, a future government might have continued it to the ex-Peishwa's adopted heir, and not provided him with a grievance: he was to become sufficiently well known as the Nana Sahib. . . . Nobody had magical prevoyance of 1857; they were glad to get Baji Rao quietly settled at Bithoor, near Cawnpore; and contemplate victoriously an India purged of Pindaris, and of the predatory power of the late Mahratta Empire.

The triumphant campaign was to George Bridges Bellasis "this vile War, in which I nearly lost my Life, in fact was given over by the Physicians, owing to incessant Marching, frequently from three in the morning to nine at night, and the Thermometer an hour after sunset 110. Enough to broil a Devil." He ended it a lieutenant-colonel, within sight at last of the full colonelcy upon which he intended to retire to England. . . . *"Who was to have gone home next year."* . . . His letters from the time of his return to India are full of this plan and goal, of calculations about his finances and his prospects of promotion. There was a certain modestly handsome house at Basildon which he had fancied from boyhood: it was called the Grotto: to this he planned to retire and live upon his colonel's pension—"in my Native Country, with all the Comforts of Life, and many of its Luxuries".

He had during these years a new correspondent, his half-sister, Anna Maria; childless himself, he felt a warm fondness towards Leah's children, and their "Amiable and excellent Mother". To the young schoolgirl he confides on one occasion that he is earning £150 a month, but finds it impossible to save. "Times will mend I hope soon though it will be many years before I shall be able to return to England with the fortune I could wish, however I am as happy as I can be in this detestable Country, and have every Comfort in Life, most particularly so in my belov'd Wife

who I'm confident you will love most dearly." He earnestly
desires that his dear little brother shall be bred for the
Church, to secure him a smooth, easy life: let them by no
means make a soldier of him: "Our life is I think the worst
that can be adopted, and did not pride induce Men to adopt
it, I should think an honest Shoemaker a much preferable
life." This kind of railing was usually part of his letters to
Lodge—almost one of the jokes between them; and would
be abruptly succeeded by: "I will now give you an account
of a Hindoo woman burying herself alive, she not being of
high caste enough to burn", or, "Is *Opal* valuable? as I have
found about a wheelbarrow-load of it"; or some remarks on
home politics—Why is Sir F. Burdett allowed at large?
—"and his friend Mr. Cobbett, who I think would look well
on a Gallows, and in time stands a good chance of gracing
one." Then wistfully back upon his own prospects: "If you
could get some great Lord or Admiral or Prince Regent, to
give me a letter to Sir Evan Nepean, saying I was a Gentlemanly fellow, or a good-tempered foolish fellow, or any
other untruth, it might be of great service to me.... Remember I have been twenty-two years in this Service, and have
been at the capture of Seringapatam and many other places";
perhaps Lodge has already sent such a letter, on the ship
that "fell in with a vile American off the Cape of Good
Hope" and threw the mails overboard. "The ship is arriv'd
safe, commanded by a Captain McQuaker—a fellow with
such a name as that, one ought not to be surprised at anything
he might do." Sir Evan Nepean is decidedly a disappointment: "as bad a man and as great an enemy to all military
men as can be conceiv'd". To be sure, this is more than a little
unjust to the dry, competent ex-Admiralty official; friend of
Jervis and Nelson, Sir Evan might prefer sailors, but he
was particularly kind to young Daniel Hutchins Bellasis,
the General's fourth son, who was his A.D.C. To Mountstuart Elphinstone, who succeeded Nepean as Governor
of Bombay in 1819, George Bellasis would need no introduction.

A coldness had occurred where all had once been har-
mony, some years after the marriage of George and Eliza:
for Edmund Lodge, in the mid-fifties, had looked up from
his heraldic scrolls long enough to fall in love. The advent
of a young bride had been a terrible blow to Charlotte, so
long his companion; and she had taken herself off with her
parrot and her pug. George wrote comfortingly that she
would soon come round, as indeed she did, before the new
Mrs. Lodge died in 1820; but meanwhile Eliza had sent her a
tactless remonstrance, and there had to be some patching up
and smoothing down. When the full colonelcy and the
longed-for day of return to England were at last in view,
Bellasis wrote: "Tell Charlotte I hope soon to give her a
kiss of reconciliation, but she will hardly thank an old Don
Quixote looking fellow like me for one."

"An old Don Quixote looking fellow": George Bridges
Bellasis at fifty: lean, swarthy, burnt to the bones, his curls
iron-coloured, but brave as ever in his scarlet, and with his
long legs astride no Rosinante, but a fine Arab. Thus Eliza
Eastwick saw him in 1817, just before he took part in
tumbling down the Mahratta Empire. He had much desired
that his sister Anna Maria should come out to him; but she,
afraid of being labelled as a "speculation miss", had hung
back. Eliza Bellasis had sent instead for Lucy's eldest
daughter, named after herself. The young Eliza, travelling
with her father, had enjoyed a wonderful journey, and after
gaieties in Calcutta, where she had been born, had set out
from Bombay for Seroor, and fallen in with Colonel Bellasis
collecting a draught of recruits at Panwell. There they all
lodged at a Portuguese tavern, known as the only one in the
Mahratta Empire; but the tavern-keeper made the sixty-one
soldiers very drunk with bad liquor, so Bellasis had him
triced up and flogged. After this slight delay, they began a
journey of 122 miles, which they covered in ten days:
Bellasis on his Arab, Eastwick with a sailor's seat on a tall,
vicious, neighing country horse, and Eliza in her palanquin
with its rhythmically grunting bearers, staring about her,

enchanted at all the strange sights—particularly at a ren-
counter with the strange wandering tribe of Brinjarries, they
who drive bullocks and carry grain all over India, so that
armies in the field might not do without them. So they went
up the Ghats, on the route travelled by John Bellasis with
the army of Ragonath Rao, forty years before: they passed
through Wurgaom, where he had reaped laurels from so
unpromising a field; and they came to Seroor, all in a
hum with war rumours, and Mrs. Bellasis waiting for her
new young companion. She cannot have expected to keep
her company long, nor did she, for Eliza Eastwick was very
shortly married to a rich Bombay officer, Major John Forde,
commanding the Peishwa's infantry.

After the fatigues and anxieties of the war, George
Bellasis was determined that his beautiful wife—for surely
she was still beautiful enough in his eyes to make them glow
when they looked at her, as his words glowed when he
wrote of her—must have a holiday in England. Soon after
she should rejoin him, they would be able to leave India
together, and for ever. . . . While she was absent, and while
the clouds of yet one more monsoon were banking blackly
up, he privately wrote down a prayer: "Accept, Thou great
and Almighty Creator, the humble and sincere thanks of a
poor mortal who ventures to address Thee for all Thy great
kindness bestowed on him. Thou, O God, hast protected
me under many and great afflictions and taught me to
believe and hope they were ultimately intended to bring me
to a proper sense of my duty towards Thee. If in any
instance, and many they must be, I have deviated from the
paths of what Thy divine law has prescribed, forgive me,
and look on me as a man subject to all the frailties of man.
I now conclude my prayer made on my birthday, 9th of
August 1821, by praying that I may once more meet my
dearest wife and that we may end our days in our native
country. I forgive all the world, and may the Almighty
forgive me. G. B. B."

His wife he did see again, but never again his native land.

He was never to live in the Grotto at Basildon. Owing to the seven years' lag in his career caused by his having "preserv'd his Honour" on that far-away morning in 1801, he attained the point for which he aimed when too worn out to profit by it. He died on Michaelmas Day of 1825.

"Death has deprived us of Colonel Bellasis, the life of every party," mourned the *Bombay Courier*, and broke into verse:

> *Bellasis the brilliant and the gay,*
> *The boon companion of the social day,*
> *The war-tried warrior and the time-tried friend,*
> *Whose spirit Fate could neither break nor bend . . .*
> *The board that spread such welcome with its fare*
> *That strangers felt themselves no strangers there.*
> *His was the voice whose laugh-inspiring sound*
> *Flung the bright halo of enjoyment round,*
> *The song whose melody each list'ner won,*
> *The jest that glanced at all and wounded none,*
> *The genuine tale inimitably told,*
> *The mirth whose influence like enchantment roll'd,*
> *And charm'd the young, and more than cheer'd the old.*

Behind the echo of that ringing laughter sounds a whisper from the voice that had cried out: "O God, Gordon, what have I done?": "I forgive all the world, and may the Almighty forgive me."

XI

THE FIVE SONS

"I HAVE the satisfaction to say all my young Men arrived in good Health on the 23rd Ulto. and are now with me. George will sell out of the Army, and I have arranged matters for his being established in the House of Bruce, Fawcett & Co. but without any share in the Firm till my worthy Friend and Son-in-Law Mr. Fawcett quits; in the mean time He will be allow'd something Monthly, and will be qualifying himself for business. Mr. Fawcett, Geo: and myself have had much conversation on the subject, and He is fully determined to stick close to it, and render himself useful in the House.

"Joseph is in the Secret Department of the Secty's Office, and getting on as well as ever He was in his Life.

"Edwd is in the Engineers, a wonderful fine young fellow, good abilities and great application; and greatly esteemed by everyone who knows Him, and will no doubt recommend himself wherever He goes.

"Daniel is a very fine modest Lad, I shall be particularly careful of Him; he must make his way in the Infantry, which is by far the best Line in the Army at present."

In the letter of August, 1801, announcing the trial for murder of his nephew George, General John, turning to a pleasanter subject, thus summarises the prospects of his sons. John, the youngest, the English-born baby, was not yet ten years old, and was still running wild at school, a halloo'ing, book-hating little urchin; but George was nearly twenty-three, Joseph turned twenty, Edward getting on for nineteen, and Daniel between sixteen and seventeen. At these mature ages, they must be considered well qualified to "make their way" in the Company's India. During their years in England, their home had been with the Carpenters at Potters Bar, some of their father's very old friends: they were lucky that it need not be with strangers and hirelings. However, the warm-hearted, unqualified gratitude which General John had been expressing towards Captain and Mrs. Carpenter this decade or so, abruptly decreased when his sons came out to him: for it would appear from their confidences that their deputy-father had proved an uncomfortable tyrant to them as they grew up, and particularly to George. Helen, returning to England in 1803, was to find them mismanaging the upbringing of young John; and her father was to write to her of Carpenter: "I never can get over his conduct towards George; duplicity I always detested, and yet I am writing as usual *Dear Carpenter* and *Dear Friend*. This Hurts my feelings much. . . . However . . . I shall ever be perfectly sensible of their Kindness to the Boys whilst *small Boys*; afterwards they knew not how to act towards them and mismanaged most dreadfully." Leah Bellasis, in the doctor's lifetime, when the lad came to stay with his uncle, had expressed the pitying opinion that "Carpenter uses him very ill"; and it is possible that some spring of energy or ambition was early broken in quiet young George Hutchins Bellasis.

This young man, nevertheless, had excellent intentions, and did his best to fit in with his father's plans. These were first for putting him into the Church; and the earnestness with which he promised to study certainly leads to the conclusion that he had been given a poor idea of his own abilities. He matriculated at Queen's when he was nineteen, in 1798; but the idea of taking Orders—"as soon as he can light upon a Bishop", as Miss Steele put it—was carried no further. Instead, a commission was bought for him as a King's officer, in the 19th Light Dragoons. This regiment was then stationed in India; and when George had joined it there, he would be able to make up his mind as to following a military career or staying in the island and advancing himself in the House of Bruce, Fawcett & Co.

In March, 1801, he and his younger brothers Joseph and

Daniel sailed in a convoy of Indiamen. Edward had preceded them, having passed out first cadet of his year from
Woolwich. None of these young men lacked parts, even
the self-diffident eldest; all were quietly good-looking—
young Daniel in particular being extremely handsome; but
they were built upon a different model from their long-
legged cousins, the doctor's sons, and were not above
middle height, indeed rather below it. Cornet George
Hutchins Bellasis had thoughtful blue eyes, under his
father's dark brows, and small sensitive features; without
saying much about it, he had grieved himself sick, to the
observation of his Aunt Leah, when the news had come of
his mother's death; and without saying much about it, he
was now leaving England very much in love with a certain
girl. . . . The *Airlie Castle*, Captain Nash, formed one of a
beautiful company, the outward-bound East India fleet.
Twenty great ships in larboard and starboard line, protected
by the frigate *Cambrian* and two seventy-fours, *Venerable* and
Superb, and with a number of South Sea whalers joining
them, would have been more of a threat than a prey to
French warships. Three years later, the China fleet returning, fifteen of the Honourable Company's ships with no
naval escort, was to form line of battle against four French
warships under Admiral Linois, and make them run for it:
Commodore Dance, of the *Lord Camden*, would get a sword
of honour and a knighthood, with £50,000 reward from the
Company, divided between him and his captains. Thus it was
to be successful; but for the captain who vainly attempted to
show fight instead of clapping on all sail to save a valuable
cargo, Leadenhall Street had no commendations. The
dilemma whether to fight or fly was one which each captain
or commodore must settle for himself, when unaccom-
panied by King's ships. It was the most probable thing in
the world that a few sea actions would form part of the
Occurrences on the Passage from Portsmouth to Bombay, 1801,
which Cornet Bellasis began to set down as soon as he got
aboard.

All those Indiamen lying off St. Helens to be joined by their escort must have been the prettiest thing to see; but they got off to rather a fumbling start: "The *Cambrian* frigate broke its capstan spindle. The *Superb* ran aground at 6 p.m. The *Windham* Indiaman ran foul of us, but we got off without damage. . . ." With repeated signals from the *Superb* to make more sail, they bustled down Channel, looking out for the French, who often came within sight of the Lizard. Sure enough, George's entry for April 5th ran: "Old England entirely out of sight! Crew very busy stowing away the Anchors and unbending the Cables; saw at 10 a.m. the *Cambrian* in chase after a French privateer, captured it about 1 p.m. At 7 saw an English brig making for the Channel. A Spanish prize under its care. Our Ship labours much and sea running excessive high." On the 6th: "Carpenter's Mate try'd and being found guilty of the Charge against him he was punished at the Gangway 3 Dozen lashes."

These successive items set the keynote of the whole voyage. It was not a pleasant one. The expectation of enemy attack might be merely an agreeable excitement for the young men, and even daily Manual and Platoon Exercise, which the cadets on board had decided to practise, at least gave them something to do; but there seems to have been an atmosphere of wartime tension and discomfort, made worse by constant bad weather. "Ports all down. Ship labouring much. Exercise small arms. . . . Sea very rough. Ports shut. A great *scrambling* at dinner, puddings, ducks and a large round of beef tumbling about, not able to save them, being so much occupied with seats. . . . Unwell. . . ." What was much worse was that the *Airlie Castle* was obviously not a happy ship, either aft or forward. As it was with Captain Nash that the passengers in the cuddy were constantly quarrelling, and as it was at his orders that the men were constantly screaming at the gangway or being clapped into irons, it is hardly unfair to surmise that the blame was his. Right at the start of the voyage the unhappy carpenter's mate was charged with theft and breaking open of locks, and got his three dozen. Just past the Cape Verde Islands: "At 2 p.m. while about to confine Boatswain's Mate in irons for mutinous behaviour and striking the Boatswain, he jumped overboard, we instantly lowered the jolly boat down and got him on board and confined him. 30th April. Taylor, Boatswain's Mate, was punished with 3 doz. lashes and was again confined and lost that office." Next, "Capt. Nash broke his Third Officer and ordered him to his Cabin." "Fifer in irons for striking a midshipman." "A Quartermaster confined in irons for refusing to do his duty."

George, a gentle and peace-loving young man, would have enjoyed the frequent dances in the evening—for there were half a dozen ladies aboard—the movements of the other ships, the occasional excitement of strange sails, the dolphins, flying-fish, and albatrosses, if his record of occurrences had not listed quarrels between Captain Nash and pretty well all the passengers in the course of the voyage: "Very unpleasant, nothing but quarreling, the least thing said provoked to enmity. . . . . Continual quarrels in the cuddy at the Capt.'s table. . . ." What with these things and an unusual proportion of illnesses and accidents, this and that man being lost overboard, or perishing of "putrid fever", or having his head stove in with a "cask of flower", all must have been uncommonly glad when the voyage drew to a term. Although stormy, it had the merit of having been short. "July 22nd. Busy packing boxes, weather very sultry, at 10 p.m. hove to, in the 2nd Mate's cabin, busy writing . . . 23rd. At 10 a.m. saw Henry and Kennery, two small isles, at 11 *Bombay* in sight, at 12 the pilot came aboard, at 3 anchored; at ½ past my brother Edward came on board, we then went to the *Worcester*, got Joseph and Daniel in the boat and at 5 landed, saw my brother Jo into a palankeen, and was ushered into my father's drawing-room by Edward at ¼ after 5. Mrs. Fawcett my sister was with him, after remaining one hour together, the coach was ordered and we retired into the Country to dinner to my sister's, found all very well. Thus concludes my Journal."

Of these four brothers, Daniel, at sixteen, was the first to be swept into the exciting operations of war which were then proceeding. Just before his personal tragedy had descended upon him, George Bridges Bellasis had written: "We have nothing but War on War in this Country we no sooner gain Territory in one part than we are oblig'd to Arm to maintain it in Another, there is now an immense Armament fitting out, God knows for what Country intended but A part of it certainly going to the Red Sea under Col. Murray and Admiral Blankett." The Marquess Wellesley indeed had intended sending an expedition to harry Batavia and the Mauritius; but had been instructed from London to send his troops instead to the Red Sea, and assist Sir Ralph Abercromby in driving the French out of Egypt. In giving General Baird the command, he sent one of his most grand and flourishing dispatches: "A more worthy sequel to the Storm of Seringapatam could not be presented to your genius and valour. I have chosen my Brother to second you in this glorious enterprise; and I rely on your giving the public the full benefit of his talents, by admitting him to your cordial confidence, and by uniting most harmoniously and zealously with him in the prosecution of my wishes . . . . May the same providential protection which accompanied you to the gates of Tippoo Sultaun's palace conduct you to Cairo. . . ." He finished by once again stressing the necessity of "unanimity"—well aware that Davie Baird was not yet cordially disposed toward the young man who had taken Seringapatam out of his hands. However, they were not now destined to co-operate in battle; Arthur Wellesley reached Bombay well ahead of Sir David, and spurred Governor Jonathan Duncan into the utmost activity, several transports had sailed by the time Baird arrived, and all were ready to leave by the first week

in April. Wellesley, however, who was staying with General
Bellasis, was now taken with a severe intermittent fever,
and had to be left behind. His convalescence must have
been agreeable, as he liked the Bombay ladies; and he
missed an expedition that certainly looked rather a fiasco,
as compared with the Mysore War.

For before Baird reached Kosseir, where he was to rendez-
vous with a European regiment from the Cape, conveyed
by Sir Home Popham, even, indeed, before he had sailed,
Sir Ralph Abercromby had engaged the greatly superior
and insolently confident French army at Alexandria, and
won his last victory. The old fighter, who was nearing
seventy, defended himself with his sword against a detachment of French horse, and paid no heed to a wound in his
thigh until the battle was won; he was then carried off the
field, covered with what was apologetically mentioned as
"only a soldier's blanket": faint with loss of blood, Abercromby roused himself: "Only a soldier's blanket! A
soldier's blanket is of great consequence. You must send
me the name of the soldier to whom it belongs." This
anecdote succinctly explains why there was real mourning
in the army when the old General died of gangrene on
March 28th.

His successor, General Hely-Hutchinson, sent General
Baird instructions for the desert crossing that was now
before him: "I believe that you will find no water on the
route; but I speak with extreme diffidence, as the minds of
men in this Country are so brutalized that it is impossible to
get just information. . . ." There certainly was no water, the
temperature was 115 in the shade, and the whole uninhabited
landscape consisted of simmering rock and scorching sand.
Nevertheless, Baird took his army of 3,600 British, and
2,800 sepoys, the whole 140 miles with the loss of only
three men. It was a nine days' march; makeshift wells had
been dug at the halting-places; but when the army came at
last in sight of the Nile, discipline gave way, and all castes,
ranks, and races, together with the horses, bullocks, camels

and elephants, rushed down to it together, and waded and drank and shouted and splashed. News came to them here that the enemy had surrendered Cairo and that General Hutchinson was marching to invest Alexandria. Baird embarked his men on the Nile, hurried them down to Lower Egypt, and fixed his headquarters on Rhonda, an island near Ghizeh and the Great Pyramid.

Young Daniel Hutchins Bellasis, who had been posted to the 2nd Battalion of the 7th Bombay Native Infantry, had to catch up his sepoys before Alexandria; and must have shared the general excitement at the novel circumstances of the campaign. That sepoys, and Bombay gun-bullocks, should have been transported across the sea, and that a half-European army should have marched across the desert, were novelties indeed. As Allison puts it: "There, for the first time in the History of the World, the sable Hindoos from the Banks of the Ganges, the swarthy Asiatics from the plains of the Euphrates, and the blue-eyed English from the shores of the Thames, met in arms at the foot of the Pyramids." The European troops, moreover, "beheld with astonishment the numerous retainers and sumptuous equipages which attested the magnificence of Asiatic warfare"—that is to say, they were struck with the uncommonly comfortable manner in which the Company's troops took the field. Disappointingly, there was no fighting for Baird's army: Alexandria also had surrendered when they got there, though of course their coming up had a great deal to do with this. It remained the gratifying fact that Napoleon had been thrust out of Egypt, violently reluctant; and that "forty centuries looked down" upon his army of veterans surrendering to a smaller force with, in general, about as much military experience as Ensign Bellasis. A campaign medal was struck in gold, to which young Daniel was entitled with the rest. He was one of the last to leave Egypt, when the Peace of Amiens brought a short lull: for the Plague, which had taken a hand in defeating the French, got into that one British unit, the Company's 7th Native

Q

Infantry: and as Napoleon's policy of poisoning the infected was not adopted they had to stay quarantined in the desert for several months after the rest of the army had sailed from Suez. They lost 250 men.

On his return to India, Daniel found himself removed to the Artillery and promoted to lieutenant. He was one of the force which escorted the Peishwa from Bassein back to Poona, and one of the detachment at the surrender of the hill fort of Karnalla; next, he was given a brigade of guns and attached to the 3rd Madras Native Infantry, with General Wellesley before Ahmednagar—the action that opened the ball, in August, 1803. This was a warm little siege: the *pettah*, or town part, from which the fort rose on a hill, according to the usual plan, was defended by excellent Arab mercenaries, a battalion of Scindia's regulars, and some horse; Wellesley, however, managed to take it in a day; and then commenced battering at the fort itself, which battered back powerfully. One who was present at the action describes how a soldier that was posted as usual to watch the enemies' fire and scream out hoarsely "Shot!" or "Shell!" as the case might be, cried first one and then the other, as the huge stone ball from a great Malabar gun approached—finishing with: "Blood an' ouns—mortar and all!" . . . But Wellesley got four of his guns in so strategic a position that the killedar thought well to surrender; and then eighteen-year old Dan Bellasis formed part of the garrison. He was detached to the capitulation of another fort in that year of victories; and Scindia being disposed of, went with Colonel Murray into Holkar's country of Malwa. Here the lad was stricken with dangerous fever, which kept him out of action for nine months, spent in Bombay as A.D.C. to his father; acquiring triangular leech-marks on his temples, since leeches, blisters, and frequent blood-letting were the most admired treatment for fever, though one school of doctors believed in burning the soles of the patient's feet with a hot iron, and making him drink a bottle of claret a day.

Edward, meanwhile, had been employed in the field as an engineer, and taken part in some successful sieges in Gujerat. He had also been hurriedly studying Persian, as his father was aiming at getting him included in the projected new Mission to Teheran. This came to pass at the end of 1803: Edward went to Mr. Lovett, the Resident at Bushire, where he joined Mr. Manesty, the Envoy, in the quality of Confidential Assistant and Officer of the Escort. It was not only a good job in itself but likely to lead to something. The Company was at this time courting Persia assiduously, though the much-publicised and very expensive Mission of Malcolm, in '99, had not produced great results. Samuel Manesty was the Resident at Bussorah, which was of importance since the Company had started a monthly Overland Mail Service via that spot, in '98. He kept great state in a very large English-style house with immense stabling, for there was no greater horse-dealer in Persia. His shooting parties were famous: the company would start at dawn, in a beautiful boat lined with red cloth, aboard which they breakfasted; then they would land and hunt, and find waiting for them a camp pitched the previous night, with a most luxurious dinner. Captain Eastwick, who had been in Persia shortly before this, has left an appreciative account of Mr. Manesty's hospitality; and the trip to the Shah's Court must have been managed "regardless". Edward pleased his chief, who placed the fact on record, in somewhat pompous form, considering that the young lieutenant was barely one-and-twenty when they set out:

"I highly gratify myself by expressing to you, on the present occasion, the satisfaction I have derived from the respectful deference with which you have constantly effected the execution of my wishes. . . . I have not failed to make such Reports to His Excellency the Most Noble the Governor-General respecting you as must convince him of my entire approval of your general conduct during the course of the late Mission, and I beg you will believe that I

shall ever recollect with real pleasure, your successful
endeavours to contribute to the social happiness enjoyed
by the individuals who formed the late British party in
Persia, by the mildness and correctness of your manners
and behaviour."

The gentleman could hardly, as the phrase is, say fairer
than that; and hopes were entertained that young Bellasis
might be made the new Resident, especially as Manesty left
him in charge when he took his departure in February, 1805,
with a special hint to the Directors of his "uniform good
sense, prudence, and propriety of conduct. . . . I am fully
persuaded that his residence here will be highly creditable
to himself and highly beneficial to the public." Bussorah,
however, was too much of a plum to fall to one so young,
and the Directors bestowed it upon a Mr. Law—who
himself told them that he thought Lieutenant Bellasis
could do the job better. "Something will turn up for
Edward in course of time", his father opined confidently;
and almost immediately the appointment of Engineer
Officer to the Surat Division of the Army turned up, and
enabled Edward to go on winning golden opinions, during
nearly ten years' soldiering up and down Gujerat.

Joseph, perhaps the least obtrusive of these correct young
men—although he wrote a very dashing hand—was
settled in his own house in Bombay, in Puzzle Row, and
improving the garden with some of the baskets of seeds
which his father, who had a passion for gardening, was
constantly obtaining from England. He was in a fairer
way to make a fortune than his brothers, for everybody
knew—certainly every "speculation Miss"—that the Company's Civil Service was far more lucrative than the
Company's Army. One diarist avers that nothing else was
talked about in company: "I am a Collector—He was a
Collector—We shall be Collectors—You ought to be a
Collector—They would have been Collectors." . . . Joseph,
indeed, was to be the Collector of Baroach, in a few years'
time—the Station where Miss King's husband had made so

large a fortune so quickly. But Joseph would not live to spend his fortune, or to marry any beauty, portionless or otherwise.

As for George, it was plain that the climate did not suit him, but he was doing his best to conform with his father's plans—little as the idea of enriching himself by a decade or two in the house of Bruce, Fawcett appeared to appeal to him. He had confessed to his father his chief reason for disliking to be out of England: he had lost his heart to Miss Charlotte Maude of Kendal, and indeed come to an understanding with her. General Bellasis, mindful of his own romance, was instantly encouraging. He had met the young lady when she was fifteen or so, and been impressed by the extent of her accomplishments—second only, in his opinion, to those of her then governess. Although her father was a man of fortune and consequence, being Deputy-Lieutenant of the county, she was the youngest daughter and one of twelve children, so that she might not have much fortune— some £5,000 or so. Nevertheless, the General determined to bring matters to bear, early in 1803, upon the occasion of the Fawcetts returning to England—Henry Fawcett should be his ambassador.

Inured to partings as any man in the Company's India must become, here was one that could cause great pain to John Bellasis. Fond and proud as he was of his sons, his daughter, it is quite plain, was always the best-loved of his children. He wrote of her, into Westmorland: "Mr. and Mrs. Fawcett have four fine children, Agnes, Henry, James, and John. . . . Mrs. Fawcett (my Helen) is an excellent young woman, and is exceedingly esteemed by everyone who knows her; she nurses all her children herself, never so happy as when at home, in short, she has innately all the goodness of disposition, and female meekness of her poor mother." . . . To her, he wrote: "You are my dear Daughter, the greatest blessing to me I have on Earth; you are everything that is good, or that the fondest Parent can wish! You are, thank God, happy in a fine Family, a respectable, kind and indulgent Husband, and I pray to God to bless and protect you in the continuance of every Earthly enjoyment."

Henry Fawcett settled himself, upon arrival in England, at 57, Portland Place; as his father died in the year of his return, he then inherited Scaleby Castle, in Cumberland, which his mother, a Miss Stephens, had brought into the family, and after which one of the firm's finest ships had been named. He had also the paternal estate of Broadfield, Dent, in the West Riding, where he had been born. He went north at once, and sent a long budget to the General, respecting his various errands. It was not possible, he reported, to buy either the living of Long Marton or "Dicky Hill's" Crackenthorpe estate with the charming situation for building, on the banks of the Eden. As to Miss Maude, she was now completely her own mistress, as her father had died; but she had referred him very properly to her elder brother, and they had discussed the financial aspect of the match. He had explained that in the new firm to be constituted on the 1st of August, 1804, George Hutchins Bellasis would become a partner, drawing about £1,000 a year to begin with, and much more later on. Thomas Holme Maude, who had succeeded his father as Deputy-Lieutenant of Westmorland, as well as on the Bench and at the family bank, was in favour of the match. So was everybody except Charlotte's mother, who was desolated at the idea of her going to India. Poor Mrs. Maude had not only recently lost her husband, but her young son Barnabas had been one of the unfortunate English caught in France by the sudden termination of the Peace of Amiens, and maliciously detained by Bonaparte: she would not see him again for eleven years.

However, the heart-rending farewells were determined upon, the young lady's outfit was bought, one more Bellasis bride was to be shipped out to Bombay; and Mrs. Fawcett in London prepared to speed her, unconscious of the fact that meanwhile the whole plan was coming unravelled at the other end.

George was very ill in Bombay, and only recovered to a series of relapses. It became plain to his father that this young man was not fit to stay and shake the Pagoda Tree; moreover, the new house, in which Mr. Remington would be chief partner—it was, indeed, afterward to be famous as Remington's, and the names of the founders forgotten— filled him with doubts as to whether it would answer. "All is not gold that glitters. . . . Mr. Fawcett is much missed, and both Mr. Law and Mr. Hadow are on the Sharp Look-out to get away if possible." . . . General John therefore decided not to put more capital into the house, and to provide for his son more modestly in some other way. "It will be George's own fault if he does not do well, and even admitting he goes into no employment whatever, by the disposition I have made he will be in retirement a much happier man in England on that small certainty than he ever would have been here on an extensive uncertainty." The *Elphinstone*, *Essex*, and *Ann*, bore the General's Europe letters, with this news, under date August 1st, 1804; the *Elphinstone* also bore George Hutchins Bellasis.

Bad news now came to the General: Miss Maude was sailing for India: George had been so very ill on the voyage that he had been left at St. Helena as unfit to proceed. "I am now quite at a loss to conjecture how it may terminate, whether George may live to get to England or not. He writes as being much recovered . . . but I am apprehensive that his life is in great danger, that he would have been dead long ago had he remained in India there cannot be a doubt." John Bellasis had the habit of always looking upon the hopeful side of things; although in "doubtful and threaten- ing suspence" as to his son's fate, he indulged a hope that he was gone on home by one of the China ships, and having the summer before him—this being written in May, 1805— would soon "get perfectly free of all complaint": moreover, that owing to the ships being late that year, Miss Maude might have got the news of his leaving India "in time to put you in as great a bustle to disembark all her packages as you have been in making all the preparations". He nevertheless is prepared to receive her at any moment; though considering the expense and danger and wasted time of the voyage "I hope to God she is still in her own country".

His hopes were justified, and his relief great upon receiving, not the young lady, but a letter from Helen to explain that a letter from George had come in time to stop the lovers from passing each other in mid-ocean; and that by what now seemed a lucky series of delays, all Miss Maude's goods except "her Couch" were still reposing in Token House Yard. George left St. Helena as soon as his strength was restored; and in the autumn of 1805 he married Charlotte Maude in Marylebone Church, both being twenty-six years old, and having been thwarted of one another by untoward fate this past four years.

They were now happy. George had no wish to be rich; and after his relations had advertised in vain for what was known as a "patent place" to be bought, which might suit him, he withdrew upon his "small certainty" to his ancestral Westmorland and a little lakeside house in the most poetical and romantic situation at Bowness on Windermere. There he presently built a charmingly pretty villa to his own fancy, called Holly Hill, after a great ancient holly tree that grew in the grounds. For the rest of his life, which was not a long one, for he died at forty-three, George lived in peace with his Charlotte, their children—four sons and two daughters—and the beauties of Nature, which he was fitted to enjoy.

For George Hutchins Bellasis was an artist. Everybody knew that he possessed a talent for drawing, not uncommon at the time, particularly in his family: but nobody could foresee that this was going to give the retiring young man a measure of fame, and even immortality, denied to his more conspicuous relations. But collectors of such matters today treasure the colour-prints made from George's water-colours of the Isle of St. Helena, during the many months that he was forced to spend there. Arthur Wellesley, staying at Randall Lodge when the quiet young man had first arrived at Bombay, had been much his friend: fifteen years later, Waterloo won, and Bonaparte boxed up on the narrow rock belonging to the Company against which he had fought and plotted so vainly—what could be a better notion than for George Bellasis to publish these drawings, and dedicate them to His Grace Field-Marshal the Duke of Wellington?

A list of two or three hundred subscribers, beginning with Queen Charlotte, the Duke of York, and the Royal Princesses, was prefixed: it contained, of course, many names from India and from Westmorland, as, Sir John Malcolm, Lord Lonsdale. There were six pictures, each with a brief but vivid passage of description; and though they aimed only at representing the scenes in such realistic detail as the camera was one day to record, they have caught the whole weird character of the place, sweetening it with period charm and a sort of ethereal prettiness. . . . Here towers the rock out of the sea "like a huge castle" with two great white-winged East Indiamen going about before it. Here is that other towering view, in the Roads, with ships riding at anchor, tiny redcoats marching along a mountain path, and a house called The Briars "said to be the place intended for the residence of Bounaparte". Here is the Castle Terrace, St. James's Town, "the grand promenade for company during the parades". There's a parade in progress —long files of red coats and white breeches, with spectators —trailing graceful ladies, leaning on the arms of officers in cocked hats. Next, we have a view of the Governor's country residence, Plantation House, in a valley of rolling meadows and plantations, with some peacocks in the foreground; and then another valley, steeply overlooked by rocks of nightmare shapes, with the sea peeping through them; the final scene is of a spot called Fairy Land, the naked rocks and sloping lawns of which are dominated by the tall white rock column called Lot: "The beauty of one part, the grandeur of another, and the horror of a third, cannot fail to astonish every observer."

The General would have been pleased and proud at George's little success; it was a pity he should not live to know of it. When telling Helen of George's return in 1804, he had added that he should not improbably come home himself by the January ships—it all depended whether that extra piece of promotion and pay was to come his way, or not: "If I should be laid on the Shelf, or any insult offered by supercession, which we are daily more and more liable to, I shall be off like a Shott!" However, a year later he had determined to stay and make a fight for it, and had entrusted Henry Fawcett with a memorial to lay before the Court of Directors setting out his claims to the Chief Command in the Presidency—the Chief Commandership of all India, no hard-working Company's Officer could possibly hope for: that was always reserved for a King's Officer. In sanguine expectation, he wrote to "my very dear Helen" that getting the Command "will make me at the least ten years younger than I am at present! With pride my Spirits will flow again in their usual Course (which I thank God are generally good) and I shall recommence the duties of high Military Command (thus honored and supported by my Honble Employers) with new zest! new ardour! and new zeal, for the advantage of the publick service; as well as for the honour, welfare, and happiness of my Family and Connexions; which will be for ever more dear to me than Life itself." He then goes on to joke about the figure he will cut, returning at length to England old and toothless: "I have only the remains of a once good set, here and there one as if Dancing the Hay! It will never do to crack nuts. . . ."

Henry Fawcett, in his solid businesslike way, arranged a good many transactions for his father-in-law, the most troublesome during these years being the affair of George

Bridges Bellasis. He must also report with regret that the *History of Dorset* was likely to be a losing concern. He now bestirred himself in Leadenhall Street, and with success: John Bellasis got the Command. Happy and busy, he wrote to Helen of his hopes of seeing her beloved face again in the course of two or three years, although he was perfectly well aware that he risked his life in staying so long—but: "I take great care of my Health". A year or two before, he had boasted to his brother in Westmorland: "I have not had a day's illness since I left England, and have almost forgot the taste of Physic." There had been an "attack" of some nature, however, in 1803, though he protested himself better than ever after it. . . . To his daughter, John Bellasis wrote more freely, in every mood, grave or jesting, than to anyone else. He wrote about music, which they both loved; about the seeds and bulbs which she sent for the gardens; about Bombay friends— too often a report of sudden death—"His Liver, on opening him, was found full of matter"—and about friends in England. He was deeply interested in her first visit to the North: "You will remember I told you what uncouth people you would be introduced to, altho' in their way they would do all in their power to make you happy, and at Crackenthorpe you would be comfortable enough, the best sleeping-room is a very good Chamber, there are those beautiful red chalk drawings by the poor Doctor . . . The best Parlour is also a good room, two bad Pictures of your poor Mother and me. . . . You would be rather crowded, it's a small House, but my Brother and Sister Hill are both very good natured; the Children would like their famous Milk and Butter which has a peculiar fine taste from the nature of Pasture they feed their Cows in, and is singular to that very spot, two Miles from thence in any direction it is perfectly different and not near so fine. . . . At Scaleby Castle I daresay you slept in the same room that I did, with the stone Balconeys to the Windows, and the Tapestry of hunting the wild Boar." He also wanted to know if a certain fine estate named White Hall, at Cock Bridge, between Carlisle and Keswick, was still for sale, if he could not build, he might buy. . . .

Helen chats back, in a charming clear hand. Relieved of the anxiety about Miss Maude, she has been down in the West, visiting her old school at Salisbury, and friends at Basingstoke—all the Deanes, Lyfords, and Digweeds who were the intimates of the Austen family: one expects the next line to produce either Jane or Cassandra, particularly when Mrs. Fawcett spends three weeks in Bath, in Great Pulteney Street. . . . There was a strength of character about this twenty-seven-year-old matron, besides her "female meekness": she disliked idling away her stay, and not only hired a pianoforte, but also a man to teach her to paint on velvet. . . .

Mr. Hallett, of Bombay, a friend and protégé of General Bellasis, and Secretary to the Military Board there, wrote to Mr. Fawcett on Wednesday the 10th of February, 1808, that the General was in perfect health and spirits; nor did he belie this description as he came across to Hallett's house on Bombay Green next day for the Thursday meeting of the Military Board, attended by his staff. It was high noon; and as John Bellasis came out of the vertical sun into the cool darkness of the house, he confessed to a slight headache, but it did not interfere with his spirits, or the activity of his spare, wiry, sun-dried person. He was a favourite with the small Hallett children, who loved to come to Randall Lodge and peer awestricken into his Camera Obscura. Young Mrs. Hallett no doubt shepherded them out of the way on this business morning; she was far gone with another child, as it chanced. In the broad front veranda, General John walked for half an hour or so, talking upon various points with the officers of the Board as they arrived. He wore his daily regimentals: no doubt something more faded than the full-dress coat which was to be preserved as a relic of him. Certainly the sash to which was hung his light dress sword must have been faded and worn, for it was the same that had been given him by his friend Mr. Lyford, of Basingstoke, when he set forth for the Indies as a young man. It was forty years since he had first put on that sash, no doubt rejoicing in its military bravery of strong crimson silk, and he had worn it constantly ever since, as thinking it a lucky piece of gear, an old friend and favourite, something associated with the battles and stormings through which he had come unscratched, and with his steady rise in life. Perhaps his wife had once been used to put it on for him, and Helen's baby fingers had played with the fringe of it. It was certainly one of those cherished habits, one of those comforting little dailinesses that are dear to men, and soothe them into forgetfulness of their own brevity. India had puckered the resolute bright eyes of John Bellasis, and thinned the hair whitened more by time than the military dab of powder; but the junior officers thought the C.O.'s step particularly brisk, as he paced up and down in that eternal old sash of his, before leading the way to the council table.

For a full hour the usual round of business succeeded, and the General worked through all that was laid before him. Some of the less seasoned must have been sweating, and furtively running a finger inside their high bullion-laced collars; half-past one o'clock in the Indian cold weather is seldom exactly cold; iced punch and the loaden dinner-tables of Bombay no doubt loomed in the minds of all. . . . Perhaps a little flushed and jaded by this time, the General began to cough slightly, a dry irritating cough that swelled the veins of his forehead as he endeavoured to suppress it. Thrusting back the handsome chair in which he sat at the head of the table, he got up and stepped outside. The assembled Board supposed that no doubt some impeding thickness needed to be hawked up genteelly in the solitude of the veranda. Colonel Spens glanced casually out after his chief—and then suddenly exclaimed: "Good God! the General is spitting blood!"

Hallett sprang to his feet and ran out upon the veranda. He saw John Bellasis rocking as he stood, with torrents of blood jetting out of his mouth. "Hallett! Hallett!" he got out, reaching a wavering hand as for support. Colonel Bailie caught up that handsome chair and brought it; the General was put into it while an incredible quantity of blood continued to rush from his mouth and nose, dyeing the faded crimson sash to a new scarlet, and causing the matting of the veranda to look like a piece of battlefield. Hallett's cry of, "Run for a surgeon!" had produced one at once, to say that there was no hope. The native servants began to wail, Mrs. Hallett ran out, and was forced back, frantically shrieking, from a scene so unfitting for her condition. All was over in the shortest space of time. John Bellasis had died in his shoes, ringed with soldiers' coats and swords, and in the midst of much blood; but at the same time, in peace, with friends, at the top of his ambition, and about his honourable business. How could the Bombay astrologers have ever combined such facts into a convincing prediction? They unarmed him, who had held to the hilt of his sword with such obstinate challenge forty years ago; his long days' work was done.

Furled and drooping marble standards, piled marble cannon-balls, escutcheon and inscription, make up a large monument to John Bellasis in Bombay Cathedral; but his body was laid with that of his loved wife, and attended to the tomb by the military pomp of slow-marching soldiers with reversed arms, loud, melancholy music, roaring guns and tolling bells, together with "a numerous concourse of gentlemen, and of all ranks and professions". To the burying of this Jangi Sahib Bahadur came the Parsee who exposed his dead to be torn by vultures on the Towers of Silence on Malabar Hill, and the Hindu who burnt them by the riverside with wood and sweet oils and sometimes living women, and the Moslem who built stone tombs over them like little mosques; these could have no idea of the homely grey churchyard under Dufton Pike where he had thought to be laid.

It is usual to speak well of the lately dead; but all spoke more than well of "this great and good man", as the *Gentleman's Magazine* was to call him: "we *knew* the General's worth, and sincerely lament his loss"; also there is the accent of real grief in the letters of his friends upon the occasion. As far as human success may be achieved, he had succeeded in the ambitions which he had brought with him to India when Hastings was Consul. Starting pretty well penniless, he had, by hard toil, steady courage, and patient endurance, made a fortune with which he had done good in every direction, and set a large family upon the road to doing equally well for themselves. Counting his nephews and Fawcett grandsons, between twenty and thirty of General John's descendants were to serve or to be born in India.

In the opening decades of the nineteenth century, there must indeed have appeared to be a Bellasis in every part of the Presidency. Peaceful years followed the extirpation of the Pindaris and the victory over the Mahrattas, except for a tiresome and expensive war forced on the Company by the Burmese, who had an erroneous notion of their own invincibility—unfortunately shared by at least one regiment of sepoys, which mutinied rather than go against them; they were disabused of this in 1826. In the same year, Lord Lake's defeat before Bhurtpore was avenged by its successful taking by Lord Combermere ("I know he's a fool and a damned fool, but he can take Bhurtpore", said Wellington); its teeth were drawn, and it was plundered "to the last lotah". Such an usurper as had endeavoured to set up there, a restless rajah inclined to prey on his neighbours, a crazed fakir promising to drive all foreigners into the sea, an uneasy conspiracy of little kings ready to take advantage of the first British reverse—these things were plenty enough to prevent the Company's troops ever rusting in idleness; but in general, the twenties were years of peace. Two years after the death of General John, his youngest son and namesake

had come out: so that there were three Bellasis brothers in the
Company's army, beside Colonel George Bridges Bellasis,
still at Poona, and one civilian, Joseph. In 1816 Joseph died
at Surat, and is commemorated by a monumental cherub
weeping over an urn; but before George Bridges died in
'25, the two elder sons of George Hutchins had come out,
and, moreover, Daniel had got a son; keeping up a fair
average of half a dozen bearers of the name in the
Company's dominions.

Daniel Hutchins Bellasis prudently did not marry until he
was thirty-six, and sufficiently advanced in the service to be
comfortably off and within sight of retirement. His father's
death had slowed up his chances of promotion, but he did
quite well, notwithstanding. After war-service with his
cousin Col. George at Seroor and Poona and in Kathiawar,
he became Aide-de-Camp to Sir Evan Nepean during his
Governorship of Bombay. Nepean seems to have found the
handsome young man not only able, but a social acquisition,
and wrote him, in his neat ex-Admiralty hand, letters of
chatting intimacy: even once condescending to a slightly
indelicate joke about a pretty woman of their mutual
acquaintance. Daniel's sparkling blue eyes under black
brows, the mischievous smile on his full lips, his dark
curls, all altered surprisingly little in the Indian years; and
his portrait at twenty is remarkably like his portrait at
five-and-thirty, apart from the thinning of the curls in
front. By that time, he held one of the best staff appointments
in Bombay, and after being Adjutant-General to the Army,
and Secretary to the Clothing Board, had succeeded his chief
and become himself Army Clothing Agent, an extremely
well-paid job. In May, 1821, he married the handsome
statuesque widow of Major Eldridge of the European
Regiment—or "Bombay Toughs". Mrs. Eldridge was
thirty-three, and had been for more than a decade a reigning
Indian beauty, having a right to look somewhat self-
satisfied in her portrait. Perhaps one dislikes her on slender
evidence: but she did come between Daniel and his devoted

DANIEL HUTCHINS BELLASIS
(1785–1836)
as a Captain of Bombay Artillery, and A.D.C. to
Sir Evan Nepean, 1812–19.

Mrs. D. H. BELLASIS
(formerly Mary—widow of Major Eldridge).

ON SURVEY IN 1840

A water-colour from Major John Brownrigg Bellasis' scrap-book.

brother Edward: and her letter home concerning her second marriage is extraordinarily like Mrs. Elton writing of her reception as a bride at Highbury. The lady who had managed to secure two husbands had been born Mary Tadman, of Gravesend; and she wrote to a sister who had not managed to secure even one: "I forgot I have not told you a word of my marriage, which by the by was the grandest affair known in Bombay, I am almost tired of the subject—visits and congratulations, etc. The Governor and Staff went with me to Church—Capt. Timins gave me away—Sir Charles Colville—Commander-in-Chief—Governor—the Members of Council and all the people of any consequence in Bombay about 100 came to a Breakfast at Randall Lodge—since which it has been one constant scene of gaiety. Last week, pity me when I tell you, how I was obliged to exert myself—we gave a dinner-party to 40 people. The Governor's family, Sir Charles and Lady Colville, and all the Big Wigs who gave me parties—the same evening 160 came at ten to a dance—afterwards a supper very splendid I assure you. The health of Major and Mrs. B. wishing them every happiness was drunk at all the parties given to us. The Bellasis are great favourites with every person in power here."

This Governor was of course Mountstuart Elphinstone. Edward Bellasis—no doubt still retaining the "mildness and correctness of his manners"—was now Private Secretary to him, and was soon to get the excellent position of Commissary-General to the Bombay Army. Throughout the upward career of the two brothers, they had been constantly doing one another good turns, and uniting to rescue their younger brother John from the consequences of his light-hearted imprudence.

John Hutchins Bellasis, youngest of the five brothers, and the only one born in England, suffered from these facts. His sister Helen was the only mother he knew; she and her husband, on their return to England, removed him from the large school where he had learnt to fight, but not much else, and placed him with a tutor who sounds remarkably like Sandford and Merton's Mr. Barlow. Even this instructive gentleman could not make him a scholar, and Henry Fawcett was afraid he would never meet the rising standard for a Company's Cadet. He, however, did so, and sailed for India in January, 1810, in the *Winchelsea*, Captain Lindsay, at nearly eighteen. He had always displayed a loving warm-hearted disposition. When he was staying at Basildon in 1802, Leah noted: "It is charming to hear with how much delight the dear boy talks of his Father; he is very affectionate to those who are kind to him; and has an amazing flow of spirits. He said to me, after making many inquiries about his poor uncle, 'I will be a Doctor of Divinity like my uncle, then I shall serve God and all my family'." The destiny of the spoilt baby was otherwise. By 1825, he was Major commanding the 10th Bombay Native Infantry, to which his nephew, George's eldest, had been posted, who sketches him as "Extremely popular, a good officer, and seen some service with Col. Prother's field force taking many strongholds from the Mahrattas. . . . Always in debt, and a jolly fast fellow, keeping open house, etc." Time and again his brothers paid his debts, making arrangements with Cursetjee Monackjee, the Bombay shroff. "My goal is to pay off Curset," he observes in a letter of mingled fondness and finance to Daniel; it was not an achievable goal for him. From England, Daniel, having returned there, reminds him, on a disconcerting rumour of his marrying, that "as you have not sufficient for yourself and Creditors you should avoid involving yourself with a Wife without she *has Money* and respectably connected—at the same time avoid encumbrances in *another way*. . . ." One gets the impression that John did not avoid them. In 1833, when he was forty-one, he suddenly married a girl of fourteen, named Ellen Maria Ashman. Her tender age and the rumour that she came of "railway people" seem to indicate that she was Eurasian; but she was not noticed by the family, and disappeared when

John died, heavily in debt, in 1837. . . . Half a century later, the Bellasis of the day, a great-nephew of John's, was amazed to receive a letter from a lady claiming to have once been his great-aunt. Although she had been since married to a merchant who had kept her in affluence and taken her "home" several times, she was now an indigent widow; and hopefully invoked the magic name of Bellasis. It is not recorded whether she took anything by it.

John Hutchins Bellasis was buried at Poona; and so India had the bones of two of the five brothers, having narrowly missed claiming those of the eldest. Daniel sailed away in 1827, retiring as a lieutenant-colonel, with his Mary and the boy and girl she had borne him. It was their intention to spend some time at the Cape, but because it came on to blow, the Captain would not put in, but went on and landed his indignant passengers on the rock of St. Helena. There they waited for Edward, who had been to meet them at the Cape; moralising over Napoleon's tomb, viewing the scenes which George had sketched long ago, and making their plans for England. These might put India gradually out of their minds; but Daniel had spent more than a quarter of a century there . . . it must be difficult not to feel that India was where he belonged.

Edward plainly found it even more difficult. Twice he had booked passage home, and twice paid forfeit of passage money; but this third time, and with his dearest friend and brother leading the way, he must go—even knowing that India would beckon him back. . . . So many men must have looked over a ship's rail as he did at the receding land of the Pagoda Tree, and felt the ache of that alien love. One should cleave to England naturally, permanently, as to wife or mother; not so to India, that temporary convenience. And yet so many of those departing would be saying inwardly, inarticulately: Oh, my mistress! my beautiful and dangerous mistress, my sordid, splendid, cruel and capricious, but most rewarding mistress . . . always in my memory I shall smell the smell of you, attar and sandalwood, corruption, and the bitter marigolds of funeral wreaths; your diamond light has dimmed my eyes, so that my motherland appears in a perpetual twilight; your burning fervency has thinned my blood, so that I must grow old and cold and shortly die, when I remove from you. . . .

XII
HIC JACET JOHN COMPANY

"I HAVE now been upwards of two years in the service, which I continue to like as much as ever, I have not, nevertheless, been able to lay my hands on a single bar of gold or any of the precious gems of East talked of at home as being so plentiful." Thus the eighteen-year-old John Brownrigg Bellasis, who was to be the family's third Indian General; but who, at the time of thus playfully writing, was an Ensign of the 10th Native Infantry—facings black velvet and gold lace—stationed at Baroach, in the year 1825.

He continues, with considerable good sense: "When a young cadet comes out from England, he has heard of Indian luxuries, like most other people, and has his head stuffed full of the fine things he will meet with; after landing, he is charmed with the variety of new sights, the faces, customs, everything so different to what he has been accustomed, but when he is posted to a regiment and ordered up country to a distant station to join, the bubble bursts. Although an officer's pay is handsome, it will go but a very short way to procure him luxuries, indeed for a few years he will but just be able to live comfortably, unless assisted at first as I was by my Uncles; promotion goes by seniority and is consequently slow—he cannot therefore expect to get a company, that is when he becomes Captain, for 12 or 14 years, and until that period an Officer without a staff appointment is but indifferently off. The pay of an Ensign is 180Rs. a month, about £18 at the present rate of exchange, from which deduct servants 40Rs., House 25Rs., In Fund 5Rs., Mess 50Rs., House-rent 15Rs., leaves 45Rs., out of which to get clothes, stationery, and little things of various kinds, so you see it must be a person of

more than common prudence to save his mite out of the
remainder."

John Brownrigg Bellasis, eldest son of George Hutchins
Bellasis and Charlotte Maude, had been born at Bowness in
August, 1806. He grew up a short, sturdy fellow, without
pretensions to good looks, but with spirit, sense, and talent.
In particular, he inherited his father's ability to draw
exquisitely detailed landscapes. At fifteen, having spent
nine months in London drilling with other cadets in Bird-
cage Walk, and taking lessons in "Equitation, Hindostani,
Persian, and also Flute and Double Flageolet", he satisfied
the India House Examiners; and in March, 1822, went
aboard the *Euphrates* Indiaman at Gravesend. Two months
earlier, his father had been laid in Bowness Churchyard,
where his wife was not to join him for thirty-five years.
Young John, faring out into the world, must have felt
important as the new head of the bereaved family; his
brother George, a year younger, was to follow him to India;
his brother Joseph was at school, and his brother Daniel was
a two-year-old toddler. If his spirits had been dashed by his
father's death, they must be raised by the excitements of the
opening prospect, and the delights of the voyage, which he
obviously enjoyed, from the sight of the beautiful crowd of
shipping in Cowes Roads, which "almost cuts out the
Windermere Regatta", to the landing from the pilot boat at
Bombay, four and a half months later. In days of peace, with
no danger of being "catch'd by the French", it could be a
charming voyage. The *Euphrates* touched at Funchal to take
in wine, and there found the *Jupiter* man-of-war upon the
same errand, and conveying Lord Amherst to succeed the
Marquess of Hastings. My Lord, who was to be the first
Governor-General to bring Simla into fashion, and whose
Consulship was to be troubled by the Burmese war, had
been appointed because the unhappy Castlereagh had cut
his handsome throat and Canning must stay and become
Prime Minister instead of going to India—as his son was to
do, a generation later. The cadets, guests of the Consul,

beheld Lord Amherst being kicked by a Portuguese horse, and listened to his daughter singing duets with "a Russian Count *Someperson*".

In Bombay, John spent a pleasant interval awaiting his commissioning and posting: staying, of course, at Randall Lodge, where "Uncle Dan has framed Papa's pictures and has them hung up on the walls", and where Uncle Dan's baby son was just able to walk, attended by the sepoy Dondoo. From some heedless caprice of his parents, this child had been named Augustus Fortunatus: not unnatural matter of regret to him in after years. All was made very smooth for the young cadet with powerful relations; John breakfasted with Mountstuart Elphinstone, and danced at Government House—"The room was beautifully lighted with large glass chandeliers and Mirrors all round—Uncle Edward, the Engineer, sees to all the arrangements, he also built Parell, which does him very great credit." However, Bombay society was at this time in even a more disturbed state than usual: these were the years mirrored in the Diary of Lady West, wife of the Chief Justice, when the resentful Company was fighting the Crown's attempt to impose King's Courts of Justice in the Presidencies. The King's Judges sent out, and particularly Sir Edward West, had to contend with violent opposition; the Bar insulted them in court, or went on strike; challenges flew about; finally ensued the strange spectacle of the Governor himself calling out the Chief Justice. Sir Edward pointed out to Mr. Elphinstone that it was impossible they should exchange shots, and taxed him with incivility at Government House in letting him walk down to dinner among a crowd of cadets, instead of allotting him the first lady in company and giving him "a seat opposite to you next to Colonel Bellasis". . . . This was the battle between "honest fellows with glittering sabres" and "quibbling quill-driving lawyers", as Malcolm put it; and when he succeeded Elphinstone at the end of '27, things grew rather worse, until he came to the point of ordering the Commander-in-Chief to put the Chief

Justice under arrest. But West was dead by then: these King's Judges died with a frequency and suddenness strange even in Bombay: it was whispered that this was not unconnected with the fact that the criminal class also resented their presence—the class accustomed to use *datura* poison. . . .

Presented by his Uncle Edward with Rs.2,500 (£200), and by his Uncle Daniel with a horse and accoutrements, the new Company's Officer went up country to join his Uncle John. With so many uncles, and a good handful of cousins —several Fawcetts and a Crosby—John Brownrigg could hardly feel like a stranger, however strange the land. He wrote home that he was very happy, and making many sketches. His other hobby, that of tootling cherubically on a wind instrument, proved to involve some danger: "The Hamalls have come running to tell me that there is a large snake in a flower-pot of pinks close to the door—I loaded my gun and found him laying coiled up close to the place I sit each evening and play on my Flageolet in the dusk, no doubt the music had attracted him there. I have just shot it (a very large Cobra Manilla, beautifully spotted) so neatly that I did not break the flower-pot." These innocent amusements were varied by riotous and elaborate practical jokes with his fellows, most of them mere schoolboys also. Here we find Outram, later to be Sir James Outram, known as the "Indian Bayard", leading the gambols at Dhoolia, whither John had gone to visit his friend Lieutenant Whichelo: "Outram is full of fun and got up a Tiger Hunt, only those in the secret knew it was a stuffed Tiger tied up in a thick bush. Whichelo, who often boasted of what he would do at a Tiger Hunt, was dared to go at it with his spear only, and proved more game than we gave him credit for, on sighting the brute crouching in the bushes, he rode right at it and speared the dummy amidst roars of laughter from the wags present. He was very wroth, and vowed to pay them off. Another joke was played off on Outram's visit to Malligaum. When at our mess, news came of wild Boar close to Camp.

The hoaxers had got a big Bazaar Pig, shaved and painted it black, I assisting at the painting, tethered it out in the plain to a bushy piece of Jungle—Skinner was the victim this time, and allowed to get ahead and spear it. He also had to be *christened* for his *first* pig killed, not a very savoury operation, but after partaking of some chops of the unclean animal which he pronounced excellent, and Outram pretended to eat, he was undeceived, when there had nearly been a serious row, but for Outram's good tact, for the hot Irishman called out all the ringleaders in the plot . . . and it was long before the matter was quieted."

John himself capped these jests with one quite as successful and rather more pleasant: "At Malligaum I and one or two others went to Morris' house about 10 o'clock one night when we knew he was at Skinners, and we cleared all his furniture and everything out of the house and locked it up in his stables. At about two in the morning he went home and found it swept and garnished and called the servants who sleepily said they knew nothing about it, had heard nothing, so Morris went off to sleep with Skinner. Early in the morning we got all his things put back again, and on one of us meeting him, he said he had been robbed of everything, was going to send for the police. 'Oh! nonsense, you must have been dreaming, or perhaps you had some brandy pawnee at Skinners, for I have just been to your house, and it looked as usual.' Morris returns home, and to his astonishment finds everything in its place. On asking the servants what they are laughing at, they confess 'Bellasis Sahib had been having a joke'."

Nobody was called out about this; but challenges were still not uncommon, though rather easier to adjust before they led to an actual meeting: the strong toils of convention which had killed Arthur Mitchell and nearly ruined George Bridges Bellasis were a little relaxing. John's next station of Sholapore—"A miserable grilling hot rocky station" abounding in court martials—was also "a great place for Duels and Drink". John, one day returning from viewing the loot of recently taken Akulcote—which included "a hatful of silver watches, and many square gold pieces, Mohurs of the Emperor Akbar"—saw an officer of the regiment drunk on the roadside: "He heard I had noticed him, and sent a young cavalry officer to call me out to a Pop! however, fearing a Court Martial he wisely withdrew his challenge, so I was not *kilt*. This ferocious youth was soon after obliged to quit the service. . . . I was next called on by the Assistant Judge of the Station who belonged to the Club of which I was Secretary, the cause was my over politeness to the ladies, to let them have the first new book just received from England. I stopped the big Civilian Carriage passing through Camp and sent the book with compliments. This was considered a piece of impudence. However, after explanations, my life was graciously spared a second time. Two other officers had a quarrel, and after firing 3 pops at each other, the seconds interfered and made them shake hands."

Frayed hot-weather tempers accounted for more of this kind of thing than did the boredom of peacetime, for there was never quite such a thing as that in the Company's India. There was always trouble, or possible trouble, big or little, somewhere. . . . "Strong detachments from every Station are out after the Ramoses, who are headed by a famous Chief, Omaji, formerly in the pay of Government, but his pension being reduced he in turn is breaking faith with the Company, and has hitherto eluded our most active pursuit, plundering and ravaging the whole Deckan—A man came into Camp with his nose cut off, and 3 Sepoys' heads were sent in a basket to the Governor as a present by the Chief, and a message saying he would serve all so whom he caught." The affair of Akulcote had recently occurred—"The ministers of a young Raja have been very refractory", and a strong detachment had been sent to chastise them: "They fell back some miles after their horse had been driven in by our Cavalry in a spirited charge headed by Captain Sparrow and Lieutenant Poole with a very few men. Captain Sparrow was killed: his horse at the same time was pierced by

two Jingal Balls (swivel) and killed too. Poole followed them
to the very gate, where several of his men were speared, and
he himself narrowly escaped under cover of some ruins,
having sabred a number of them. I visited the Fort a very
short time before, it is a very strong place, and from some
sketches was enabled to give the Engineer who accompanied the party a good idea of the works. . . . A non-com-
missioned officer discharged from the 1st Cavalry had a large
command in the Fort at its investment, and our officers
could see with their glasses the gun-lascars in their divisions,
sporting the Company's uniform! and showing by their shots
they had not forgotten their practice, many of the balls
coming into Camp. This comes of *reduction*, the poor
fellows set adrift will fight for whoever will pay them, the
whole country swarms with discharged men. Many old
officers think there will be a General rise."

It is surprising for how many years the Mutiny was
expected, while at the same time every tactless blunder was
committed that could invite it. Those who remembered the
affair of Vellore could have foreseen the very pattern: a
clumsy mismanagement concerning the most powerful
human impulse, the force which has caused every major war
and made and unmade empires: religion; this coming atop
a heap of grievances, and a sudden conviction that the overlords, in so minute a minority, were not invincible. The
defeat at Bhurtpore had impressed this fact on the India of
1806; the far worse disaster of the Afghan war was to make
it clear to a later generation.

Young John, who had sketched the recalcitrant fort and
also its Rajah in his days of friendliness—"a fine little fellow
who received us with a gracious Salaam; he had on a little
sword most beautifully inlaid with precious stones"—
sketched all of the beautiful terrible country that presented
itself to his steady artist's eyes. Rajahs were part of the
picture, like tigers and idols. At Baroda: "The Native
Prince here is fond of Elephant Fights with men, in which

the latter are often killed and the noble animal hurt and tormented, he is a great wretch and murdered two children himself in some rite to the gods." . . . At Sholapore, the Rajah of Sattara—"of whom I have a good likeness . . . being called out to receive him and kept standing in the sun waiting for His Blackness for hours together is no joke"—won general approval by generously heading the subscription list for the widow of Captain Sparrow. There was little harm about this nominal head of all the Mahrattas, except his haughty conviction that too much honour could not be paid to him as the descendant of Sivaji; these overweening ideas, and the fact that he was clay in the hands of any wizard or adventurer who came to court, presently made him tiresome. At last he took to drilling all his women on the barrack square, instructing them in the management of guns and war-elephants; and as European nations did not do this for another hundred years, the Company concluded he must be mad, and deposed him. . . . As to tigers, John was no fanatic sportsman, though he enjoyed a little pig-sticking: he neither killed tigers nor was killed by them, like many of his brother-officers: he preferred to keep one as a pet and draw it—until the day when it sprang on his shoulders and tried that bite at the back of the neck which is the death-stroke to a buck. John, however, was wearing his regimentals, with a very high, stiff, laced collar, and escaped with a scratch.

Those scarlet coats with the choking high collars and tight waists, above long, elegant blue trousers, and below the glazed shakoes with their plumes, occupy the foregrounds of many of his exquisite sketches: groups of officers, animating in tiny detail a scene of jungle or sunset lake or ancient crumbling city—Bijapur of the Adil Shahs, Cambay, Ahmedabad: and refusing, like the generations before them, to make any concession to the climate in their attire. John's brother, who had his father's name, George Hutchins Bellasis, had immediately followed him into the Company's army; they were often able to meet, and even to nurse one another through different bouts of fever; while for several years John was stationed with cousins, one of whom, John Fawcett, had a strong religious influence upon him. As for "Cousin Crosby"—the grandson of Hannah Bellasis, the General's sister—he was "expecting a wife out from England" with the ship that brought Sir John Malcolm in 1827. "I do not admire the plan of commissioning a wife out," John observed sagely; and with reason, for Miss Crosby—she was another cousin, and a beauty—met aboard ship somebody whom she liked better, and was, as Uncle John chuckled to Uncle Dan, "*spliced* to a Major Vaughan at the Cape!!!" Crosby, very sore, wrote to beg Daniel not to notice them there: "For she has brought disgrace on her family. . . . It may turn out a fortunate thing for me that she never became my wife." It might have been fortunate also for pretty Miss Crosby—who reported herself as "very happy" at the Cape—for her intended husband had stiff, unsympathetic handwriting, and was becoming addicted to a very austere form of religion. This was the matter in which Fawcett was leader: and young Bellasis was very ardent in it. Every week, about a dozen of these young officers met to read the Bible, expound and pray; and they also did their best to instruct the natives: "I have a Brahmin who comes here to work," recounts twenty-three-year-old John, "and have lent him a book to read . . . and by talking and arguing with him on adoring stocks and stones cut out like monkeys and other animals, he has entirely left off worshipping them." . . . "At this moment there are some thousands of natives viewing the eclipse of the moon which is at full tonight. The Brahmins tell them that one of their gods, the moon's brother, is angry and in the shape of the Snake (Nag) is trying to swallow the moon . . . all the crowd are calling out *Chor do!* let it go!—that the snake may not swallow it. Can you believe such stuff!!"

Anyone familiar with the lives of the Mutiny officers will recognise their Cromwellian note of Bible-and-Sword; but the new piety had reached the Company's army considerably earlier. In the 'forties, John Nicholson was to write home offering to contribute anonymously to his sister's Sunday-school, and recommending an excellent commentary on the Scriptures: John Bellasis was doing these things in the 'twenties. While the first enthusiasm lasted, his letters displayed patches of what a non-sympathiser would have called Methodistical jargon—phrases that would have acutely embarrassed a later generation of *pukka sahibs* who left their vague religion entirely to the padre, and that would have equally shocked the young man's immediate forebears, on different grounds. Certainly for any sermon upon European morals in India, he had plenty of examples about him. The Resident at Sholapore was old Meadows Taylor, who maintained a large harem, in the style of days gone by . . . and there was "jolly, fast" Uncle John; even handsome Uncle Dan, a bachelor on his marriage-licence, somehow had a grown daughter returning from education in Europe, who married a Bombay civilian, and died, poor girl, of consumption. . . . John earnestly states that it requires great resolution to resist the temptations of a Camp; and even when his evangelical ardour has waned, he seems to have kept up his resolution manfully. Missionary zeal continued to spread, especially in Bombay, where the successor to Malcolm, Sir R. Grant and his Lady were much inclined that way. It was a very praiseworthy thing, to be sure: but a good deal more dangerous than anybody seems to have realised.

Young John Bellasis had the politics that went with evangelicalism, and was defiantly a Radical. In the year when mobs were yelling for "The Bill, the whole Bill, and nothing but the Bill!" and burning down half Bristol in their enthusiasm for Reform, he wrote from Sholapore: "The most intense anxiety prevails in this country regarding it, and the papers are devoured the moment they arrive"; as to Abolition, "It will be a great thing, the downfall of the West Indies, that sink of iniquity and foul stain on England." "You say our friends are all moderate reformers, that is, they are for moderate reform of glaring abuses! . . . I myself know little enough about politics, because our rulers and superiors think that soldiers ought not to think . . . but I humbly consider every Christian ought to interest himself in the welfare of his country. . . . As for that beautiful fabric the Church of England, she must come down. . . . I see the Bishops are making a great stir, but it is too late, they must be clipped." He adds that there are "foul blots" on the Company's rule which must be done away: Government support of idolatrous shrines, and Suttee. As this last rite was abolished by Lord William Bentinck when Governor-General in 1829, it shows what a long labour the enforcement of such a reform must be: for our officer concludes: "A poor woman quite young was burnt alive before my door not a fortnight ago." Moreover, he is writing in 1836 that "Infanticide, Suttee, and rebellion are worse than ever".

By the year 1838, however: "You will not be sorry to learn that I am not such a violent Radical as I used to be. . . . I shall now be content with what you must allow is very moderate, namely to remodel the Bishops more to primitive times, abolish the hereditary Peerage, vote by ballot, and triennial Parliaments." At the age of thirty-two, John considers it time to sober down: he has been in India seventeen years. He had intended to have taken his furlough after the first ten years, and then come back to serve the rest, but one of those staff appointments, now grown so rare, had dropped into his lap, purely because he happened to have learnt surveying while at school. This, with his grasp of the native tongues, and gift of drawing, made him just the right man to be detached on survey of newly acquired territories; so he was able to "say good-bye to parades and court-martials, and lay by red coat and sword", and be off into the heart of the Deccan, dressed in broad-brimmed hat and jacket, shifting camp every few days, making many friends among the village headmen, and hardly ever seeing a white face. Next year his plans for going home are held up by the operations taking place in Kabul, Sind, and Burma: he is rather disappointed not to have been ordered to Kabul—little knowing what he would prove to have missed. However, disaster had not yet overtaken Shah Suja and his British backers at the beginning of 1840, when Captain Bellasis at last started homeward, puzzled by the strong pull of India: "It is very odd, I have a secret aversion to going home which I cannot account for, as I long to see you all again."

In March, 1840, Helen died—the last survivor of the children of General John Bellasis, except Edward, who would die three years later, a General himself. None had lived to a great age: Helen was sixty-two. She had been widowed at thirty-eight, Henry Fawcett having died in 1816 at Portland Place, after being several years Independent Member for Carlisle. As a handsome, rich widow, she had married again, three years later, a well-connected Army officer named Barrington Tristram; and by him she had two more children, William and Mary Ann. Thus her family had learnt to think of her for twenty years as Mrs. Tristram, and not under the name for which she had quitted her own, with all due female meekness, as a schoolgirl of sixteen.

On their return to England, Lieutenant-Colonel Daniel Hutchins Bellasis and his lady had been duly presented at Court, in the memorable summer of 1832: just ten days after the final passing of the Reform Bill. The mobbing and shouting was over; the alarming Lord Durham was being packed off to Russia; the good old Sailor King could take breath and turn to at the terribly hard work of levees and drawing-rooms. In the report of this occasion—"Their Majesties kept up an animated conversation with their Royal relatives, attendants, and some of the company"— one can hear his loud quarterdeck voice uttering tactless and unroyal remarks; however, the band of the Life Guards below was loudly playing "various fashionable pieces". "The Duchess of Kent came in state, attended by Lady Charlotte St. Maur and Sir John Conroy"—but not with the little Princess Victoria on this day. Classical simplicity had long been dead, and a Drawing-room in Reform year would

SKETCH OF A SAP-HEAD AT THE SIEGE OF MULTAN, 1848–49

From Major John Brownrigg Bellasis' scrap-book.

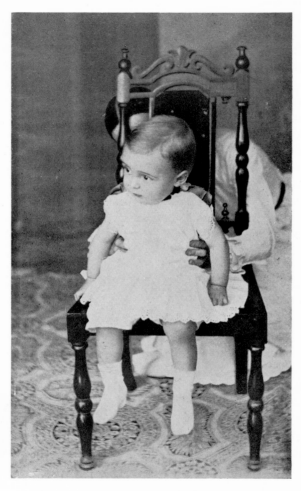

"The little white child . . . held up by loving black
hands, the hands of Gulab, or Jemdani, or Amina,
the Ayah" (p.279).

be a paint-box jumble of colours, vulgar with flounces and feathers and too-heavy jewellery, but very pretty. Mrs. Colonel D. H. Bellasis contributed to the general effect: "A rich mauve figured gros de Naples dress, beautifully embroidered with floss silk; mantille and sabots of rich blonde lace: manteau of emerald-green moire lined with rich white satin, elegantly trimmed with leaves of satin. Head-dress, feathers, rich blonde lappets, a superb tiara of diamonds, emeralds, and pearls; necklace, earrings and bracelets to correspond."

Brother Edward had no wife to bedizen, though he was about acquiring one; when he made his bow to William IV it was alone, except for an old comrade—"he and I had our first campaign together in 1802 at the Siege of Kunee"; also, under a certain disadvantage: "By some accident I sprained the great toe of my right foot, and at Night it became so bad I despaired of reaching the Levee. I however sent for a Doctor and by his applications and attention, we got the Toe in sufficient trim to get on the Boot without a Stocking. . . . My Leg was very painful the whole time and it seemed as if I had a Cork Leg, which Major Livingstone said had a good soldierlike effect." All went well, however; Colonel Edward was to be presented by Sir Henry Blackwood, a Bombay friend then in waiting on the King. Continuing the graphic account which he sent to Helen Tristram from the Oriental Club, he goes on to tell how Sir Henry, standing on the monarch's left, read aloud his names and titles, and then murmured to His Majesty: "I present Colonel Bellasis." The King responded breezily: "I know you do. You know, you told me you'd do so"—and offered his hand to be kissed, saying, "I'm glad to see you, Colonel Bellasis, glad to see you"; "I said, I thank Your Majesty, and making a low bow retired backwards. . . . When I got home the Boot was a pretty pulling business, Leeches etc. were applied, and with great care I was fit for duty yesterday." This was attendance at the Drawing-room, which did more good than the leeches, for "the enchanting fairy scene

s

operated as a soothing balm": to one who had been in India since his schooldays, the feminine part of London Society was even overpowering: "The animating beauty and loveliness the Forest of Feathers exhibited under their graceful wave was certainly the most fascinating display of Nature's most perfect work I ever beheld." The enchanted Colonel, however, had enough presence of mind to make the proper bows to the King, who cleverly recognised him, to the Queen "who returned the compliment, which she certainly does very gracefully", and to the Duchess of Kent and the young Princess Victoria.

Fifty is rather late in life to marry, but Edward was now determined upon it, and selected a Miss Anne Susan Powell, an amiable creature; they had two children, who died. Since his first setting foot in India, moreover, he had been wedded quite as indissolubly to a grievance; which must have made him, of all the elderly officers at the Oriental Club, quite the most tedious. It concerned the fact that by a Company's order he and a brother cadet who had passed out of Woolwich first of their year, had been granted special precedence, and that the Bombay authorities had paid no attention to this, thus setting them back several steps. He had been memorialising the Honourable Court of Directors ever since; and now made a special effort, with a view to being appointed Chief Engineer of Bombay. Perhaps the Directors felt it unreasonable that they should be required to undo their entire scheme of precedence for the past thirty years; they rejected his appeals; and he went back to India for a year in 1838, to see what could be done at that end—obtaining at last the honorary distinction of having his promotion to Major-General antedated. There was nothing else to stop for: nothing else that India could give him in the way of rank, wealth, or employment . . . he might as well go home and resign; and he did.

John, of course, had died at Poona in 1837; and in February, 1836, Daniel had died, in circumstances particularly distressing to Edward: for Mrs. Daniel had been carrying on a quarrel for some weeks which had kept the brothers from meeting. When the younger, after complaining of some slight indisposition, and as usual, of the cold, the terrible cold of England, fell dead out of his chair after dinner, the news was a shocking blow to Edward. However, when his own time came, he was to share a vault with his brother and their sister Helen in "the new Cemetery off the Harrow Road"—Kensal Green.

Mrs. Colonel D. H. Bellasis was left with a very pretty lawn-surrounded house in Grove End Road, Regent's Park, in which to bring up her son and daughter, Augustus and Flora. The Regency charm of its rounded bows, French windows, and frivolous little balconies, did not in the least appeal to the younger generation, however; and when Flora married Captain Oliver, R.N., it was rendered unrecognisable at great expense, with new wings of varie-gated brick, an ornamental glass-roofed entrance with encaustic tiling, stained glass, and every other horror in which the nineteenth century strove to forget the eighteenth.

Augustus Fortunatus Bellasis became a Company's Writer, and after two years at Haileybury, arrived at Bom-bay at the beginning of 1843, when he was twenty. He was neither tall, distinguished-looking, nor particularly hand-some, but he had a good brain and a sensitive imagination, and he did his work well. Before he took a year's leave in 1851—and how the Company's servants must have blessed the Overland route and the steamships that made a short furlough possible—he had been Third Assistant Collector and Magistrate of Tannah, Deputy Registrar of the Sudder Dewanee and Sudder Foujdaree Adawlut—the Company's Civil and Criminal Courts at Bombay—and after being appointed Assistant to Outram at Baroda, had changed over to a Fawcett cousin, Collector of Surat. "My report on the Southern Districts was ordered to be published by Govern-ment, and will be found among their selection of public records," he boasts mildly; and he also published a collection of cases from the Adawlut records in which decisions had been given on one moot point or another, summarising them with a cool precision which shows how good a magistrate he must have been. The detail of these cases sheds a good deal of light on native manners: endlessly repeated are the murders of little children for the sake of the golden ornaments with which foolish parents bedizen them according to custom: the murders of old husbands by young wives and their paramours: occasionally a Suttee, with a defence of ignorance of the law: and, with a lofty comment on such "gross ignorance and superstition", the clubbing to death of a *Bhootali*, or witch. Augustus Fortunatus had been nursed at the breast of a Hindu girl of fifteen, and spoken her tongue before he could speak his own; it was so with most of his colleagues; they ruled in no strange land.

The 'forties were not years of peace in India—beginning as they did with the shattering disaster of the retreat from Kabul, and ending with the Sikh war and the siege of Multan. Augustus came to India in the year when the British flag was hoisted for the first time on the great tower of Hyderabad in Sind—not to be confused with its southern namesake in the Nizam's country; and the eagle-beaked Napier paced the battlefield of Miani by moonlight, declaiming Scriptural texts. . . . Meanwhile, John Brownrigg Bellasis had taken the first part of his furlough after the new manner, in a tour through Europe, after viewing the Pyramids; and had spent the latter part in getting married. His bride was Miss Louisa Eames, who had not at all a Radical background, being, indeed, daughter to an Equerry of the late Duke of York. He returned to India as a Major, and was to be Colonel of his regiment in time to command it at the Mutiny—when it remained loyal. His brother George had been unable to take a furlough at the same time as himself, as his was one of the Bombay regiments ordered to go and take Aden, and he was still there when John passed by that "dreadfully barren hot hole". The operations had been successful, as John had noted the year before. "The taking of Aden was a very spirited affair, no Officer killed, and only a few wounded—The beautiful brass Turkish guns, eighty pounders, taken, and some stands of colours sent home to be presented to the young Queen."

All the officers of George's Regiment had dined, before setting out for the Red Sea, with General Edward Hutchins Bellasis, then on his brief return to Bombay, drinking to their success; and George had found particular favour in his uncle's eyes: "George Hutchins Bellasis came on board, grown and well, indeed a very nice Young Man, and is Adjutant of his Regiment, he has the stamp of a Soldier. I was greatly pleased with him."

George was at this time thirty-one; and he did not go home until two or three years later, being then resolved to find a wife, as his brother had just done. As he was a little, upright man, with bright blue eyes and soldierly ginger whiskers, he was naturally attracted to a tall, stately black-haired young lady. He met Fanny Skelton while staying with his mother at Holly Hill. The Skeltons had removed to Bowness, as they thought Dover "grown pretentious and expensive"—a great consideration with five grown daughters to be disposed of. . . . Captain Daniel Jones Skelton had indeed a difficult row to hoe. Independent of his being a Marquess's nephew, he had gentlemanly tastes and a most sociable disposition: and he desired to see his girls making thoroughly suitable marriages. However, he was not rich, and it was a puzzle where to settle: Bath and Cheltenham were delightfully genteel, but far too expensive: Cockermouth and Whitehaven, in his native Cumberland, were not expensive, but then they were not genteel—people dined there at 2 o'clock. It ended in Dover, and the purchase of No. 6, Clarence Lawn in 1835. Dover was the height of gentility in the nineteenth century and the very place—one would suppose—in which to marry off five daughters. The band played in Clarence Lawn, gay balls were given at Batcheller's Rooms, tight-waisted, scarlet officers from the Castle and from Deal and Canterbury clustered at private parties, noble connections came to stay; but, however, by 1841, nobody had married Eliza, Maria, Mary Dorothea, Fanny, or Sophia Henrietta. . . . Tragedy also had overtaken Captain Skelton's two sons. Charles had gone to Addiscombe on the Cornwallis nomination, and had sailed for Calcutta in the *Roxburgh Castle* in 1831. It was a period of dauntingly slow promotion in the Company's Army; Charles was not pleased with his prospects, or with India, and he died five years later at Lucknow, aged twenty-three, an Ensign in the 47th Native Infantry. He had been very handsome and promising. Henry now, at fourteen, "urgently requested" to be sent to sea; and his father hoped that a voyage to India in the *Walmer Castle* might cure him of the fancy. It did; "He dislik'd his situation so much that he would not return in the ship, but quitted her the evening before she left Calcutta, and we never heard of him afterwards. . . . There was always something peculiar in the disposition of the Boy, he was restless and of a wandering turn —liked liberty—hated constraint—and always expressed a strong desire to sail round the world." . . . The boy may have died one of many strange deaths in the bazaars of Calcutta; but it was pretty clear that the distant tiger country had crunched the bones of both sons; and Daniel Skelton must feel that a change of scene was needed to recover his own spirits.

The family removed to the Lakes in 1841, letting the Dover house, and hiring Rayrigg Hall near Bowness, a fine old place with which they were much pleased until they found that it was full of rats. They were also disappointed in a local cousin, Sir Richard Fleming, who was a baronet, and also Rector of Bowness and Grasmere; for it turned out that "owing to the irregularity of his conduct . . . his acquaintance was not desirable . . . he was not noticed by any of the Families". These families, living at Storrs, Belfield, Ferney Green, Colgarth, The Craig, Ecelbrig, and Mr. Curwen's house on the Island, are of names grown familiar to Wordsworthians; and upon one July day, Skelton notes: "Introduced to Wordsworth the Poet and drank Tea in his company—found him a very agreeable old Man, 73, in possession of all his faculties." . . . Three daughters now married in rapid succession: certainly the move had answered. One married James Burrow, son of the disappointing baronet's sister who had made a bad match with a mere "statesman" or yeoman farmer, and had a large family; James was the eldest, and perfectly genteel, being at Oxford. As soon as he had taken Orders and secured a curacy, Maria was bestowed upon him. A Mr. Browne Ponsonby then carried off Eliza; and finally, Fanny accepted Captain George Bellasis, and married him in Bowness Church in August, '45: "The Church very full, and Fanny look'd very well and prettily dressed." There had been another Bellasis wedding there recently, when one of the two girls, Helen, had been married to the Rev. Robert Perceval Graves, elder brother of the Bishop of Limerick: a family whose lively talents were to be traced on the shelves of every circulating library a hundred years later, and to add a name to the roll of English poets. To this Helen Bellasis had descended, by the by, the Queen of Cannanore's emerald, set into a brooch.

All now travelled to London, to fit Fanny out for India, where Captain Bellasis was to be stationed at Dhoolia with the 24th Native Infantry. The Skeltons carried with them, rather endearingly, a pet known as "our Dear Dog Fly": this animal pervades the Captain's Diary for more than a decade, until sorrowfully laid to rest in a friend's garden at Dover. For, having now only two daughters left upon hand, it was decided that the Lakes, however romantically beautiful, were very dull; and the Skeltons were happy to return to Clarence Lawn. From thence Mary eloped with a rakish middle-aged Colonel, and Sophia eventually married a stockbroker, and old Daniel was borne to the grave with fatal gout, having lived to shake his head over the Mutiny and the Crimea—"alas, we had no Duke among our Generals, all without Talent. . . ."

John Brownrigg Bellasis, in a brisk Radical diatribe against "rascally Lords" had complained that Sir Charles Metcalfe was thrust aside for Lord Auckland in 1836. Certainly, had Metcalfe been Governor-General, instead of that pleasant-mannered, well-meaning and ill-judging Whig, there would have been no calamitous Afghan war. It is a long, unhappy story, how—in a fit of alarm about Russia's designs on Afghanistan—the "Army of the Indus" was dispatched to place upon the throne of Kabul Shah Suja who had been thrust off it thirty years back, instead of Dost Mahomed who had been governing very well for a barbaric chieftain, and was perfectly willing to be friendly with the Company: of how the treaty with the Amirs of Sind, providing that armies should not pass through their territory, was coolly broken: of how, as soon as the Commander-in-Chief marched off again to congratulatory banquets in Bombay, the whole thing came unstuck: of how the English were obliged to evacuate Kabul under a safe-conduct which was a typical Afghan joke: and how, of the 16,000 soldiers and camp-followers who set out for India, but one wounded man came alive through the passes. . . . Of course, it was necessary for the English to return with a victorious army, retake Kabul, release the captives whose narratives, particularly that of Lady Sale, created excitement in England, and subsequently fight two campaigns, one with the Amirs of Sind, and one with the great Sikh army of the Khalsa. Sir Charles Napier took Sind—without making the *Peccavi* pun, for he thought it a very right and proper thing that the province should be delivered from its former oppressive rulers, and set in order by himself after his model victory of Miani. General Gough made a very bloody business of the Sikh war: "Another such victory and we are undone!" cried the Governor-General after the battle of Ferozshah; followed Sobraon, which also put many English homes into mourning, owing to the aged Gough's habit of hurling his men against the Sikh guns without adequate use of his own artillery, but at least ended the war. The chief cities of the

Punjab were now garrisoned with British troops, and Henry
Lawrence became Agent at Lahore, where a little boy, with
his cruel and depraved mother as regent, had succeeded the
great Ranjit Singh. The jewels taken as indemnity included
the Koh-i-Noor, which Ranjit had squeezed out of Shah
Suja, whose ancestors had looted it from the last Moguls.
This symbol of Imperial dominion was sent to the young
wife at Windsor.

Sind, as well as the Punjab, now needed British garrisons
and Residents; it was fortunate that the Company's servants
included some administrators and warriors of real genius—
such as the Lawrence brothers, and John Nicholson who
was to save India ten years later. Bartle Frere became the
Commissioner in Sind, and when Augustus Bellasis returned from his year's furlough, he was to be appointed
Frere's Judicial Assistant; two years later he was to be himself Collector and Magistrate of the great Sind stronghold
of Hyderabad—a post which Henry Lawrence himself had
desired. Meanwhile, in the year 1849, Captain George
Hutchins Bellasis was stationed at Hyderabad, with Fanny
his wife, and their little son, George Montalt. Augustus had
been godfather to this baby; and to Augustus Captain
George wrote with high praise of the place: "The climate
here is truly delightful at present, we wear *cloth* all day, and
have only just dispensed with our evening fire! . . . We have
the finest vegetables I have seen *out of England*! especially
pease and cauliflowers." George, who has more than his
share of the mid-Victorian habit of underlining his words,
continues in his neat little long-tailed hand with an account
of his brother John's part in the taking of Multan. The
second Sikh war had broken out quite unnecessarily in the
summer of '48. Mulraj, the Governor of Multan, had
neglected to send a tribute due at Lahore, and on being
pressed had pettishly resigned his post. He had not
expected to be taken at his word, and to have two English
"politicals" arrive to discuss his replacement. However,
there were Sikh fanatics in the city who did not like English

politicals: Mr. Vans Agnew and Lieutenant Anderson were murdered, their escorting force having mutinied; and Mulraj decided to put himself at the head of a general Punjab rebellion. This could have been nipped at the outset if the Government had sent forces to assist the tiny army with which Lieutenant Edwardes had driven Mulraj into Multan and kept him there "like a terrier barking at a tiger"; but the old generals wanted the war put off until the cold weather. The Resident at Lahore, however—unfortunately Henry Lawrence was on furlough—sent an army under General Whish, which sat down before the city in due form, and was shortly deserted by the Sikh detachment under Sher Singh, who moved off to the enemy, beating the *Dhurum kha dosa*, the Khalsa drum. This defection caused the raising of the siege in September, until reinforcements arrived in December. With them was John Bellasis, and his sketch-book. He drew Multan and the horrible hot wastes of sand that surrounded it—the place was celebrated in vernacular verse for dust, dogs, beggars, and graveyards—the mud-walled town, and the strongest citadel in the Punjab. He drew, one minute after it occurred, the great explosion when the enemy's magazine was hit by a shell. He drew dead Sikhs lying beside their great brass guns with their long hair in the dust; and living Sikhs fighting with sword and shield to the war-cry of *"Wah Guruji ke Khalsa!"* He drew the immense variety of uniforms in the besiegers' trenches, from the gorgeous fancy-dress of the Sind Horse to his own plain scarlet—a frock or tunic, now that officers were no longer wasp-waisted. Shells and cannon-balls fell about him from time to time, as he plied his pencil. At last, Mulraj having been given an ultimatum, all was prepared for a storm, as George recounts to Augustus: "Intimation was sent in to Mr. Mulraj that he had but *24 hours* of his earthly existence remaining! On the morning of that day (the 22nd January) 2 hours *before daylight*, and amidst *torrents of rain*, the storming parties went forward and moved to their positions, the *Bombay* portion being under the command of *Major Bellasis*! By daylight they were all ready to commence operations, when *soon after* out came *Mulraj* with 4 or 5 thousand fine Sikh soldiers, and laid down their arms to General Whish!! The command of a storming party, I daresay you know, is *no joke*! and the leaders on such occasions are 9 times out of 10 cut down or desperately wounded, especially when opposed to such brave troops as these Sikhs! . . . Lucky that Mr. Mulraj thought better of it. John wrote me rather an affecting letter the day before, which of course made us *extremely anxious* for next day's post! His firm trust and confidence, however, were with *Him* who giveth the victory . . . Hobson remains as prize-agent, and they report 2 *Crores* of prizes!! or something enormous. . . . The remains (*headless*) of poor Agnew and Anderson have been *disinterr'd* and buried up top of the Fort with military honours. . . . The troops cannot occupy the Fort yet on account of the still fearful stench from the heaps of slain."

The Company's pattern of war was still much the same as it had been in the days of General John and Colonel George; indeed there were officers then serving who had seen the brigades of De Boigne broken at Laswari and Assaye. This was one reason for Chilianwallah, which had taken place a week before the surrender of Multan: Gough was too old: so was the Colonel of the regiment which ran away. Gough joined battle at a wholly unsuitable time and place, because, he said, "The impudent rascals fired on me! They put my Irish blood up." George Bellasis comments: "You of course *have heard* of Lord Gough's *awful* battle (some call it *victory*!!) and through his *blunderheaded Irish blood*, the fearful sacrifice of life! The behaviour of the 14th Dragoons is incredible! . . . and unless this affair is cleared up it will *go hard* with them at the *Horse Guards*."

It was well for all concerned that there were young men like John Nicholson ready to cope with the storm which was to come in the next decade. Meanwhile, Gough used his artillery for once, and contrived to win the battle of Gujarat, and the war ended.

The Koh-i-Noor was placed upon show to the British public in the Great Exhibition at the Crystal Palace, and disappointed everybody much: it looked like glass, they said, and dull glass. However, the public was for the first time really conscious of India: the new illustrated papers had brought pictures of the late wars to many breakfast-tables: the Indian splendours in the Exhibition began to be viewed with a personal interest. The tone of public feeling was to wonder at the continued existence of the Company. Surely it and its wars were sad anachronisms in this wonderful year of new beginnings, 1851. . . . There are moments in history when we can almost see the hour-glass being inverted, when we can almost hear the turning of an enor-mous page. The least imaginative must have been conscious that something like a new era was beginning with the new half of the century: the dullest must have been stirred by the scene on that clear, blue May day when the steeples rocked with bell-ringing and all London was in Hyde Park. Under the huge glass arch among all the light and space, colour and grandeur, the trumpets and the cheering, the 25,000 invited guests saw the little Queen glide with her superb gait to a blue-and-silver throne, wearing pink satin and masses of diamonds which copied the rainbows playing in the central glass fountain. The triumphant Prince Consort was at her side in the uniform of a Field-Marshal. Soon, such a uniform would become a mere fancy-dress; war would surely be obsolete very shortly, vanishing before progress, "the appliances of Steam and the wonder-working powers of the Electric Telegraph", as Mr. Paxton put it. A gentleman in the Company's service, on leave from Bombay, viewed the scene, and must have felt something of its meaning. Certainly the eighteenth century had died hard; but it was dead at last. Should not the Company die with it?

Augustus Fortunatus Bellasis went back to India next

year, and presently found himself at Hyderabad with powers of life and death, exercising which, he hanged Rana Singh, the brigand chief, above the gateway of the Fort of Omerkote. He altered the manner of collecting the revenue, entirely revised the irrigation system, discovering and cleaning up the usual corruption; he also made several hundred miles of roads, including the first metalled road ever seen in those parts, from the city to the Indus; this was planted with a double avenue of trees, and called by his name. No doubt he ruled better than the Amirs, a little pale, spruce gentleman, with neat whiskers and thoughtful blue eyes, who sat in the seat of power because his grandfather had come to give a modest shake to the Pagoda Tree.

His friends had all advised him to bring back a wife from England, but he had not done so, and never would; it was his fate to fall in love but once, with a woman who would not marry him. Nevertheless, he thought a good deal about the future of the family to which he was proud of belonging: such matters appealed to his imagination. . . . If he were to have no son, and since his sister's sons must be Olivers, the only descendants of General John Bellasis to carry the name into the next generation would be the sons of John Brownrigg and George Hutchins Bellasis; their two brothers at Bowness, Daniel and Joseph, had made no figure in the world, and had not married. It was, alas, a family grievance that Long Marton, after so many centuries, had slipped through the hands of Hugh's descendants: parcelled and portioned off here and there, until that which had stretched from Kirkby Thore to Dufton was dwindled into a smallholding; moreover, the family had dwindled with it, there was but one impoverished male survivor. It was from the line of the General's elder brother, however, that the family had most to hope: from that baby with which Leah had comforted the old doctor's death-bed. Edward Bellasis might be said to owe his existence to his uncle, as it was General John's generosity which had made it possible for him to be born, and which had helped his widowed mother to bring him up becomingly, as his stepfather Maude was not rich. A little money was never better spent; the boy grew up as tall, handsome, and distinguished-looking as the half-brothers who had died in India; and on leaving Christ Hospital, he took a first-class brain and unlimited application into the law. "A great Parliamentary lawyer", says the *Dictionary of National Biography*. By the year of his cousin Augustus's first furlough, he had been a Sergeant-at-Law for six years, earning an income of better than £10,000; and had just caused shocked paragraphs in the papers by being received into the Catholic Church. This step he had taken, not because he thought it was a picturesque link with the family past, or anything of that sort, but from conviction coolly worked out over a series of years. It was, indeed, a most unpopular step to take immediately after the great howl about Papal Aggression, and would be likely to bar his way to any further distinction, Bench or baronetcy; but he was already famous and rich, and he had a large and increasing family: perhaps some of them might carry on the name in India.

Augustus took his next furlough in 1856, after deputising for Bartle Frere in Sind, and there enlivening Karachi—that "regular dust-hole", as his cousin called it, expressing the general opinion, past and present, with a very splendid ball on the Queen's birthday. No dancers could have had less idea what the next year was to bring forth. . . . In company with his friend and colleague Charles Manson, Augustus spent five months travelling in Europe: they visited the Crimea, where hostilities had only just been concluded, and moralised over the disastrous battlefields which had broken the dream of universal peace with which the 'fifties had opened. It was, however, a good thing to know that Russia had received a check: fear of Russian designs had haunted the Company ever since they ceased worrying about the French: India would now feel safer. The gentlemen proceeded to England, at the beginning of the London season, and had scarcely had time to wonder at the prodigious size of the latest crinolines, when they received a message of recall from Bombay.

"*Most alarming* news from India," old Captain Skelton was tremulously inscribing in his journal. Fortunately Fanny and George had come home two or three years before, he being obliged to sell out on account of ill-health: they were now at Bowness, tending the death-bed of old Mrs. Bellasis, once Charlotte Maude. John, however, was commanding his sepoy regiment at Hyderabad; and poor Louisa, who had been invalided home with her children, was in wild anxiety for him. He wrote that "the trouble is only beginning. . . ."

Manson was murdered in the South Mahratta country, Augustus Bellasis spent some months expecting to be murdered at Karachi. . . . "Bungalows began to blaze round us nearer and nearer till the frenzied mob reached that next our own. . . . The stables were first burned, we heard the shrieks of the horses. Then came the mob to the house itself with awful shouts and curses. We heard the doors broken in, and many many shots, and at the moment my servant said they had been to bring away Mrs. C. but had found her dead on the ground, cut horribly, and she on the eve of her confinement." That was a lady's report from Meerut in May, and it was the pattern for the whole. Mutiny spread like fire, or, as John Nicholson said, small-pox. The outer world heard with helpless horror the stories that came out of India. None was worse than the story of Cawnpore, with the massacre of the boats and the massacre of the well. It is said that a woman of the Nana Sahib's harem insisted on the murder of the two hundred and ten women and children whose remains were found when Havelock's men marched in. The place was swimming in blood, in which fragments of dresses, collars, bonnets, children's frocks and toys lay sopping. The walls were marked with bullets and the wooden pillars with sword-cuts, aimed low, at women crouching to shield their

children. The well was filled up and brimmed over with
bodies. All that terrible year and into the next, the English
fought off the tigers unloosed against them; but the worst
was over when John Nicholson, having secured the loyalty
of the Punjab, began to strike here and there with his
Moveable Column—a Captain by rank, a Brigadier by
courtesy, to the dismay of all the aged Generals. When
he died at the taking of Delhi, aged thirty-four, the back of
the Mutiny was broken. The Sikhs had worshipped him
as a god, and the Punjabis sang heroic ballads about him.
Lord Canning, the Governor-General, now began to be
angrily nicknamed "Clemency Canning" from his attempts
to combine justice with mercy in pacifying the country: for
the first wild reaction among many of the English when
they began to be victorious was to requite massacre with
indiscriminate massacre. "Our indiscriminate severity has
raised such a feeling of enmity and hatred against us among
the better classes and the love of plunder is so strong among
the lower orders that I fear it will take long before things
settle down into order and peace," wrote Augustus
Bellasis, in October, 1858. "In Scinde we have, thanks to
God and to Mr. Frere's good management, been pretty
quiet, but all around us is unsettled and disturbed, and the
disorder is very contagious." He goes on to recount how
that a spy has come to him in disguise and offered to deliver
the escaped Nana Sahib for eleven lakhs of rupees; but he has
clapped the man into jail. He also has in his charge the
Rajah of Kolapor's brother, in strict custody on an island
in the harbour; and an ex-Queen, "a horrid intriguing old
woman who intended to massacre all the Europeans about
this time last year; and now when I go to see her, which I
have to do about once a week, she always in tears appeals to
her injured innocence. Whenever the Queen cries, it is
Court etiquette for all her female attendants to cry too, so
you can imagine what a perplexing position I am in sometimes. . . ."

Not until another year had passed was Lord Canning able

to progress through the country holding durbars at which the loyal chiefs were publicly rewarded; but already, when Augustus wrote, one more Mutiny casualty had taken place: in August, 1858, an "Act for the better Government of India" had been placed upon the Statute Book: John Company was dead.

T

XIII

FULL CIRCLE

"THIS is a fearful hurricane, Willy my boy—we cannot weather this!" . . . The great tempest with which the year 1865 shrieked its way out of the world was battering at the London houses; and Captain Robert Eastwick, dying with the dying year—his ninety-fourth—thought himself once more on the deck of his ship, instead of between the curtains of a four-poster. He had been bearing great pain with the utmost fortitude; it was only at the very end that he lost hold upon reality, in the roaring confusion of the storm, and the total darkness—for he had been stone blind these five-and-twenty years.

"The old blind Captain with the gold-headed stick", walking as firmly as a seeing man, had been a familiar sight about his home in Brompton, and about the East India houses in the City. Something of a romantic sight also: speaking to a solidly secure mid-Victorian world of other and more adventurous days and ways. Rich England, powerful England, safe England, fat England, where no man but a few professional soldiers had seen the face of war, nor was to do so for another fifty years—this had been, in Robert Eastwick's youth, an England of paper-money and food-rationing, of expected revolution and imminent invasion, an England with the world leagued against her, and the Corsican's bayonets glittering across the Straits. The shadow of the insatiable little man in the cocked hat had not only extended over the narrow seas, it had fallen upon India, where his ships of prey put all the coasts in peril, and the Tiger of Seringapatam looked for the coming of his armies . . . The India to which Robert Eastwick had first voyaged was an India of which the English were not yet masters; he had seen the conquests of Wellesley confirm the conquests of Clive, and the traders, upon equal terms with the people of the country, become a sacred ruling race. Even the ghost of John Company was beginning to fade out of memory; the Koh-i-Noor was set in the Crown of England, and the Queen was to be Empress of India.

In India, the sons of Robert Eastwick and Lucy had made fine careers: Edward was a famous Oriental scholar, and now a Member of Parliament: William had been an East India Director and a Member of Council. Lucy was forty years dead—she had died while he was captaining the *Asia* to China, in the Company's gold buttons. He had tried to fill the gap in his life, when he settled down ashore, by marrying a friend of hers. This wife had given him two daughters, great comforts to his age, though he had seen them only as infants. He had never seen Victoria's England at all. Just before the young Queen's accession, his sister-in-law Eliza had died: that liveliest of the seven beauties, whom he had convoyed across the highwaymen's heath and all out to India to marry, something irregularly, her tall and handsome soldier. She lay far enough away from him now, buried at Walmer, which saw very few Indiamen towering in the Downs, in these days of steam. Eliza had lived her remaining decade after leaving India with her sister Hannah Gordon; the Gordons had come home about 1820, had settled at Walmer, and after twenty years of childless married life had suddenly been able to rejoice in a son. The faces of Eliza, and Hannah, and Ann for whom a man had been killed, and long-dead Esther, and his own Lucy, all the faces of those days of his youth, must crowd back upon the dying old man in his blindness. Perhaps, after he had fancied himself driving before a hurricane with Lucy's son, his mind might wander still further back and back, to the roar of the wind in tattered canvas and the boom of cannonading, while the *Endeavour* ran down the Straits of Sunda with Lucy at the helm.

For many years before the final extinction of the

India Company, the Crown had been gradually taking over its powers, though each step of the slow change had been resisted. At the last, when there was not much of the old Company left to abolish, the Directors defended its rule and record with dignity and a great measure of truth. A grocer's shop that should turn into an Imperial Satrapy must display anomalies and make-shifts, and be something less than perfect; but despite the dazzling glitter of the Star Pagoda, and the shaking of that tree, the manner in which

> . . . *ennobling thoughts depart*
> *When men change swords for ledgers, and desert*
> *The student's bower for gold*—

there had been nobility in that rule, more than sufficient to outweigh the baseness. For some very great and good and brave men had been the servants of the Company: and it had well begun upon the work which it handed over to the nation at large, of bringing peace and good government to the land which had been a jungle of predatory tigers before the coming of Clive.

"The Indian Civil Service is still the best service in the world," protested Augustus Bellasis in 1866: he was attempting to persuade his cousin Serjeant Bellasis to send a son to India—pointing out that when he himself retired in a few years' time, there would be no Bellasis left there: "a thing which has not happened for a hundred years". No son of the Serjeant's came, but his daughter Katherine, who in 1867 married Lewin Bowring, C.S.I., Chief Commissioner of Mysore and Coorg, and lately Secretary to Clemency Canning. At Bangalore, which Lord Cornwallis had taken in 1791, at Seringapatam, where George Bellasis had secured his grim lock of hair in 1799, the Chief Commissioner, walking with his Bellasis bride, meditated his book on Tipu Sultan; and India was to claim their sons and grandsons.

The eldest son of Edward Bellasis, indeed, who was being looked to as the future head of the family, became conscious of another call; he was ordained a priest, the first Bellasis priest since the last Bellasis nobleman, the Abbé Charles. A younger brother did likewise; another followed the path of his father's early friend, Sir Edmund Lodge, and became a Pursuivant at Arms, Bluemantle, and Lancaster Herald. Only one of the sons married, but he had a very large family. Of the daughters, several became nuns. That little coterie of lawyers, Bellasis, Badely, Hope-Scott, and the rest, who so badly shocked the 'fifties by returning to the faith of their fathers, were all dear friends of Newman, particularly Bellasis; and the Serjeant's name, as well as his status as a distinguished convert, took him right into the close cousinhood that was English Catholic society at the time of the Second Spring. He was, indeed, of the same name and race as the mother of the Catholic leader, the Duke of Norfolk, however remotely distant the connection. . . . "The Duke and Duchess of Norfolk and half of the Catholic world lunched yesterday with Mrs. Bellasis at Prince of Wales Terrace, Kensington, to meet Cardinal Newman": this social item does not mean that some two hundred million people came filing up the steps, but only that a small selection of the very small cousinhood attended.

Augustus not only "was to have gone home next year", but actually was on his way out of India by the new Suez Canal, when he died, at the age of forty-nine, and was buried at Suez, leaving instructions for one of his nephews to take the name of Oliver-Bellasis. A tablet to "Augustus F. Bellasis"—he had hated his silly second name—with his arms, and mention of his "long and distinguished service", was set up in Bombay Cathedral, near to that of General John. The other General John came home after the Mutiny, and settled down happily at Holly Hill, very busy as Secretary of the Army Scripture Readers and Soldiers Aid Society. He also married again late in life when his delicate wife died; and rather unexpectedly, considering his Low Church views, his benevolent features and flowing white beard got into a stained-glass window, as a patriarch, when

one was put up to his memory at Bowness. His two surviving sons—India had claimed the other two as infants—
did not represent the family in India. It was the sons of his
brother George who went to India, one in the Army and
one in the Civil Service.

The India of Major George Montalt Bellasis, Bengal Staff
Corps, and of Edward Skelton Bellasis, Punjab Irrigation
Department, was an India more exactly pigeon-holed even
than the Company's territories at the height of its
monopoly. Everybody was there for some reason, and
not for the reason that had brought their forebears; nobody
made fortunes now, either swiftly or slowly: they made so
much *per mensem*, and everybody knew the sum. Then
they retired on a pension to Cheltenham, if they did not die
suddenly. They worked, through fever and prickly heat,
mosquitoes, the smiting sun and drowning rain, at keeping
the land in order and guarding the passes . . . for beyond
the passes still lay danger: robber tribes impossible to tame,
and huge ambitious countries. They had cloaked unchang-
ing India in an immense fabric of mails and telegraphs
and punctual trains and quiet safety; but they too were much
the same people as their predecessors of the dangerous
days: in 1894 Edward Bellasis did "the maddest thing"
his brother George had ever heard of by spending his leave
exploring in the Himalayas with his young wife and two
small children, and going into Little Tibet, or Baltistan, by
ways which no white woman had ever traversed before.
Nobody enjoyed it more than the young wife, who wrote
gay letters home about the snow and the precipices and
other hazards: "At one place the path went round the edge
of an immense granite cliff, and the river had cut it away for
60 yards or so. There was nothing for it but to go through
the water. Two Baltis carried the children and kept them
dry, though the water was nearly up to their shoulders.
Then came my turn, I rolled my habit up round my waist
and climbed onto a Balti's back and went in. Of course my
riding breeches were soaked to my waist, and I rode along

with them hanging on to my saddle to get dry—oh, it was
so funny!" The wife of Major George died of the cholera,
and the little only son was sent home to England, being
photographed before he went: one of those photographs of
which every such family has several in old albums, taken so
that there will be something to remember the child by,
should the parents never see it again: the little white child,
too white, too thin, held up by loving black hands, the
hands of Gulab, or Jemdani, or Amina, the Ayah.

Which was the country of those children? Which, indeed,
the country of their parents? Perhaps, when the Roman
official had worn through his tour of duty at Lindum or
Verulamium or on the savage Frontier, cursing the climate
and the food, and had returned to the wine and olives of his
home, he might remember English primroses and singing-
birds and soft rain, while he sat in the sun-hot circus—and
wonder which was home. . . . But when half a dozen
generations have taken the milk of India's breast, and
manured her dust with their blood and bones, there can be no
real cutting asunder. Whatever time may do to the material
and immaterial fabrics built when England ruled, England is
for ever part of India, as Rome is part of England.

In the church of Houghton-le-Spring, County Durham, a
Bellasis in the King's Coat looked at the stone knight who
had borne the same name. There was a certain likeness in the
helmeted stone face to those of the pilots who had waddled
out to the take-off in their bulky flying clothes during
the war that was now ending—the war that had confounded
the wise men by proving no inhuman scientific combat of
machines, but fruitful of individual valour: armoured
tourneys in the sky, knots of brave men picked for forlorn
hopes. This was the face of war, familiar now to all in the
land; but there were things one only learnt in wearing
uniform: the inner meaning of the speech about St. Crispin
and Crispinian: the something incommunicable, indescrib-
able, that is the soul of all armies. Many descendants of the

stone knight had learnt it, and this descendant had learnt it also, these five hard years; having now a memory full of the faces of young men going into battle, not upon the earth: of nights of fire and noise and death: of fatigue, hardship, routine, considerable physical danger, riotous scenes of pleasure, long spells of monotony, vivid bursts of action, history visibly in the making—and compounded of all and above all, the particular essence of being a soldier. It would now be easy to understand those forebears, if we could ever meet, the Corporal must reflect: though they would be puzzled at my pride in my two stripes: and very much puzzled at the Royal Air Force: and more puzzled than all to find me a woman. . . .

That one should be posted to a light bomber station in County Durham was surely too sharp a coincidence for fiction: next door to the spot where "Belasise" was marked on the map, indistinguishably muddled into Middlesbrough; and within reach of the stone Sir Rowland de Belasise, and the brass to the pious memory of Margaret, widow of that Richard who first enriched the family with ill-gotten lands. Surely the wheel was come full circle . . . The Corporal considered that perhaps she might spend her next leave going over the border into Westmorland, which she had never seen, for she lived in the South; but now she had other things to think upon. Her thoughts were out of England, and gone into the Far East—not, like those of many, because a bomb had lately been dropped there that was expected to alter the course of human history, but because the captives taken by the Japanese were now to be delivered.

In the Cathedral of St. Thomas at Bombay, a Bellasis in the King's Coat looked at the stone banners and cannon upon the monument of General John. The uniform of this officer in the Royal Air Force was motley and irregular, his tall person was gaunt with privation, and his eyes had seen many horrid and terrible things; he and his fellows, indeed,

regard sixty million of his fellow-Hindus as untouchably outside the human pale; and leave the Moslem free to cut the Brahmin's throat.

Mr. Henry Beveridge, Liberal Mid-Victorian historian, rejoicing over the death of John Company and the Queen's proclamation concerning the intended policy of education and emancipation in India, ends with: "Should the day ever come that India, in consequence of the development of her resources by British capital, and the enlightenment of her people by British philanthropy, shall again take rank among the nations as an independent state, then it will not be too much to say, that the extinction of our Indian empire by such peaceful means sheds more lustre on the British name than all the other events recorded in its history."

Assent is easy here; but will that day have come, the right and proper day, when they haul down the flag over the Residency at Lucknow, and saw off the flagstaff at its base, and the pipes play a lament, and the troops march down the Apollo Bunder?

Or, after the going of the Legions, will there not be a redness in the sky and in the streets? . . . And what will presently come over the passes?

APPENDIX

A LIST OF THE GOVERNORS OF BOMBAY UNDER THE COMPANY

The Honourable Sir GEORGE OXENDEN. 1668. *Headquarters at Surat.*

The Hon. GERALD AUNGIER. 1669.

The Hon. THOMAS ROLTE. 1677.

The Hon. Sir JOHN CHILD, Bart. 1681. *Headquarters at Bombay.*

Captain RICHARD KEIGWIN. 1683. *Usurped Governorship.*

The Hon. BARTHOLOMEW HARRIS. 1690.

The Hon. DANIEL ANNESLEY. 1694. *Acting.*

The Hon. Sir JOHN GAYER. 1694.

The Hon. Sir NICHOLAS WAITE. 1704.

The Hon. WILLIAM AISLABIE. 1708.

The Hon. STEPHEN STRUTT. 1715. *Officiating.*

The Hon. CHARLES BOONE. 1716. *First President of Council.*

The Hon. WILLIAM PHIPPS. 1720. *Dismissed.*

The Hon. STEPHEN LAW. 1728. *Acting Governor.*

The Hon. ROBERT COWAN. 1728.

The Hon. JOHN HORNE. 1734.

The Hon. STEPHEN LAW. 1739.

The Hon. JOHN GEEKIE. 1742.

The Hon. WILLIAM WAKE. 1742.

The Hon. RICHARD BOURCHIER. 1750.

The Hon. CHARLES CROMMELIN. 1760.

The Hon. THOMAS HODGES. 1767.

The Hon. WILLIAM HORNBY. 1771.

The Hon. RAWSON HART BODDAM. 1784.

The Hon. ANDREW RAMSAY. 1788. *Acting Governor.*

The Hon. Major-General Sir WILLIAM MEDOWS, K.B. 1790. *C. in C.*

The Hon. Major-General ROBERT ABERCROMBY, K.B. 1790.

The Hon. GEORGE DICK. 1793. *Officiating.*

The Hon. JOHN GRIFFITH. 1795.

The Hon. JONATHAN DUNCAN. 1795.

The Hon. GEORGE BROWN. 1811. *Acting.*

The Right Hon. Sir EVAN NEPEAN, Bart. 1812.

The Hon. MOUNTSTUART ELPHINSTONE. 1819.

Major-General the Hon. Sir JOHN MALCOLM, G.C.B., K.L.S. 1827.

Lieutenant-General the Hon. Sir THOMAS SIDNEY BECKWITH. 1830.

The Hon. JOHN ROMER. 1831. *Acting.*

The Right Hon. JOHN EARL OF CLARE. 1831.

The Right Hon. Sir ROBERT GRANT, G.C.H. 1835.

The Hon. JAMES FARISH. 1838. *Acting.*

The Hon. Sir JAMES RIVETT-CARNAC, Bart. 1839.

Sir WILLIAM HAY MACNAGHTEN, Bart. *Assassinated at Kabul.* 1841.

The Hon. GEORGE WILLIAM ANDERSON. 1841. *Acting.*

The Hon. Sir GEORGE ARTHUR, Bart., K.C.H. 1842.

The Hon. LESTOCK ROBERT REID. 1846. *Acting.*

The Hon. Sir GEORGE RUSSELL CLERK. 1847.

The Right Hon. LUCIUS BENTINCK, Viscount Falkland. 1848.

The Right Hon. JOHN LORD ELPHINSTONE, G.C.B., G.C.H. 1853.

Later Governors served under the Crown.

HONOURABLE COMPANY

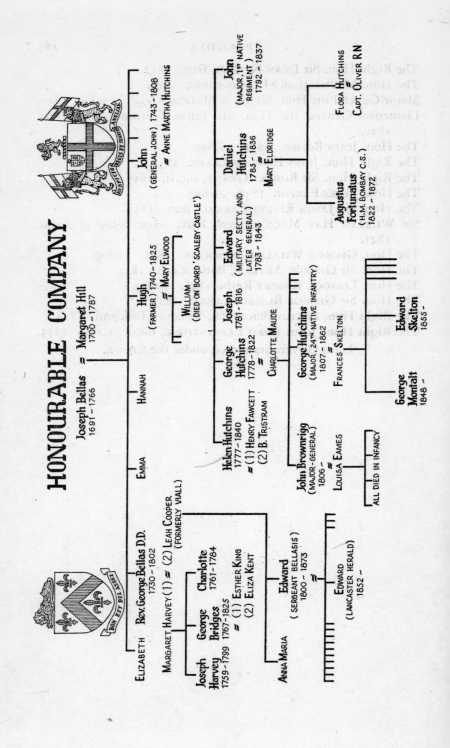

Joseph Bellas
1691 ~ 1766
=
Margaret Hill
1700 ~ 1787

Elizabeth | Rev. George Bellas D.D. | Emma | Hannah | Hugh | John
1730 ~ 1802 | | | (FARMER) 1740 ~ 1825 | (GENERAL JOHN) 1743 ~ 1808
Margaret Harvey (1) = (2) Leah Cooper | | = Mary Elwood | = Anne Martha Hutchins
(FORMERLY VIALL) | |

William
(DIED ON BOARD 'SCALEBY CASTLE')

Joseph | George | Charlotte
Harvey | Bridges | 1761 ~ 1784
1759 ~ 1799 | 1767 ~ 1825 | = (1) Esther King
| | (2) Eliza Kent

George | Joseph | Edward | Daniel | John
Hutchins | 1781 ~ 1816 | (MILITARY SECTY. AND | Hutchins | (MAJOR, 1ST NATIVE
1778 ~ 1822 | | LATER GENERAL) | 1785 ~ 1836 | REGIMENT) 1792 ~ 1837
= Charlotte Maude | | 1783 ~ 1843 | = Mary Eldridge

Helen Hutchins
1777 ~ 1840
= (1) Henry Fawcett
(2) B. Tristram

George Hutchins | | Augustus | Flora Hutchins
(MAJOR, 24TH NATIVE INFANTRY) | | Fortunatus | = Capt. Oliver RN
1807 ~ 1862 | | (H.M. BOMBAY C.S.)
= Frances Skelton | | 1822 ~ 1872

John Brownrigg
(MAJOR~GENERAL)
1806 ~
=
Louisa Eames

Edward | Edward Skelton
(SERGEANT BELLASIS) | 1855 ~
1800 ~ 1873 |

Anna Maria

Edward
(LANCASTER HERALD)
1852 ~

George
Montalt
1848 ~

ALL DIED IN INFANCY